T0354600

CHUCKLES AND CHALLENGES

by Charlie McOuat

iUniverse, Inc.
New York   Bloomington

Copyright © 2010 by Charlie McOuat

All rights reserved. No part of this book may be used or reproduced by any means, graphic, electronic, or mechanical, including photocopying, recording, taping or by any information storage retrieval system without the written permission of the publisher except in the case of brief quotations embodied in critical articles and reviews.

iUniverse books may be ordered through booksellers or by contacting:

iUniverse
1663 Liberty Drive
Bloomington, IN 47403
www.iuniverse.com
1-800-Authors (1-800-288-4677)

Because of the dynamic nature of the Internet, any Web addresses or links contained in this book may have changed since publication and may no longer be valid. The views expressed in this work are solely those of the author and do not necessarily reflect the views of the publisher, and the publisher hereby disclaims any responsibility for them.

ISBN: 978-1-4502-6725-0 (sc)
ISBN: 978-1-4502-6726-7 (ebook)

Printed in the United States of America

iUniverse rev. date: 10/08/2010

CONTENTS

Part VI: Fiction, Poems

PART I
Rochester and Buffalo

Life

On September 1, 1939, Hitler attacked Poland starting World War II. Two years later, he marched towards Leningrad. On Dec 7, 1941, Japan attacked our ships in Pearl Harbor forcing the United States to enter the war. The world was in sad shape, people were frightened, panic was rampant, but then, on June 15, 1941, a ray of hope. I was born. I'm not taking credit for the defeat of the Nazis, but let's face it, within four years of my birth, the war was over, there was peace in the world, and a new optimism in the United States.

I was born into a middle class family in Rochester, New York. Three older sisters preceded me, possibly preparing my parents. We had no car, and wouldn't buy our first one until eight years later. This is a Scottish family and we didn't spend foolishly. Our next door neighbor and uncle used to drive my mother to the hospital for her deliveries but he warned, after the third girl in a row, "If the next one isn't a boy, I'll not drive you again." I was wanted. I'm sure my father and many neighbors gave a sigh of relief when the boy finally arrived, but I think later, they wondered.

I don't remember much about those first few years but most of the well worn pictures from that era have me eating chocolate, sucking my fingers, or just looking confused, with three sisters constantly hovering over me. I assume that no matter what I did, the three sisters hovered, wiped, scolded, teased, and pampered with the intruder- me.

I came into the world with all the advantages given to the first born son, but I know I cried a lot. Was I colicky? I know I had some kind of Rh factor problem that endangered my early health but after much consternation and answered prayers, I rallied and now live to tell about it.

In 1941 there was a lot of military research taking place. I entered the world via Strong Memorial Hospital, where some of the babies born at that time were intentionally exposed to radiation doses to test for unknown effects. I missed this experimentation by a few months but maybe learned that this is a tough world and I would have to watch out for myself. Years later, in adolescence, we all thought it was great fun to go to a certain shoe store and see our feet X-rayed by this new machine "Yuck, I can see your skeleton." We got first glimpse of the bones in our feet while inside our blood cells mutated. It's amazing that the species survives with all our scientific advances.

I'm sure being the only boy had its advantages. Saturday night bath night we all were washed in the same tub, but because of my masculine anatomy, I got to go last and the girls had to go together and then clean the tub, just for me. Resentment? Who knows?

It didn't seem like a small house then, but a family of six with three bedrooms, one toilet must have produced a lot of competition for space and recognition. A large upright piano dominated not just the small living room but the whole house. Even though my oldest sister Betty was the only pianist, she implanted "Malaguena," in my brain.

My first real memory was playing house under the dining room table with my middle sister Mary. I usually felt left out of things because I was the youngest and only boy, but this time I was included. She made all the rules with her as the mother while I was confined to secondary status as the garbage collector. Now there's nothing wrong with being a garbage collector but when it's my very first significant memory, it shows where I put myself in the family hierarchy. My self concept as the last, youngest, and the different one, was established early.

Mostly I remember crying a lot. For example, the first Sunday I had to leave my parents and go to Sunday school with the rest of the kids, I cried. I can remember screaming, grasping a rung of a stairway and not letting go, my howls piercing the church. Some old well meaning lady urged me to "not embarrass my parents like that. Let go the staircase and be a big boy." Big boy hell, I wanted no part of it. I wanted my Mommy and no one or nothing else. "Gimme my Mommy, right now or I'll rip this place apart," was my mantra. Of course, I only weighed 35 pounds so "ripping the place apart," was not a realistic option. Being a spoiled little brat was my method of coping with the hostile world beyond my mother's apron strings.

My grandfather pleaded with my mother to not "baby the lad," but she waited for a son and wasn't going to allow common sense or an interfering father in law to get between her and this beautiful boy. Beautiful? Yes. People would stop and admire me, the lad, and say, "He's too beautiful to be a boy. It must be a girl. Look at those long eyelashes." At times though, untangling my eye lashes from my eye balls became an issue and another excuse to cry.

My crying scene at church was a mere warm up to the day my mom left the house to go shopping and by mistake left me inside, looking out the window at her disappearing frame. She walked only a few feet away and then remembered her treasured son, but in the interim it took her to walk those few feet, I screamed like my world was ending. Indeed it was. Mommy was leaving me alone for a whole minute and I'd have none of it.

I don't know where those insecurities came from. I know I wasn't breast fed, and years later, when I was a more mature five year old, a baby cousin from the country came to visit and his warmed milk bottles were lined up on the kitchen table in front of me. I felt like attacking them. "Where's mine?" I wondered. I may have been weaned too early because those bottles represented to me everything I ever wanted or needed. "Gimmie those, all of them right now," I thought.

From Teddy to Parades

And then, there's the Teddy incident. Teddy was my childhood doll and best friend ever. I remember his distinctive smell that was pleasing only to me, his wooden head, and humanoid eyes with lashes that opened and closed as I tilted him back and forth. Those were the days. My doll was a friend, comforter, and a scapegoat all in one loved package. We were inseparable. We said our evening prayers together, "Thank you God for my Teddy," I hugged him all night and then we greeted each morning together. Through the day I dragged him around the house or left him abandoned in a corner, it didn't matter. It only depended on my mood. Unlike humans, he never rebelled at rejection or needed anything himself. He was totally mine to reject or love. Those were definitely the good old days, never to be repeated.

After many years, I'm sure Teddy's odor and appearance became obnoxious to the whole household. His cloth arms became rags, one eye failed to open and the smell-phew!- lets just say that his smell preceded him into a room.

One day, when I was still too young for school but totally attached to, and dependant on Teddy for everything, my mother decided to do some renovations. I'm sure this was after all attempts at reason failed, like, "I was a big boy now and should think about getting along without Teddy," ("No way," was my response, "Not today, not tomorrow, not ever, no way will I ever abandon my alter ego"). Somehow my mother manipulated me into agreeing that we could make Teddy happier by a coat of paint for his face, a few stitches for his arms, and maybe some nice new shoes. She must have snuck him away in one of my weak moments, like nap time, and took him down in our cold dark basement for his very impersonal and insulting paint job. Reality hit when I awoke from my Teddy less nap. "Where's Teddy?" I asked.

Mom held my hand and led me out of my bedroom, down the stairs, through the hallway and into the kitchen. The next leg of the journey was through the cellar door, down the forbidden cellar stairs, into the darkness, around the corner to a card table, which was covered with newspaper and there, laid out like a cadaver, were the remains of Teddy. His face was no longer dotted with my teeth marks, but sanded and repainted a hideous pink. His beautiful arms scared with stitches, his whole persona altered, gone, and dead. He smelled like paint instead of three year old vomit and drool. I screamed, "That's not Teddy. Where is my Teddy? He's gone. What did you do with my Teddy?" Tears and screams drowned out my mom's pleadings that "he is still Teddy; he just needed a new suit and a bath."

I insisted that was not Teddy and I hated what he had become- respectable. I could never accept that face, that body, or its sterile non-stink. My loving mother held me, stroked my head, and whispered softly, but there was no going back. Teddy was gone. This was the first of life's disasters and my screams of horror did nothing to alleviate the empty feeling. I'm sure the incident and my reaction were the subject at the evening meal. My sisters' life went on with their usual teasing and heartless fun. They raced each other to see who could gulp down their glass of milk the fastest. They didn't know or care that my first experience with Hell began that afternoon in our own basement. Nobody realized that I was sitting there, with oatmeal running down my chin and wondering, "Is my life over already? Is this what life is like without Teddy? Do people just run around, getting and spending, yakking and carrying on without a Teddy to love?"

"I don't want Teddy anymore," I screamed throughout the meal and through everyone's sleepless night that followed. The next day, exhausted but persistent, I stood on the living room couch and watched with my guilt ridden mother, while the garbage men took Teddy away. They threw him high on the truck, alongside our discarded garbage and tin cans. Gone. My life changed. The house became quiet, lifeless, and empty. I plodded on, ate, slept, took my naps but the core, my comfort, and joy drove off in the garbage truck. If this is what it felt like to grow up, I wanted none of it. I was shocked like a switch going off, left with an emptiness that hides the panic beneath. Teddy was there, loving, constant, and totally dependable and then in a split second, was gone, abandoned, discarded, but not forgotten. Only a convenient socially acceptable covering over a painful scar remained. I later learned the word for the process is called "socialization," or "maturation." I'd rather say, "Oh Shit."

My parents dated for eight years before they agreed they had enough money for marriage and a house. My Aunts joked that they had to push my shy, indecisive father into proposing before my mother became discouraged and looked elsewhere. My Uncle Alex lived next door and built our house. It was a warm, loving house but we were never allowed to use the shower. Before my time, while the house was brand new, someone turned on the shower and the water rushed through some fault and flowed on down the stairwell, soaking the ceiling. I guess they patted it dry but no one dared to confront the uncle-builder. It was just easier to take baths and not use the flawed shower. I took my first shower when I was eight years old at the YMCA. We did not like conflict.

Many of our good times centered on Scottish Celebrations like Robert Burns Day, weddings, or parades. My father was bag pipe major of Rochester, N.Y. and was in constant demand. When he practiced his pipes in the kitchen, my sisters would complain about the noise permeating the house, but I liked it. I marched closely behind him and when social pressures, like a quiet house, forced him down to the basement, I followed. I was proud and happy to be with him. He seemed to stand taller when blowing his pipes and I was impressed just by the volume. All that energy came from lungs to fingers to chanter to bag to drones to the outside world. At times, I'm still in awe of people who make a lot of noise.

My three sisters dressed in kilts and marched in parades with my father's bag pipe band. They didn't play an instrument or dance but made the long trek through the city while I watched with my mother. I always waved to my Dad but don't remember seeing my sisters. I was probably jealous and didn't want them to know how much I envied them. I was pre-kindergarten, but may have questioned the sanity of guys wearing skirts.

Another attraction in the parade was Jimmy Hart, the oldest living Civil War Veteran. That was 1950 so Jimmy had to be over 100 years old. I wonder now why they called the centenarian "Jimmy," instead of "Mr. Hart," but that's friendly Rochester.

The highlight of the parade for everyone was the tremendous display of our armed forces, recently arrived home from their victory in World War II. Bands, tanks, canons, jeeps, and an endless line of uniformed soldiers, Army, Navy, Marines and Air Force, marching in perfect unison, while planes flying overhead, brought everyone to their feet. Patriotism and pride were rampant, tears and cheers resounded from every corner, shaking the ground for these well deserved war heroes. I waved a little flag and yelled along with everyone else, without realizing at the time, that these men did indeed save the world. Those same men are now bent double, not from the packs on their backs, but from age. They remain heroes and I make a point of thanking them at every opportunity.

My own back is now bent, sore, and stiff, not from being a war hero or any other kind of a hero. It's just from all those years. I thank God they were good years, mostly very good years.

Elmerston Road

Our house on Elmerston Road stood alone, with a vacant lot as we called them on each side. We thought that gave us some distinction, something that set us apart from our neighbors. My father bought the lot along with the house in anticipation of a large family and had the immigrant idea that any land was precious. Our neighbors on the other side, the Wagner's, sold real estate and knew it would be a good investment.

Huge elm trees reached out across the road, making a green canopy of beauty. Each spring their white blossoms signaled that the long Rochester winter was finally waning. In the summer they provided shade, keeping our bodies and houses cool. In the fall the green leaves turned to various shades of red, yellow and brown and sprinkled their treasures over the earth. In the winter they were stark naked, but stood strong and reliable against snow and ice. All seasons they stood invincible against wind, ice and frigid temperatures until the sixties when a tiny bug attacked with a vengeance and wouldn't let go until the last tree died and was carted away. Overnight, the Dutch elm disease struck and turned the stately trees to pitiful piles of sawdust.

I knew we weren't rich. Our family didn't own a car until I was eight years old and I was definitely the last one in number Forty Nine School to have a TV set. School mates talked about Howdy Doody, Buffalo Bob, and Cookla Fran and Ollie, while I sat in ignorance. We probably could have afforded one earlier, but my Dad thought they would interfere with our studying and threaten family togetherness. Experience has proved him right. Families today sit mesmerized in front of the "idiot box," seldom speaking to each other.

Our house was small for a family of six but I never thought of it as undersized when growing up. My three teenaged sisters fought for time in front of the mirror in the only bathroom. Our phone was centrally located in the kitchen and there was no possibility of privacy. Even now, I like to take one of our phones into remote areas even when talking about trivial things, like when are we going rowing in the morning.

We gathered around a huge radio in the living room to be frightened by the Shadow, with the cackling Lamont Cranston, or reassured by the efficiency of crime fighters in True Detective Mysteries, or excited by The Lone Ranger and the William Tell Overture. My father's favorite was Jack Benny; probably because Jack's characteristic thriftiness matched his own frugality.

Crabby old Mrs. Rooney lived across the street. We couldn't let a baseball roll in her yard or she'd come out and yell, "One more time like that Charles and I'll keep that ball." Her daughter, Elinore, "wasn't too bad," but Donna, the oldest, smoked and later necked with guys in their driveway. She was grumpy like her mother.

Old Mrs. Keifer lived alone down the street in a big house with all her cats. I had to sit quietly while my mother listened to her complaints about aches and pains and listen to her gossip about beloved neighbors. She was bitter and boring but my Mom felt compelled to be friendly and dragged me along. Her cats prowled the house, scratching, meowing, and pouncing on me from dark corners. In her last days on Earth, she requested to have my dad come and take her excess coal for our family. He took one step into the coal bin, found it reeking of cat urine, and came home deciding that free coal wasn't worth the odor.

My Aunt Mabel and Uncle Alex lived next door. She was my Grandmother's sister. That whole family of eight siblings came from Scotland within a few years of each other. Uncle Alex was a builder, with long curly white hair which he said came from eating carrots. He was the only person I heard of who belonged to a country club. I liked him because he smoked and was always ready to talk sports. They had two children. Alec Jr. was a frogman in WWII and a family hero. He married a pretty woman and had three daughters, two of them were twins. Their daughter Jean was our childhood baby sitter. She never married but when she was in her thirties, she had one fling with a divorced man. Both parents ganged up to discourage her, "Why do you need to get married now, Jean? You have everything you need right here at our house. Food, shelter, what else do you need?" She cried a lot and never dated again. She died young of breast cancer.

Graham Rice lived up the street. The first day I met him. I was playing peacefully in the side yard when this new kid came from nowhere and hit me over the head with a two by four. My enraged father dragged me and my bleeding head to Graham's house where we met his father who satisfied us all with a few hard licks to Graham's behind. We became fast friends playing baseball, basketball, and baseball daily, each in its own season.

Graham always came to the house on the first snowfall. He'd throw a snowball at our window and beacon, "Hey Charlie, come on out. It's good packin'." Something I still cringe at when I think of him is how one day a third friend persuaded me to play a joke on Graham by abandoning him in a down town movie theatre. To this day I think of disloyalty to a friend as a lowest form of behavior.

Across the street from Graham, in the "yellow house," lived Jimmy Hughes. Jimmy's pants always hung down to his knees and his nose dripped its residue to his chin. He never carried a hanky but wiped it on his sleeve or just let it flow. Jimmy wasn't athletic in those early years but later set a scoring record for his freshmen high school basketball team.

His father was a cop. When I was a teenager, I hitch hiked each summer to Nantucket to get away from long boring Rochester summers. When I returned one September, Jimmy was one of many neighborhood boys who were arrested for stealing cars and taking them on joy rides. I was a follower in those days and probably would have gone along with such foolishness if I hadn't escaped to my ocean paradise.

About that time the Hughes's moved out of our neighborhood and we lost track of each other until college days. He had been kicked out of his house for some reason but put himself through the University of Rochester by being a bookie. He worked at a race track called Batavia Downs, where he got inside information and shared with wealthy bettors around the city. I went to the races with him one night and was distraught when I lost twenty dollars. Jimmy lost thousands but bought us each a steak dinner on the way home. He carried rolls of money with him and packed a gun.

I was saddened years later when I saw him wandering the streets like a homeless man, ragged pants again hanging to his knees and mucous dripping from his nose. Gambling had been kind to him for a few years but ultimately took everything from him and left him just another homeless victim.

Next door to the crabby Mrs. Rooney lived the Wilsons. Dr. Wilson did research at the University of Rochester. He brought home a white rat for his young son Jay to enjoy as a pet. Jay loved the rat and named him Judy. Jay was still sucking his thumb and talking like a baby when one day he brought his precious Judy over to show it to our family. He let the rat out of his cage and we all watched him crawl around our front yard. Our neighbors, the Wagner's, had a dog named Spot, who took one look at the freed rat, attacked, grabbed him by the neck, shook and wouldn't let go. Jay screamed and cried, "'Pot, you let go my Dudy." Despite Jay's pleading the dog shook harder and harder until the life was gone from the rat. We all chased the dog but nothing saved his pet. Days afterwards, Jay roamed the neighborhood in a daze, crying and telling the world, "'Pot killed my Dudy. I hate 'Pot.'" His young doctor father soon moved from our modest neighborhood and I assume Jay still remembers that day.

The Wagners lived next to us for years but I don't remember much about them besides their rat killing dog named Spot and their phone number. Our phone number was Monroe8-011J while theirs was Monroe 8-011R. If my Mom wanted to talk with Mrs., Wagner she just asked the operator, "Hello Operator, this is 'J' would you please ring 'R' for me?" I sometimes long for those days with human phone operators when I dial so many times and only connect with a mechanical voice. "Press 1 if you're in pain, 2 if you want to pay a bill, 3 if you…"

Mr. Wagner worked hard all his life as a builder of houses. He saved his money, retired, then immediately took his wife on a drive across country. They got as far as Oklahoma, where a drunk driver ran a red light, and killed them both. Spot, the breaker of little boy's hearts, had died years before.

Mrs. Rooney never did carry out her threat to "keep my baseball," Jay Wilson, I'm sure recovered from "Dudy's" tortuous death, and my head long ago recovered from Graham Rice's introductory crack with a two by four. I hope he's now happy and throwing snowballs at his grandson's window, beaconing him to "come on out. It's good packin'." Scars run deep but most of them heal and make the area stronger. I'd like to thank all these good people for enriching my life, but they've moved on or passed on as we all will do. I smile when I think of these incidences and smile again anticipating the great adventures awaiting tomorrow. The years gallop by and I have to hang on to enjoy the ride for surely some malady will hit someday and turn me into a pile of dust, like the Dutch elm disease did to our precious trees.

Charlotte

Charlotte is the beach to go to in Rochester, New York. From our house, it required two public bus transfers, an hour of patient waiting until the bus went over the last hill and revealed the blue waters of Lake Ontario beyond. Even though the driver warned all passengers to "sit down," I couldn't resist standing on my seat to get my first view of the lake. The airbrakes hissed, the bus stopped, I grabbed my pail and shovel, took my mother's hand, and followed my three sisters, who were already running off the bus towards the beach. My father walked behind, counting heads, making sure we were all together.

My sisters disappeared into the woman's changing area while my dad herded me to the men's locker. He let me have my own basket to hold my clothes. I yanked off my pants and shirt and threw them on the wet floor. "Pick up your clothes; put them in the basket," he ordered. "The beach is going nowhere. Don't worry." I hated waiting while he too slowly untied his shoes, took off his trousers and sport shirt, fussing over each button, one at a time, then folding everything up and placing each item in his basket. "Charles, go to the bathroom before we head for the beach." *Won't we ever get there? Why is he always so slow and fussy?*

We left the dark bath house and I squinted in the bright sunlight and ran to the beach. My sisters were already running to the water by the time I yelled to my Mom, "Hey this is great. Look Mom, I can't even see across the water. Is this the ocean?"

Betty, Mary and Flora were splashing around, yelling, laughing, throwing water on each other when I waded in behind. The water was cold and the waves broke up to my chest."Move in closer," warned my Dad, "You're already out too far." I trudged back towards the shore, watching them have fun while I retreated. Flora paddled a blue life ring around, kicked her feet and screamed, "I'm floating. These waves are huge."

Mary agreed, "I'm glad we brought these life rings."

Two giant boys, almost as tall as my oldest sister Betty, but with dark black skin, ran passed me, splashing water on my face and running out towards Flora and Mary. Their size and dark skin startled me. "What was that?" I wondered.

The biggest one stopped near Flora, stood for a second and said, "I wish I had a life ring like that. Can I try it?" She jumped off the ring, ran to my dad and put her arms around his neck. She held tight and yelled, "Daddy, Daddy, I don't want them to use my life ring. They'll get their black goo all over it. They're dirty." This was our first contact with a black person.

My dad patted Flora on the back, walked towards the two Negro boys and in a calm quiet voice said, "Here, do you want a turn? It's OK."

He held the ring steady while the boy jumped on, paddled around with his hands, kicked his feet and squealed with delight, just like my sisters had done before him. Flora looked on in horror as she watched him sitting on her

19

precious ring. The boy soon got bored, hopped off and said "Thank you." He ran through the waves to the deeper water where his friend was floating on his back.

Flora frowned at her abandoned ring. The corners of her mouth turned down, unsure whether to touch it or not. My father took her hand, gently set her back on the tube and said, "They're just like you, honey. Having fun. Just like us. They're no different than us except their skin is darker. Come on Flora, you're OK. It's a beautiful day. It's your ring. Thank you for being a big girl and sharing. Have fun."

He pulled her around while she kicked her feet. She flicked water from her face and soon forgot the incident. I haven't. My Dad never looked so big and l and I never forgot the lesson. Thanks Dad.

I Always Knew
What was Coming

Christmas dinners in my preschool years, were reserved for Grandpa and Grandma McOuat's house. Homes on Springfield Avenue were crowded together, old like their owners, with tiny front lawns, buried under two feet of Rochester snow. Huge elm trees, branches laden with snow and ice, bent over the street, forming a crystal canopy to greet us. This was the boyhood home of my father and his sisters, covered with the same phony brick that passed out of fashion forty years before. Change doesn't come easy to the McOuats.

Inside the house, I took off my heavy coat and made a b-line for the front porch where a familiar friend, a mounted deer head stared down at me from his wall entrapment. I stood transfixed, wondering why he didn't come down and join the party. His sparkling eyes welcomed me again this year, but I couldn't relax because I always knew what was coming.

Cousins crowded together on the living room rug to play card games like Old Maid, Crazy Eights, or War. Aunts and Uncles sat in chairs, entertained by their offspring, and wishing each other a Merry Christmas. I joined in the action but couldn't have fun because I always knew what was coming.

Aunt Mabel noticed my long face and asked, "Charles, what's wrong? Come sit by me. I'll read you a story." She read from the familiar book that personified good and evil. Good was symbolized by two innocent children lost in the woods, seduced by an old witch, representing evil. The witch had a pointed nose and prominent chin that come together over her toothless mouth. Gray witch hair straggled over her wrinkled skin of her face, while she cackled in an old rocker, licking her lips in anticipation of the meal ahead. She fired up a big black stove behind her, preparing to roast and eat the innocent children, who shook in fear in front of her. I snuggled closer to my Aunt, comforted by the warm fat under her arms but I kept thinking about what was coming.

At dinner we held hands around the table, saying a Bobby Burns grace, and then enjoying Grandma's mashed potatoes and gravy, succulent roast beef, and string beans drenched in butter. My favorite dessert was Grandma's apple pie, topped with a scoop of vanilla ice cream that slid down my throat in a sweet mixture of cold and hot. I loved the smells and the tastes but I couldn't digest the food because I always knew what was coming.

After dinner we sang Scottish songs like "Roamin' in the Gloamin', Ye Take the High Road, and Scotland the Brave." My favorite was "Charlie is My Darlin.'

When it was time to say goodbye, we put on our coats, hugged again, and this was my signal to hide. It was futile but I tried. My father found me huddled under the table in the pantry. With a firm voice, he beckoned, "Come on

Charles, stop this foolishness, it's time to go next door and visit Grandma Duckett."

The moment was at hand. As slowly as possible, I put on my boots and mittens, buttoned my coat, and pulled my woolen cap down over my ears. I trudged next door after my father, through the waist deep snow, up the icy back steps, through the creaky wooden door that banged shut, cutting off any possible escape. I was now trapped in the kitchen with Grandma Duckett. She was a hundred years old and looked every minute of it. Her toothless mouth, hidden between prominent chin and pointed nose, was barely visible between lifeless lips. Her too frequent attempts at talking emitted a hissing sound like an angry snake. Gray witch hair, hung hideously over her cadaverous face, matched the picture in the book. Behind her rocking chair, I stared into an opening in a big black stove just big enough to squeeze a child like me into the blazing fire. I took a step back but my father's firm hand pushed me towards her. His words sealed my fate. The dreaded end of day was here, "Charles, kiss your Grandma." Oh no, this clear assault on my distant manhood had already ruined my day and now there was no escape.

I smelled the decaying meat odor emanating from her death like body, tried to look beyond the dried up drool caked in the corners of her mouth, ignored the creaks and cackles of the witch and her chair. I went into survival mode, stepped forward, held my breath, put my mouth within an inch of her wrinkled skin, and made a kissing sound by smacking my lips together. My last shred of dignity was preserved for another year. My lips never touched the mean old witchy skin but I had satisfied my father and avoided a spanking. For now, there was peace in the family at Christmas.

Grandpa McOuat

Grandpa McOuat died when I was eight years old. It was my first experience with death and I didn't like it. My father, who seldom showed emotion, sneaked off into secluded corners of the house to cry. One night I saw him sitting alone in the car. I asked my Mom, "Where's Dad?"

She pointed to the car, sitting in the driveway, "I think he's in the car. Crying over Grandpa." This scared me; I wasn't used to sadness like that in our house, and my father, the strength of the family, never showed tears, interpreted by the times as a sign of weakness.

The funeral came in a few days. I remember sitting up front in the service, between my Mom and Dad, wanting all the sadness to end. Grandpa was old, in his eighties, but had been healthy. I could always tell he was coming because his shoes squeaked. One leg was shorter that the other, from some "old country" Scottish disease. One shoe was built up but he still walked with a noticeable limp. He was short, had a mustache, and talked funny, with his Scottish brogue. He was never sick but when he went on a trip with my Aunt and Uncle, he died. Pernicious Anemia they called it.

I sat in the front row during his service, my tie cut into my neck, my pants cramped my crotch, and my shoes were tied too tight. I sat trying to behave, determined to be brave and not cry, but I kept thinking of my Grandma. What would she do now that she was all alone? Her husband was dead and she was left by herself. I sat there, playing with my fingers when I heard someone moving into the seat behind me. I turned around and there was Grandma with a sad, desperate look on her face. She leaned over my seat and gave me kiss on the cheek. I started crying, a few sobs at first and then a flood of loud, wailing screeches. I felt sorry for Grandma and the tears wouldn't stop. My Mom grabbed me, hugged me, and I said, "It's OK Charles. You loved Grandpa. It's OK." I think she may have led me from the service because I remember seeing my cousins starring at me and thinking I had done something wrong. *They didn't cry so why did I have to? Am I different? They're big and I'm small.*

At the gathering at our house later, my teenaged cousin, Bruce, tried to make everyone laugh by saying, "When Charles started crying at the funeral, I felt like calling Noah for his arch."

Another cousin Al, who was a navy frog man and a hero to me and my family, came over and said in a soft, soothing voice, "Never mind Charles, You loved Grandpa. You did great," and he gave me a hug. I remained quiet but felt like screaming to everybody that I cried not because I loved Grandpa; I just didn't want Grandma to have to live alone. That's what was so sad to me. Why couldn't they understand?

I got over my Grandfather's death, my family survived, and my Grandmother lived on for twenty more years before she joined her departed husband at the age of ninety five.

I don't remember thinking much about him until twenty five years later when I was a dentist with a busy practice. An old man named David Wilson, came into my office, who had recently moved to Cape Cod from Rochester. He spoke with the familiar Scottish brogue and asked if I was Bill McOuat's son. I said yes and he told me about his strong connection with my family. Mr. Wilson said he used to host Scottish festivals in the city and was a friend of my father and grandfather. He had been a prominent banker in Rochester and he joked, "I hated to see your grandfather come into the bank. Whenever he came in, he lectured to anyone who would listen about the great economic inequalities in the United States. Some people had much more opportunity than others," he preached, "and it wasn't fair." David's banking friends shuttered and accused him of hanging around with Communists. "Your Grandpa talked often about a trip to Washington, D.C. and the wonderful monuments and parks but he emphasized his horror at the slum areas alongside all this wealth. He never had much formal schooling but he read all the time. He read college text books on economics and history, loved classic literature, and music. He was outspoken and always ready for a debate. He was a little guy, with squeaky shoes and a very big heart. My banking friends hated to see him coming."

My father was the first one in his family to go beyond fourth grade. When you reached that age in Scotland, you went into the mills if a girl, or the mines if a boy and stayed there until death. I'm thankful my Grandfather had the courage to leave and bring his family to the USA.

He was a railroad worker in Scotland and when he decided to immigrate to Australia, his coworkers gave him a farewell dinner and a gold watch with the inscription, "Good luck on your passage to Australia." His plans were made, he said good bye to friends and family but when he arrived at the docks to board his ship, something happened that delayed its passage for a few days. My industrious grandfather found an alternate ship that was leaving immediately for the United States. He boarded, came to Ellis Island, made his way to Rochester, and found a job as a janitor in a church. Later he worked for the railroads in this country and after a year, brought his family to him. That watch wishing him well in Australia has been passed to me. I'm thankful he left Scotland and his ship to Australia was delayed.

Catch

My Dad liked to hide behind a newspaper when he came home from work. He was tired. His job was demanding and a small house with four young children was not a place to unwind. He was thirty seven when I was born so by the time I was ten and exploding with energy, he was ready to sit back in an easy chair.

I hated that newspaper. It may have been a source of information for him, but for me, it was strictly a barrier between us. I stood in front of it, pounding my baseball rhythmically into my glove. I tried to make the whack, whack, whack sound of the ball hitting the glove as loud as possible. If that didn't bring a response, I tried the more direct approach, "Hey Dad, do you want to play catch?" Most often he would peer from behind the paper, like he just became aware of my presence, smile, neatly fold up his paper and say, "Sure, I'd love to. Let's go."

He led the way down the cellar steps to where two baseball gloves rested on the shelf. The new one was mine. It was a three fingered Bob Feller model that I had bought with $6.98 of my own money at Sears and Roebuck Co. His was an antique catcher's mitt, overstuffed with padding that went back to the days before Babe Ruth. It had no flexibility like a modern glove, but was designed to stop the ball while you used your free hand to trap it against the well worn leather. It was impossible to catch one handed like everyone does today.

I followed him out to the side yard where he crouched down in the catcher's position while I fired away with my best assortment of curves, knuckleballs, and high hard ones. He called balls and strikes with the gesticulations of a major league umpire. We had invisible men on the bases signifying the imaginary batters who I had walked on four balls. His calls were generous so I usually got three strikeouts before a runner reached home. This game of catch was only for fun and encouragement, no technical instruction or negativity.

In the fall, when the evenings turned cooler and the leaves began to fall, we put our baseball gloves away for the winter and brought out a football. Our "side yard," as we called it was one of the few vacant lots left in our rapidly developing neighborhood. It was full of tall weeds with mounds and crevices that were an embarrassment to my Mom but gave our property a distinction in that time of yard conformity and perfect lawns.

We went to one end of the lot and huddled together like I saw the Cleveland Browns did on a neighbors TV set. He'd say, "Where are you going?"

I answered, "I'll go straight to the Milk box, slant to the right and you hit me on top of that mound in front of the street light."

"Sounds good," he said and then took his quarterback position while I crouched in the three point stance of a tight end.

He waited while I ran my deceptive pattern towards the mound and every time when I looked back, he threw a perfect spiral to me. I often made a heroic dive off the mound, grabbing the ball at the last second, just before it hit the ground. I could almost hear the crowds cheering. I knew my father was a great passer because he never missed. On TV, I watched the great Johnny Unitas hit his receivers but sometimes he missed. Not my Dad. He was perfect. I often wondered why he wasted his time behind that desk, day after day at Eastman Kodak Company, when he could be playing football in front of thousands each Sunday like my heroes.

Maturity taught me that there is a big difference between a father and son having a casual game of catch and a real football game against skilled players. I too soon realized that my Dad wasn't as good as Johnny Unitas. He may not have even been the best in the neighborhood, but I know I had the best father.

Stan the Man and Me

In a small city like Rochester, N.Y, the Red Wing baseball team is as important as the Yankees were to the Bronx or the Red Sox to Beantown. I knew each ballplayer's batting average, height, weight, where they were from, whether they batted right or left handed, and their wife's first name. The Red Wings were a St, Louis Cardinal triple A farm team, which meant that the players were one step below major league caliber and if they succeeded they would be sent up to the Cardinals. It followed that St. Louis was my favorite major league team and their star, Stan Musial was my favorite person in the whole world.

I knew everything about Stan the Man. He was born in the coal mining town of Donora, Pennsylvania, began his career as a left handed pitcher, but hurt his arm, and was convinced by a friend, named Dickie Kerr, to become an outfielder. His wife's maiden name was Lillian Lambesh. He became a great hitter, and actually played a few months for my Red Wings in 1941, the year of my birth. Stan had a lifetime batting average of 331, played both outfield and first base, and led the league in hitting seven times. He was also reputed to be nice to everyone; kind to his family, fans, and friends.

When I was eleven years old, still too young to be side tracked by my later obsession with girls, my baseball fanaticism was at its peak. I skipped meals to play baseball in the playground at #49 School. I awoke each morning, headed straight to the sports section of the Rochester Times Union to see how many hits Stan Musial got last night against the Dodgers? Did they win? Is he still leading the league in batting? Usually, my day started well because he was almost always successful the night before.

My Dad played baseball in college, shared my interest, and was amused by my compulsion. One June morning he casually mentioned that the St. Louis Cardinals were coming to Rochester to play an exhibition game against the Boston Red Sox and "maybe I'd like to go."

"Like to go?" Did he say? "Like to go?"I had to go. "Are you kidding Dad? Of course I want to go. Just you and me, no sisters? Will Stan Musial be here?"

"Yes Charles, just you and me. And yes, Stan Musial will be here. Also Enos Slaughter, Marty Marion, the whole team."

I didn't care about the whole team. I cared about nothing but Stan the Man. He was every hero, real and mythical, condensed into one talented person. That three week's wait between being told about the game and its arrival, took forever. I watched the clock, checked and rechecked the calendar, hardly slept at night, fidgeted during the day, and didn't care about food. My quiet self became loquacious and all about one subject, Stan my Man.

The night of the game was perfect, no threat of rain, no traffic jams, no problems. I ran into Red Wing Stadium, dragging my Dad, talking, gawking, and running at the mouth. Our seats also were perfect, ten rows up from the box seats, behind first base. My thrifty father even splurged 50 cents for a souvenir program so I could keep score. We made sure we were in our seats an hour before game time. I didn't want to miss a minute of batting practice. "Hey Dad, there's #2 Red Schoendinst, and Country Slaughter #12, and Marty Marion and…" Every seat in the stadium was filled. The crowd was already on its feet, cheering, yelling, screaming as each Cardinal took his swings.

"Hey Dad, why are all those people gathering in the box seats?" I asked. They seemed to flock around this one player patiently signing autographs. He was standing along the first baseline, talking to kids who leaned over the box seat railing. He turned his back for a minute so I could read his number. It is, it actually is number six. Stan Musial, here in Red Wing Stadium, a few feet away from me, signing autographs. "Dad, there he is. It's him. I'm goin' down there." I didn't wait for permission. I grabbed our scorecard, jumped over seats, pushed away anyone in front of me, and ran into the crowd. I pushed, squirmed, slithered around and underneath, and made my way to my hero. I couldn't speak but held out my program. He took my pen and said nothing. He didn't have to. I looked into his face, down at the program, back at precious uniform, his faint smile. Someone snapped a flashbulb. I whispered a "thank you."

I floated back to my seat, showed my Dad our treasure, snuggled closer, and stared at the scribbling on the inside page. I didn't let go the whole game except when I stood up and clapped when Stan doubled off the right field fence in his one and only time at bat.

The next morning, my mother came into my bedroom smiling, carrying the newspaper. "Charles, you don't want to sleep in today. I know you were up late last night but I think you might want to look at this morning's sports section. Here it is. Look who's on the front page."

My jaw dropped, my eyes widened, and I let out a huge, "Wow!" There on the front page of the sports section was Stan Musial signing a scorecard for a skinny kid wearing a white T-shirt and a distinctive grin. It was me, all aglow, getting an autograph from the man himself. My big day could now be preserved in my scrapbook and in the archives of the Rochester Times Union.

Newspapers turn yellow and fade, but Stan the Man is still my hero. That priceless photograph survived moves after high school, college, dental school, the army, and on to Cape Cod. Somehow it was later lost but remains a clear picture in my mind, like it was taken yesterday.

Conesus Lake

When my Uncle built his cottage at Conesus Lake I was too young to hammer nails but old enough to stay out of the way. As I stood back and I watched my father and two uncles sawing, pounding, and fitting pieces together, I had no idea this modest structure would have such a major impact on my life. My Uncle Harris made so many good choices when planning this camp that if he wanted to create a perfect haven for young boys, he accomplished his goal.

He picked a great location. It was right in the middle of an eight mile long lake about an hour drive from our house in Rochester. A footbridge adjacent to the camp led across a creek to a path to Long Point Park where kids could play arcade games as long as their coins lasted. On Saturday nights in the summer black and white movies flashed on a screen high over the crowd. We watched Tom Mix chase the bad guys or Flash Gordon dash through space to save our world. Often they were serials where the hero was left falling over a cliff at the end while we had to wait a whole week to see him jump and swim for safety. The hero prevailed by the end of the month proving again that crime doesn't pay and we had better behave.

For two pennies we could buy five by three black and white baseball cards of Ted Williams, Joe DiMaggio, or my favorite Stan Musial. If I had only saved those penny treasures I could now sell them and buy each of my kids a new car. On special occasions, or maybe when we hung around too long annoying my Aunt Jean, she bribed us each a quarter to play miniature golf. My cousin Art was a full year older than me so he usually kept score and managed to win the contests. A nickel was enough for an ice cream cone with a choice of vanilla, chocolate or strawberry. We weighed ourselves on a scale that also told our fortune-"You will have some tough times ahead but will succeed if you persist and work hard." I had to stand on a box to peek over the window ledge to watch teen agers roller skate around in a circle to the accompaniment of popular music, like Patti Page's "The Tennessee Waltz" or a Bing Crosby love song.

The creek next to the cottage was full of water runoff from nearby hills in the spring but mostly dried up in summer. Deep pools were a great place to catch Polly wags, tad poles, and croaking frogs. On an especially lucky day, minnows got trapped in a pool and we delighted in catching them in a tin can and setting them free in the lake. As we got older and more adventurous, we walked up the dry creek bed into the dark woods where strange animal sounds sent us scurrying back to the cottage and the safety of the adults. Art once claimed he really did see a bear. I wondered at the time if he was just tired of walking and wanted to see how fast we could make our retreat to the camp.

Meals were served on paper plates at a fold out table near the large picture window facing the lake. I tried to wedge in close enough so I wouldn't lose sight of the precious lake. Hot dogs, either red Texas or white Porkers, smothered with chopped onions, relish, mustard and catsup never tasted as good as they did in that cottage. Fresh corn on the cob bought from a local farm went down easily, painted with butter and sprinkled with salt. Juicy watermelon when in season dripped down our chins so we usually had to take them outside and spit the seeds on the ground. Cousin Art took pride in showing he could spit his farther than mine.

My second set of parents and always my favorite relatives were the owners of the cottage, my Aunt Jean and Uncle Harris. They taught me how to have fun and enjoy the moment. They enjoyed each other and whatever they did they did with zest unique to them. Even in the winter, I was sometimes treated to an overnight at their house where I could stay up and watch profession wrestling. Our family didn't have a TV set but I kept up with the antics of Gorgeous George or Yukon Eric at my second home, their house. Friday night boxing introduced me to Kid Gavilon, with his bolo punch, the lightening fast Sugar Ray Robinson, and Archie Moore.

I can't remember Aunt Jean without a smile on her face and that joy radiated to others lucky enough to be around her. It didn't matter if the weather was rainy, sunny, cold, or stifling hot, her mood was always sunny. She belly laughed over little things like a cute remark from a child or one of her own mistakes like over cooking a hotdog and watching the contorted face of her husband as he faked agony to eat the charred remains.

I had more fun with Uncle Harris than any other person in that period of my life. He went beyond being a mere role model, companion, and friend. Most of my relatives were conservative and quiet in social situations. Not Uncle Harris. We often had to delay lunches while we searched the neighborhood and pried him loose in mid conversation with a neighbor.

I caught my first bass with him, a 10 ½ inch beauty that jumped three times before he scooped the net underneath and brought him aboard our motorboat. One night we fished with the aid of a Coleman lantern and I caught two walleyed pike on some spinner worm combination that he sold in his hardware store. Before we sent the baits overboard he rubbed this special fish attracting oil on the worms. When I pulled in the second one he exclaimed, "Wow It works. That stuff really works." After he caught one, he remarked, "You know Charlie, You catch all these fish. If I went home with nothing again, people would wonder if I know how to fish."

One day, after he picked me up at the house, we drove to this isolated creek not too far out of the way to his cottage and dragged a trap for small crabs. The next day we used those crabs to catch a stringer full of delicious perch on this special place on Conesus Lake where the larger fish laid under the sea weed. I learned from him. After catching this mess of fish, he said, "You know some people have to go a long way to catch fish or have fun. We caught these right near our cottage instead of going off to the end of the lake. Fun is where you make it. We could've built the cottage in the Adirondack Mountains but here we are close to home. You make your own fun in this world and you don't have to go half way around the world to do it." He was an expert at having fun.

I had a rite of passage with him the day he let me steer his motorboat. It was a 14 wooden scow propelled by a 10 horsepower Johnson outboard. It may have been one of the slowest boats on the lake but I knew I had passed a certain age milestone when he moved over and, said, "Charles, why don't you take us home." He even let me steer into the dock. I couldn't say, "Yes," fast enough when he hopped out and asked, "Would you like to take it out by yourself." He trusted me with that precious motorboat. My chest swelled when I returned home after that weekend and bragged to my friends what I had done.

One of my sister Betty's boyfriends and I invented a new sport just off my Uncle Harris's dock. We liked to snorkel and fish so we combined them into one sport. With our snorkel and fins on, we floated on an inner tube and fished with an old rod and reel. We looked down into the water through our masks, found the largest perch, and then dangled our worms in front of him. We watched him swallow the bait, swim to try to dislodge the hook and then reeled him in. If it didn't swallow too much of the worm, we took him off the hook, stuffed him in our bathing suit and went after another one. We swam, snorkeled, fished, and floated all at the same time.

Uncle Harris and Aunt Jean square danced together. They also raised chickens, traveled, and even worked together. Their hardware store was so successful because they enjoyed each moment with each other and with their customers.

When I got a few years older, I was more interested in sports like baseball or basketball than fishing. He sold me my first very own baseball glove- a three fingered Bob Feller model that I cherished for years. He also constructed a wooden bang board so I could shoot baskets indefinitely in my back yard. The True Temper fishing rod and reel he sold me lasted for fifty years. My gratitude to these two special people will last forever. They were always there, always on my side, teaching me how to enjoy life.

Genesee Valley Park

Genesee Valley Park in Rochester. New York is not a long way from the house I grew up in. Today if you drove from 149 Elmerston Road to Genesee Valley Park you'd arrive before the engine of the car heated up. It wouldn't take more than ten minutes and pennies worth of gas, but in those days before we owned a car, it took days.

It took at least three days just to plane the trip. We had to decide what snacks to bring, whether hot dogs or hamburgers, whether to bring sweat shirts for the cold Rochester summer breezes or prepare for rain that often attacked on the day of a picnic sending us scurrying for the shelters. We didn't have to decide who was going because we were all going, my mother, father, three sisters and me. Me? I'm Charles, the youngest and only boy. When we started out in those days, I pictured myself at the end of our single file family hiking unit. My father would lead, followed by my three sisters in order of birth, Betty the first, the oldest, smartest and prettiest. She was my favorite. Mary followed her, struggling behind trying to keep up; she wore thick glasses, sometimes with an eye patch, and was always nice to me. Flora, the cute freckled face one followed. She was so cute she sucked her thumb like a baby right up until junior high school when her first boyfriend shamed her to stop. My mother came next, always nurturing, following my Dad, keeping everyone happy. I tagged along with her. She was my friend making sure I didn't get lost in the family pecking order assuring us all that we were loved, that we were important

We filed down Elmerston Road, passed Castleman Road, the 'busy street" and then through the woods towards the park. We passed construction on the right which was the "New apartments" and my first look at clustered housing. We owned our own house and I felt sorry for people who had to live in those small places. Beyond the woods we came to a clearing where we walked alongside the Barge Canal for a few paces. The locks smelled. It smelled like sewage, like a combination of feces and garbage, something rotten beneath the maggots in our garbage can, something to avoid, not touch, something very dirty and sickening.

There was a man in a little house that tended the locks and pushed a lever that opened and closed them when boat traffic passed by. I think the whole thing was an anachronism because I never remember any boat traffic on the canal. It was a throwback to the "Old days," the days of navigation on the Erie Canal. "Low Bridge everybody down" low bridge for we're goin' through a town, Have you ever known your neighbor have you ever known your pal If you've ever navigated on the Erie Canal." Less colorful railroads, trucks, and later airplanes put an end to the Erie Canal. For some reason it was renamed the less romantic, "Barge Canal."

Alongside the canal a narrow dirt path led past some real danger. There was a tall metal column that held high tension wires and "if you touched them you could get electrocuted." I didn't know what that meant but they said it was a terrific shock that could kill you. I didn't want me or anyone in my family to touch that edifice.

After the locks and the edifice, came the railroad tracks. We all had to stop, wait for the last in line which was me and scramble over the tracks without getting our foot stuck. If you get your foot stuck, "you might not be able to free it when the trains came and you'd get run over, maybe die or worse, lose your leg." I also don't remember ever seeing a train pass. I heard them from my bedroom window in the middle of the night. It sounded exciting, like an invitation to see the world beyond my house.

Also the tracks were a place where "bums hung out." I didn't know what bums were but pictured them as bad old men who did evil things to little kids. I was born in 1941 so most of the so called "bums" from that era were more than likely unfortunate unemployed men from the depression era. All those sophisticated insights would come years later with maturity at Monroe High School.

Over the tracks and through some more woods we finally came to Genesee Valley Park. We still had to hang together because "bad guys can hang out in parks. We don't want them to get any of you kids."

"What's a kidnapper," I wanted to ask, but when I did I always got some kind of an evasive answer. It was never defined but I knew I shouldn't talk to strangers, don't take candy from anybody, and don't wander away. Wow! I didn't know the world was so dangerous in those innocent, halcyon days until I started to write about these picnics in the park.

My favorite times in the park revolved around my father's bag pipe band practices. His Scottish John White Johnson Bagpipe Band had to practice there. Twenty pipers going full blast with kettle drums and a big base drum were not welcome near civilized neighborhoods. My dad was the pipe major, the best piper in the band, always near the front in a parade, the one asked to play at weddings and funerals, He was good. Whenever he was near his fellow Scottish bagpipers, he started talking funny like them, with a brogue. He was born in Scotland but his brogue only became prominent when he was near his friends from "the old country." I thought he was putting it on but my sister Betty called it "a phenomenon." What's a phenomenon?" I wondered at the time.

I had my first crush years later on a Scottish girl named Jeannie Archibald. Her father or grandfather played in the band and I found myself staring at her. She was pretty and was able to dance the Highland Fling. I don't know if she could do the Sword Dance but even the big base drummer wearing the leopard's skin followed her every movement. Her bottom gyrated around in a circle when she walked. I think she necked with guys without even marrying them. I never did get to talk to her. I was too shy, too young, and she was too pretty.

One time I remember I was alone in the park with my grandmother. I don't know how it happened but we were walking back home over the tracks, past the dangerous edifice to just before the locks when she said, "Charles, you stand here, I'm going into the woods, I'm OK but don't come in and don't look." She went into the woods, I turned around and looked, her pants were down and she was going poopy." It was my first look at a woman with her pants down and it wasn't pretty. I think I've had a normal life so I guess I wasn't seriously traumatized.

Another incident with using the woods as a toilet happened years later when I was in dental school and I brought home my first ultra-serious girl friend, Marilyn, who later became my wife. My dad and mom walked with us to Genesee Valley Park over much of the same terrain we passed as a young family. I had an attack of diarrhea and told Marilyn I had to go into the woods. She giggled and thought it was funny. I told my parents to wait for us. I did my business and when I came out my Mom asked "How did you wipe yourself?"

I turned red and whispered my confession that I used my underpants and expected the issue to be ended.

My loving wonderful Mother persisted, "Well what did you do with your pants?"

"I left them in the woods Mom. They're ruined. They stink. Forget it."

"But Charles, they can be washed. You go back and get them." In an effort to be a good son, I did go back, wrapped them in a towel, and my Mom washed them out. This was indeed a Scottish family where absolutely nothing was thrown away or certainly not wasted. Marilyn got a preview of what she was getting into before the wedding.

The park was a happy place. Besides bagpipe practice there were scheduled band concerts in a shell. Tubas, trumpets, brasses of all sorts blasted out their patriotic rhythms to clapping crowds. We couldn't stay up late to see the finish because we tried to march home to the music before dark. We would never ever spend the money to take a cab.

I was eight years old before we purchased our first car. I was proud of our new Nash Rambler with white sidewall tires and fancy hood ornament, but I didn't realize at the time that we paid a heavy price. It signaled the end of walking through those dangerous, exciting passages to family fun in the park. We joined the fifties generation with cars and TV sets later than most families and I'm glad we waited.

Father's Dilemma- Me

My Dad always gave up his seat on the bus to a woman, tipped his hat when they passed by, and pulled out their chair at the dinner table. He was kind, seldom spoke against anyone, and never complained. Besides being the world's nicest man, he was also the straightest. He always wore a bow tie and suit to work, seldom missed church on Sundays, and never cursed. On the golf course, he might say "darn it," when a drive went into the woods but nothing stronger. He sang church hymns loudly but off key, changing pitch when the notes went beyond his range. He closed both eyes when he prayed, switching into his Scottish brogue in reciting The Lord's Prayer with the congregation. He refused communion, either because he rejected the ritual or maybe because of its association with wine. The Baptist Church substituted grape juice for wine but he still abstained.

In an expansive mood one day, he confessed to me that he tried beer once with his father, didn't like "that smelly stuff," and never touched alcohol again. Two of my sisters had fancy, formal weddings, but Dad rejected my sister's pleas to loosen up. "Sorry, no alcohol." When guests arrived and asked, "Where's the booze?" the negative response was sobering.

One of Flora's high school boyfriends put a couple of "Birch Beers" in our refrigerator and Dad threw it out, mistakenly thinking it contained alcohol. His uncompromising beliefs and my quest for independence naturally produced major conflicts during my teenage years.

New York was the only state at the time to allow eighteen year olds to drink. I was shy with girls and took to beer drinking to ease dating stress. Returning home from one of my first nights "out with the boys," I had no front door key, so had to knock for help. As he approached, I straightened up, put on a serious face, said "Hi," and hiccupped in his face. Maybe he was sleep walking, or maybe he just fed up with confrontation with his rebellious son, because he said nothing. I slept without a fight.

A night I still feel guilty about was on one of my first vacations home from college. I barrowed his almost new Mercury Marquise and told him I was double dating with a friend and going to a movie. Instead, we went directly to a "Gay Nineties Bar," and drank enough pitchers of beer to get us all feeling very good. I was only eighteen, hadn't driven much, and definitely had a strong reaction to a few beers. While driving our dates home, I put my arm around the cutie snuggled next to me. As I reached over her head, my steering hand jerked the car to the right, over the curb, and sideswiped a 'NO PARKING" sign. No one was hurt but we sobered up fast. Steve, my friend, staggered out, viewed the crashed in right side of the car and announced, "Charlie, you're absolutely screwed. The McClung Mobile (our pet name for my father's car) is dead, and so will you be."

The accident was witnessed by no one and the damage didn't prevent me from driving our dates and Steve to their houses. I returned home, drove slowly into our driveway, eased the car into the garage, and surveyed the damage. "Shit Charlie, you are screwed," I said to myself. There was no broken glass but the fender and front door on that side looked terminal. I tiptoed up the stairs, not bothering to brush my teeth, fearing the sound would wake my parents. I didn't sleep that night and the first thing I heard in the morning was, "Charles, what happened last night. The car is ruined?"

I jumped out of bed, feeling like a cornered animal, grasping at any distant hope, knowing that the truth was not an option. "I'm sorry Dad, we went to the movies last night and when we came out, someone hit the car. It was parked. I'm sorry."

My wonderful, trusting father chose to accept that explanation and merely answered, "We'll have to fill out an accident report for the insurance company." God was with me again because I was returning to college the next day, escaping more questions and possible accusations. In a phone call two weeks later, he revealed, "Charles, our insurance man said the damage was pretty extensive to be from a crash into a parked car, but they're paying the claim, anyway. We've never filed a claim with them before, this is our first." Despite my best efforts to lose his trust and screw up my life forever, he stuck with me. He seemed to know when to confront and when to lay back. I learned from him and hopefully, walk in his footprints today.

Another time I tested his patience with me was my trouble in Mrs. Murphy's science class. Mrs. Murphy had a well deserved reputation as the worst teacher in the school. She had been teaching too long, didn't like kids, and they didn't like her. My three sisters preceded me at Monroe High and warned me about this horrible lady who taught tenth grade biology. They told how all the cool kids in the school tormented the poor woman and I wanted to be cool. I was agonizingly shy with girls but longed for their approval. I assumed that the way to gain their attention and be a cool guy was to be cruel to this pathetic old woman.

I was lucky because three of the most popular girls at Monroe were in biology class with me. A favorite sadistic trick of obnoxious teen agers like me was to have someone in one corner of the room start humming loudly. Humming doesn't require lip movement so she couldn't tell who was doing it. She would turn sharply towards the distraction and demand, "Stop that humming, right now." That hummer would stop then another sadist in the opposite corner would start. Soon the whole room was humming and the distraught old woman would be frantic, turning in all directions, completely losing control of the class and herself.

Since this was biology class, the shelves of the room were stocked with skeletons, frog diagrams, and an aquarium with live fish. I loved fish and all living creatures even then but I needed the attention of the young beauties even more. Those were the pre ballpoint pen days of inkwells and fountain pens. While Mrs. Murphy wrote something on the blackboard and turned her back to the class, I strolled over and to everyone's delight, poured black ink in her fish tank. The class roared, I retreated to my seat and Mrs. Murphy snapped to attention, "All right class, what's going on? Stop this foolishness right now." The more she bellowed, the more everyone laughed, and again there was chaos

This time however, I, we, went too far. She looked at the darkened fish tank and demanded to know, "Who poured ink in my fish tank? This class will not proceed; we will not be dismissed, until I know who did this horrible deed." The class was silent, no one spoke but I, already feeling remorse and not wanting to involve my innocent classmates, stood up and confessed, "I did Mrs. Murphy. I poured ink in your fish tank."

She didn't wait for an explanation because there was none. She pointed to the door and said, "Charles, you get out of my class right now and never, ever come back. Go to the principal's office. I never want to see you again." That was a serious threat because I was college bound. I was from a family where my going to college was an accepted fact, like puberty, and if I didn't pass high school biology, no decent college would accept me. I sat for one week in the principal's office, contemplating my misdeeds, and confronting my own cruelty to her. When others went to their fourth period classes, I sat with the principal, feeling guilty, and worrying for the first time about my future.

After a week of stewing, feeling like a hardened criminal, Mr. Lowell, the high school principal, said, "Charles, you've never been in trouble like this before. You've always been a good kid. I don't know what's going on but I will see if Mrs. Murphy will take you back in class if you apologize to her and bring your father to school for a conference with me."

"Oh damn," I thought, "Now I've got to drag my long suffering father into my foolishness." I had no choice however so two days later my Dad came to school to try and bail out his wastrel son. He took time from his job, sat across from Mr. Lowell, both wearing bow ties and both with very serious expressions on their faces. I cringed and wanted to die. Mr. Lowell did all the talking, explaining about teen age rebellion, confusion of maturation, Oedipus Complexes and other psychological terms I didn't understand. My poor father nodded in agreement and said little. I was too intimidated to speak.

After a lifetime of talking, Mr. Lowell revealed that Mrs. Murphy had reluctantly agreed to permit me back in her class but if I did anything the least bit out of line, I would be suspended and receive a failing grade in biology. I assured them both that I had learned my lesson and I would never again be a problem to her or anyone else.

The next day when I walked in the classroom door, everyone stood up and cheered like I had just scored a touchdown. Mrs. Murray looked at me and said, "Charles, I won't tolerate any more disturbances like this. If you can't behave, you can go right back to the principal's office."

I said, "I'm sorry Miss Murphy. I didn't say anything. I assure you my friends and I will cooperate."

They did, I got a B in biology, and eventually was accepted into college. I again thank my Dad for sticking with me. He had an immigrant's serious attitude toward education, and surely didn't understand how his son, offered every opportunity to learn, could choose to squander it away. It wasn't the last time I risked everything for the approval of a woman.

A Date with Jean

I finally had a date with Jean. I had met her between classes, carried her books, ogled at her continuously, and day dreamed about her all day, every day. She was a perky, blond cheer leader, with huge blue eyes that made me swoon. I was the basketball player she gave a personal cheer for before every game. She was a freshman, I a sophomore which was a perfect fit into unwritten social mores of high school. The only problem was that I was painfully shy, especially with her. I knew she liked me but my brain was reduced to jello by excessive teenage hormones. I couldn't talk to her or look her in the eye. She'd smile and my head would go down and my mouth dried up, leaving me speechless. Worst of all, my face blushed red.

Somehow I did conjure up courage enough to ask her to a movie for the next weekend. She accepted with enthusiasm and now the Friday was here. My first challenge came before I left home. I wore my best Chino pants but they weren't dressy enough for my very conservative father. "Wear your good charcoal gray pants, Charles. Treat this poor girl with respect." This fashion advice came from a man who wore an outdated bow tie to work every day. We fought and I eventually compromised with something between Sunday best and everyday school clothes.

I walked to Jean's house where she met me at the door and she was beyond cute. She was a beautiful, charming love goddess. She smiled and winked and talked with ease while I froze. The only thing I could think of to say was, "My Dad and I just had a fight. He wanted me to wear a suit. I couldn't"

She spoke up, "I think you look great. I'm glad we're finally going out on a date. I've been looking forward to this."

"Me too," was probably my only contribution to our conversation on that long walk to the theatre.

She rambled on, "My Dad sometimes gets on my nerves too. He's really a good guy but has funny ideas about kids. My Mom's my best buddy in the world. She helps me a lot. I thank God for both my parents. I know they love me and that's what's important." She continued talking, praising her parents, delighting in the world while I became more intimidated with each word.

The movie was, "Bridge on the River Kwi," with William Holden and Alex Guinness. As soon as the lights went out, I stretched my arm around the back of her chair and actually got nerve enough to touch her right shoulder with my hand. I wanted to kiss her but that was impossible so I held my right arm in that position until it not only went to sleep but cramped from my shoulder to the tip of my fingers. Before the Bridge over the river was finished I lifted my paralyzed arm down with my left hand and sat innocently while circulation was restored.

My next move was to touch her left hand with my right one. We touched and she grabbed onto my hand and held it. I was ecstatic. I even managed to look her way in the darkened theatre and force a smile. *Life is good I thought* or at least it's good until that hand cramped up again. There came a time in the movie when the bridge was blown up and everyone in the theatre clapped. I used the time to withdraw my hand and restore its normal function.

After the show, she suggested a coke at the nearby restaurant. It was fine except I now had to sit face to face with her in a well lit booth. My panicky shyness came on strongly and I choked. She talked about everything while I fidgeted. "Did you like the movie, Charlie?"

"Yeh, I liked it."

She bubbled on, "It was so realistic. The jungle, the strength of the men. I can't believe what those poor guys went through to win that war. I'll be humming that music for weeks I'm sure. And William Holden was so handsome and brave. Don't you think, Charlie?"

"Yeh, he was," I agreed.

With effort I managed a few utterances about English class or the next basketball game but everything was forced, monosyllabic, and in hushed tones.

I paid the $1.50 bill and then we began the long walk to her house. The words just did not come. I felt too inadequate to try to hold her hand and assumed she had lost interest in any form of affection. *How could she want to hold hands with me when I was being such a dork?* My self abuse was in full blossom until we mercifully reached her house. She maybe wanted a hug or a kiss but all I could muster was a faint, "Thanks a lot. I had a good time," and shuffled away, head down.

In retrospect, if that "was a good time" I don't know what torture would feel like.

Animals Invade
the MIT DU House

I picked up the phone near the front door of the Tufts University Delta Upsilon house and a voice identified himself at the other end as a member of the MIT DU fraternity. He was inviting us over for what he clearly described as a house wrecking party. They were going to tear down their house and were planning one last wild party before the wrecking ball came to complete the job.

That sounded like a unique chance to have some fun and enhance our own reputation as our campus animal house. I passed the word that Saturday night we were all to get dates, go to MIT and help them wreck their house.

A friend and I picked up our dates from the girls dorm and then drove into Cambridge to the fraternity house. It was already loaded with students from any school in New England that had a Delta Upsilon Chapter. The house looked in good shape to me and I couldn't understand why they needed to tear it down but it wasn't my decision. We arrived early but the huge party room was already jammed full of drunken college students. It was difficult to move in the smoke filled room. I could hardly recognize my date standing next to me. I didn't know her well and after my first beer, I was more focused on having fun than impressing her.

A guy with a bull horn announced the beginning of the Chug-a-lug beer contest. Each school picked a team of four fast drinkers for a relay contest. Each participant drank a 16 ounce beer from a paper cup, turned the cup over on his head to show it was empty, and then the next in line did the same until all four were finished. The winner of that round went on to challenge in the next.

I was chosen as point man on our team. Five teams lined up, each participant held a cup filled to the brim. The horn sounded, I downed the whole 16 ounces in two gulps, put the empty cup on my head, the next guy extended the lead, and the four of us finished way before their last member started. We were good. We congratulated each other like we had just done something significant. My eyes were hazy from beer and smoke, my stomach was full of Budweiser but I sipped some more as I watched the next two contests. Teams were eliminated and then the three winners challenged for the championship. I had no idea where my date was, who she was, or what she thought of the show. I was focused only on winning the contest and contributing to the wrecking of the house.

We lined up, the horn sounded and despite my slow start, our team won. We were champion beer drinkers of the New England DUs.

I don't remember clearly the details of the rest of the party but certain images appear like shadows through a fog. Bobby Gold thought it was fun to throw ink all over a bedroom wall until someone came and convinced us that wasn't a fraternal thing to do.

Later, I stood on a winding stairway, with my back to the wall, trying to get enough leverage to kick down the banister. I was so proud of my efforts that when someone came and asked what the hell I was doing and why, I bragged, "I'm Chuck from Tufts." and couldn't understand why he wasn't helping me. He asked what I was doing it for and I said, "Because this is a house wrecking party." His plea of, "No it isn't." didn't really register at the time but I didn't resist when a friend came and hustled me off the stairway. I was sober enough to remain silent when people hunted through the crowd yelling, "Where is Chuck from Tufts?"

The last image penetrating the haze was the grand farewell. A beautiful chandelier hung in the foyer. I grabbed hold and swung across the room like Errol Flynn in an old swashbuckler movie. This time someone stated emphatically, "Charlie, this is not a house wrecking party. You're being a big jerk. All you're doing is fucking up somebody's house."

I jumped down and thought *Now they tell me. What took you so long*? I had enough sense hold on to my date and stagger directly to the car, without saying good night or begging for forgiveness.

"Shit that was fun," were the only parting words I could muster at my date's dorm. I didn't consider a good night kiss. I'm sure that was our one and only date.

Years later, when I was a responsible dentist, father, husband, and somewhat respected member of a Cape Cod community, a patient came into my office and together we laughed about the new John Beluchi movie, "Animal House." We agreed that it was a comedy classic. He volunteered, "You know I was at a party like that once."

I said, "Was it by any chance at the MIT DU house?"

"It sure was. Were you there too?" I felt an immediate bond but didn't go into detail about being, "Chuck from Tufts."

Fall in Love

Marilyn and I had been dating for a month when I thought it was time that she saw my apartment and meet my roommates. I lived with four other dental students in six rooms above a laundry. It was on the corner of Merrimac Street, a short walk from the house where she lived with her family.

Five busy guys, crowded together in tight conditions can accumulate a lot of clutter. A friend warned me that this special woman would be repulsed by a mess so I spent the afternoon cleaning. I scrubbed the shower, scrapped the mildew off the walls, washed the dirty dishes that were piled in the sink, hid the mousetraps, and made my bed. I wanted her to like me and be impressed by my roommates and our apartment. That evening, we were on our way to the library to study together when I casually asked if she'd like to see where I lived. She said yes so we took a little detour upstairs. She charmed my roommates and politely complimented us on how neat we kept everything. We stayed only a few minutes. We both had a lot of work to do.

A long straight stairway was our only passageway in and out of our living area. Its steepness was probably the reason that the rent was so cheap and limited the possible renters to young students. There were no landings or breaks in the steady descent down to Main Street. When we stood at the top of the stairway, I put my arm out to support her and the other hand reached for the guard rail. Instead of helping her, I took one step into an abyss. With nothing to catch me, I fell like a bouncing ball down the twenty plus steps to the bottom. I never felt myself going; the world just went out from beneath me. I rolled, tumbled, fell, gathering momentum all the way until I crashed into the door at the bottom.

I didn't realize what happened. My body parts moved without too much pain so I assumed that I was all right. Marilyn came down with a startled look on her face. "Are you okay?" she asked.

I rubbed my back and shoulders, "Yeh, I guess so."

I stood up slowly, grabbing onto the hand railing that I had missed coming down. She started chuckling, shyly at first, and then broke into full belly laughs. She was soon out of control and had to struggle to say, "I'm sorry for laughing but you looked so funny rolling down those stairs. It was like those Saturday morning cartoons. Maybe the Three Stooges." The more she tried to stifle her laughter, the more she lost control. Tears flowed down her cheeks and her face was a bright red. She tried to speak but couldn't. She calmed down slightly and said, "I'm sorry. Really. You could've been hurt."

I laughed too when I envisioned a body, mine, free falling down the stairs. "I'm glad I entertained you. C'mon, let's get to the library." Any attempt to regain my lost dignity was futile.

We went outside into the cold Buffalo winter. The sidewalks were icy, piles of snow lining both sides of the street, the wind blowing in our faces. She pulled her wool scarf around her neck and mumbled, "It must be genetic-laughing in a crises I mean. My sister and I were cooking breakfast in our kitchen one morning. I leaned against the stove and the back of my shirt tail caught on fire. I couldn't stop the fire. I jumped around, rolled on the floor, rubbed against the walls and finally got it out. My sister was standing right there but instead of helping, she was bent over laughing at me. She apologized, 'I'm sorry Marilyn but you looked so funny rolling around like that, on fire. I can't help it.' You Charlie, looked just as ridiculous tumbling down those stairs."

I put my arm around her shoulder and we laughed together. I dismissed the hard hearted aspect of her reaction and just admired this unique person who could find such humor in a crisis. I melted right there in those freezing Buffalo temperatures. I wanted to kiss the snow resting on her eye lash but instead we continued walking to the library. I never did cool my passion for her.

Months later, she accepted my marriage proposal, but told me that I had to formally request her parent's permission. My initial reaction was, "Are you serious?" but I would have done anything for her.

One Sunday morning after going to the Unitarian Church together, her Mother and Father sat with us at their dining room table. We enjoyed a nice dinner together and talked easily about everything except our marriage. We all knew what was coming but I still had to go through the process. The dessert was finished, the plates were cleared and after a long silence, I squirmed in my chair and I asked, "With your permission, I would like to marry Marilyn."

Her mother leaned towards me with a very serious expression and replied, "As long as you love our Marilyn, you may marry her."

I almost interrupted her in answering, "I do. Oh, I do I do love your daughter."

I did then and I still do.

We shared many more laughs in our too short time together.

PART II

Cobleskill

Job Interview

This was the big interview. I was getting out of the Army in six months and needed a place to go. Re-enlisting was not an option. I didn't want to be separated from my family. Half of the dentists were shipped to Vietnam for one year but I had been lucky. I couldn't press this good fortune any longer; I needed a place to settle down.

I had been to Cobleskill before, met Bill, liked him and the beautiful little village in the Catskill Mountains. I had mentally committed to him and the town but I still needed to impress him enough that he would hire me. Marilyn drove me to the airport that morning and now I was about to land at the Albany Airport where Bill would meet me for the hour drive to Cobleskill. My hair was neatly combed, my shoes shined, I checked my deodorant. This trip, I would meet Bill's wife and three children and I had to impress everyone. "First impressions mean everything," Marilyn had reminded me. I was glad to be landing because I was getting airsick from all that flying. I wasn't afraid of planes but all those ups and downs and the turns would often send me scurrying for an airsick bag.

I was glad to be on solid ground again. No more flying until my return trip in two days. "Hi Bill," I saved my warmest smile and sincerest handshake for this moment.

"Hi, Charlie. How was your flight? You look great."

"My trip was fine. You look well, too." And he did look well. He had been a college football player only a few years before and now was an avid skier which kept his body young. His blonde hair was neatly trimmed, his clothes immaculate, he looked like he was prepared for the sterile conditions of a dental office right there in the airport.

"Hey, Charlie. This is my son Billy. He wanted to be the first to meet you."

I reached out and shook the hand of the handsome, smiling 6 year old boy. "I'm pleased to meet you Billy. Thanks for coming all this way just to pick me up." He backed up a step as if he was trying to appraise this new guy who might be working with his Dad. I picked up my small traveling bag and said, "Where's the car."

Bill answered, "Oh, I didn't drive. I brought my airplane. Come on. It's parked over here."

I took one look at his small Piper Cub and shuttered, thinking of more turbulence in that small plane. I managed to say, "Oh, that's great. What a surprise."

"Here," said Bill, "We'll put your stuff in the back, with Billy. You ride up front with me. You'll get a bird's eye view of Schoharie County."

"Are you sure? Maybe Billy would like the front." I was not so much being polite as trying to get as far away from my prospective boss as possible if I was going to throw up my breakfast along the way."

"Oh no. You'll see so much better from up here," said Bill with great enthusiasm

"If you're sure it's OK." I was trying not to be negative but the first thing I looked for when I came aboard was an airsick bag. I saw none and realized that this was going to be a challenge. My job, my family's future, my ego were all dependent on me controlling myself on this flight. I could feel every bump on the runway as he taxied out to our take off point. The roar of the engine sounded like two jet planes. I fastened my seat belt and wondered if I had paid that last life insurance premium.

"Pilot to tower. This is B708 ready for take off." He spoke with authority into the radio microphone. The engines roared even louder. It did sound like he knew what he was doing. I was getting into some pretty fancy company here with this young dentist already owning an airplane. The engine roared, Bill turned a few gadgets, pushed wheel forward and we were air born.

"That was nice. Smooth. How long have you been flying?" I asked just for conversation.

"I've been flying for months but I just passed my solo exam. Come on we'll dive down to Howe Caverns"

"Oh God," I thought. *"Why have you forsaken me?"* He pushed the stick forward, the plane dove and my stomach heaved. But I said, "You sure know what you're doing. This is wonderful." I thought, *"Where is that damn airsick bag? What good is a plane without an airsick bag? I think my good luck has just ended."* I started to taste the eggs that I had eaten hours before. *"Why the hell did I have to eat breakfast this morning? It's Marilyn's fault. She insisted on those damn eggs so I would be sharp for my interview. I knew I shouldn't. Now I'm screwed. Damn it."* Bill said something about root canals or impacted molars. *"What the hell do I care about someone else's troubles,"* I thought. *"I've got plenty of my own right here"* But I said, with commendable control, "Oh yes, I like to do root canals but I still have a lot to learn about molars."

Now the eggs were well out of my stomach and gathering for takeoff in my esophagus. Bill looked at my colorless face. "Are you OK?" he asked.

"Well, Sometimes I get sick in airplanes," I said in the understatement of a lifetime. I made the quick decision that my eggs and everything else that I'd eaten in the last week would within seconds be splattered all over this beautiful new airplane which was his pride and joy. I was beyond hope. It was too late for bargaining with God. He must be busy anyway. If I had my travel bag with me I could let go in that, but that was in the back seat with Billy. I reached up, grabbed my shirt by the collar, took it off and everything erupted immediately into my pressed shirt. I was exploding. My shirt was filling and I couldn't stop. I had visions of the shirt overflowing and maybe I would keep vomiting until I brought the plane down. Tears flowed down my cheeks. The noise, the smell made me sicker. Finally my stomach was empty but the noise of my stomach was louder than the airplane. My breakfast, my pride and probably my job were gone.

I imagined Billy in the back seat thinking, "I hope my Dad doesn't hire this jerk. Anybody but him." My stomach was now empty, my shirt full of a week's worth of partially digested food, and my pride, gone.

Bill said, "Sorry, Charlie. I didn't know you had a problem. We're almost there. Here's the runway." I looked down and saw that the "runway" was nothing more than a cleared farmer's field next to town. Bill's skillful landing brought us safely to my favorite place, Mother Earth.

I climbed out of the plane, bare chested, hair disheveled, with a wild look like Rambo. I carried my shirt carefully by the corners, so as not to spill the reeking contents. Before me stood Bill's beautiful wife Betsy, trailing two of the most all-American, apple pie eating kids imaginable. Billy lagged well behind, keeping a safe distance from the obnoxious intruder-me.

Bill tried to stay positive, "Come on Charlie. I'd like you to meet my wife, Betsy."

Instead of extending her hand, she stared, retreated two steps, forced a smile and said softly, "Welcome to Cobleskill."

Despite the auspicious start, we had a nice weekend together. After a long shower and a few drinks, Bill hired me. When he took me to the Albany Airport on Sunday, we drove.

The Ambulance Hearse

My last few months in the army were spent mostly anticipating our move to Cobleskill. I looked forward to being a civilian again, starting a new career and a new life. I was 29 years old with a wonderful wife and two perfect children. Bill and Betsy were very helpful to us in settling into Cobleskill. We bought our first house. It was a picturesque two story near the town square so I could walk to work and Marilyn could leisurely stroll around town with our two kids.

Bill had a second floor dental office over looking Main Street. Its central location and his professional expertise made him so busy that he had to hire me as his associate. It was the match made in heaven; I needed a job and he needed help. We were both young, ambitious, and happy in our profession. Our future was bright. All I had to do was build a good reputation in town and the business would skyrocket.

I had been there about a month and was getting comfortable in the practice when an emergency toothache came in for me to treat. I sat the old man down in the chair, took an X-ray and then went back to my scheduled patient while the X-ray developed. When I returned to the emergency patient, he said, "I don't feel well." I double checked his medical history and found nothing significant.

"How are you doing Mr. Cormier?" I asked.

"Not well Doc. I feel pretty weak." He was now moaning rather than talking.

I hadn't done anything yet so knew it wasn't from medication or a procedure. "Mr. Cormier, I'm going to lean you back in the chair and put this cold towel on your forehead." I noticed his skin was pale. "Do you feel any better?"

"Not really, Doc. I feel like I'm going to pass out." Drool was forming at the corners of his mouth and his glassy eyes stared off into the distance.

"Don't worry Mr.Cormier. You'll be OK." My heart was pounding. After about five minutes of him just getting weaker and me running out of options, I called my partner, Bill, into the room. He went through the same procedures I just had just done, without response, and then said, "Charlie, I think we ought to call an ambulance."

I agreed with him. We had no choice but in a small town like Cobleskill, the ambulance is the same vehicle as the hearse. It's a big black limo. People would confuse whether it was an ambulance that acted as a hearse or a hearse that acted like an ambulance. It was totally both so you could not tell if the client inside was going to the hospital or the morgue.

The ambulance driving mortician responded quickly to our call. His flashing red lights and siren blaring announced to the town that there was big news somewhere and when he parked his hearse at our front door on Main Street, everyone knew the source. A small town begs for the unusual to happen just to break the monotony but when the hearse pulls up to the dental office where that "new guy," just came to work, this is earthshaking. Crowds gathered and gossip started. "I hear that new dentist killed a guy in his office."

"Really? Wait until I tell Mildred." Etc.

The mortician and his assistant carried a stretcher up the stairs and into the office. While he took a pulse and analyzed the patient's condition, the other patients in the office whispered and stared. My own patient gave me a dirty look. The mortician didn't say a word but quickly lifted Mr. Cormier onto the stretcher and then carried him down the stairs, out the front door, into the waiting hearse. It seemed like the whole town was jockeying for a better view. The hearse sped off to the hospital with sirens blaring. "Were they signaling the end of my career?" I wondered.

When I returned to my patient, still in the chair, he looked at me like I was the Grim Reaper. He grabbed my hand as I approached with the drill and said, "Hey Doc, before you stick that thing in my mouth, Are you sure you're OK?"

I stopped shaking long enough to answer, "Of course, I'm fine, Open wide." Just like falling off a horse, you have to get back on.

Bill was completely cool and supportive throughout the crisis. Mr. Cormier was admitted into the hospital where they found that he was suffering from a bleeding ulcer. He had taken aspirin to alleviate his toothache and this aggravated his ulcer. In a few days, he was stabilized enough for me to go to the hospital and extract the offending tooth. The rumors subsided and the business kept coming and I enjoyed many happy days with the Lancaster family and the good people of Cobleskill.

PART III

Cape Cod

Seward House

I was thrilled to move to Cape Cod. We traded the six
months of harsh winter in Upstate New York for the steady
pounding of surf on Nauset Beach. A real estate salesman
sold us a beautiful old house he said was built by a sea
captain in 1820. He was a tight lipped Yankee and didn't
have much else to say about it. Marilyn and I both fell in
love with the place and were ready to spend the rest of
our lives there. Our dream house was a yellow Victorian,
perched on a prominent knoll, overlooking a marina across
the street. It sat on an acre of land, less than a mile from the
ocean. We were home at last.

A great house in a great location necessitated a lot of
debt, but I was young and confident. Within one week an
actual live patient came into my office to have some dental
work done. She was one of the grand old ladies of the town,
with weather scared skin and a kerchief tied over her head
to cover windblown hair. She squinted through thick glasses
that looked like they were ready to slide off her red nose.
"Welcome to Orleans," she said, and then added without
pause, "Did you know your house is haunted?"

I stiffened to attention. "What?" I said. "What did you say?"

"Your house, its haunted. Check it out. It's known as the Old Seward House. It's haunted. Don't worry, lots of the old houses around here are haunted. Most people don't pay much attention to that stuff nowadays. You'll be fine. Relax. Welcome to Orleans."

I thought, "Wait until Marilyn hears about this. We left the security of Cobleskill, with all that business, to come here, to the end of the Earth, with few patients. And now I've bought a haunted house." I feared that my impulsive move from our picturesque mountain village might be putting my family at risk.

After six years of marriage, I should have known how Marilyn would cope with a crisis like living in a haunted house. At first she shrugged it off and then started chuckling. Her chuckles soon progressed to gut tightening, eye watering, laughter.

I said, "Marilyn, are you all right? Sometimes you worry me. I just told you we are living in a haunted house and you think it's the funniest thing ever."

She slowly gained composure, pointed at me, and said, "Look at you. You're actually shook up over this thing. You don't really believe this house is haunted... Do you?"

"No. Of course not," I snapped back, trying to regain some dignity.

Despite her casual attitude, we did go hand in hand the next day to check the records at the town hall. We found that our new purchase was known as the Seward House, and a Judge Seward presided at the Salem Witch Trials centuries ago. The condemned witches supposedly put a curse on the judge and his relatives for all generations. He came to Orleans, built this summer house, and it had remained in his family, until we came along and bought it, one hundred and fifty years later. Our real estate salesman had omitted that bit of information from his sales pitch.

Was it haunted? Only if someone wanted it to be. This was in the days before bulldozers hit the Cape like an organized army, developing everything from the bridge to Provincetown. We had few neighbors, no street lights and by 6 o'clock in the winter, it was totally dark. The constant whistling sound of the wind invading our walls was interrupted only by the bashing of bare tree limbs lashing against our windows. Stores closed by 5PM and most restaurants were boarded up months before when the tourists left at the end of the summer. An old house standing alone against cold weather, with gray skies and trees bent double with the wind is a good backdrop for any ghost tale, especially when the seeds have been planted by local legend.

One winter night Marilyn and I were lying in bed listening to the howling wind when we heard a large animal, like a fox or a wolf attacking our walls. Marilyn shook my arm, "What is that?" she asked.

We moved closer together. I listened, then did the only thing a non macho guy like me could do; I pulled the covers over my ears, buried my head in the pillow and snuggled closer. "I don't know what that is and I'm not going to find out now. Let's hug. It can wait until morning."

I ignored her groans of disappointment and went to sleep.

In the morning, I consulted with a neighbor, who told us those "large animals that attacked us," were actually just tiny field mice caught between our walls. They scratched and squealed and their tiny feet running up and down made a thunderous racket. The next day we went to the SPCA and invested in a hungry yellow cat. Royal, the wonder cat, solved the mouse problem.

The house was the greatest place to play hide-and-seek. On cold dark winter nights, as a special treat to the kids, we turned off all the lights and burned one candle in the living room and one in the kitchen. The flickering light and distorted shapes made everything spooky. The kids thought it was fun. They were more secure in the dark than I was. To impress the kids, I faked courage until some shadow dancing against the wall would send me scurrying for a light switch.

One night we were playing when the dark house became stone cold silent. That was unusual because the kid's giggles and shouts of "here I am," normally produced enough noise to keep me calm. I looked out into the kitchen and saw this large humanoid form hulking over the candle. It cast a 12 foot shadow against the wall and made a "Whoooo," sound, like in a horror movie. I screamed and ran to the kitchen, "Rob, Heather, Where are you?" The figure turned slowly towards me revealing a smiling Marilyn with a trench coat pulled over her head. She had come home from work, seen the darkened house and realized we were playing our game. She decided, with the aid of our kids, to play a joke on her easily spooked husband.

Was that house haunted? We were much more blessed than cursed in that creaky, drafty, wonderful, old Seward House.

Neighbors

Good advice from Benjamin Franklin urges us to, "Love your neighbor but don't pull down the hedge." His wisdom is as timely today as it was in the era of "Poor Richard's Almanac."

When we moved to East Orleans, our neighbors on each side were retirement age and that was all they had in common. The Fletchers lived in a white house on the right side and were about as liberal as possible while the Savages, towards the beach side in a green house, were their direct opposite. They seldom spoke to each other but when talking to us, the Fletchers would ask, "How are your crazy neighbors on the other side?" The Savages asked about those "communists," who lived next door.

Bald, paunchy, pipe smoking, Jack Fletcher had one time been an engineer with the Manhattan Project during World War II and now supplemented his retirement savings by refinishing old furniture. We liked them. We dined together at some of the local restaurants and Jack encouraged our young kids to come over and watch him put new life into antique chairs, but there were certain aspects of their lives that remained a mystery. They disappeared on weekends without a word and never talked about what they did. Four years later, without any forewarning, they suddenly put their house on the market and moved to Kissimmee, Florida, hardly saying "good bye."

We missed them but I didn't think much about their abrupt departure until 5 years later when I took the kids to Disney Land in Florida. Kissimmee was nearby so I called them. "Oh Yes," they answered, "of course we'd love to see you but you may not want to bring the kids. We live in a nudist colony."

A nudist colony? I thought, *Maybe that's where they disappeared to every weekend.*

I explained to the kids that they couldn't accompany me to a colony of naked people and encouraged them to have a night of television watching in the motel free of any interference from me. They were about 12 and 13, fascinated by nudity but bribes of popcorn and coke had them munching away in front of Leave It to Beaver and Love Boat. I drove on.

Kissimmee at that time was still small and isolated. The deluxe four lane super highway leading past the town was devoid of business development and came to a sudden end near a forested area. A 12 high fence surrounding it signaled that I had arrived. On the solitary drive over, images of beautiful nude women lounging around a swimming pool stimulated my overactive mind until I balanced that with the realization that the Fletchers were now at least 70 years old. That scenario of me sitting down with them, sipping coffee, starring at their well traveled bodies, kept me well within the speed limit. *What about eye contact? And proper etiquette? Is a visitor obligated to disrobe or could I just ogle?*

I parked the car and walked through a maze of passageways to a uniformed security guard. Jack met me at the gate in a golf cart, wearing a sweat suit, and we sped away to his house. I turned my neck in every direction trying to find the perfect body, but everyone was covered, like Jack. Unusual freezing temperatures were threatening the Florida fruit crop and if oranges were at risk, so were naked bodies. It was both a relief and a disappointment when I realized that even nudists wear clothes in frigid weather.

When Alice greeted me at her front door with a warm hug, I could feel her mature nakedness through her bathrobe. It wasn't fun. They invited some friends over, all covered, all old, and curious about the stranger in street clothes. After an amiable cup of coffee and some small talk, I used my kids being alone in a strange motel as an excuse to leave. There were no thrills, no arousals, but the strange behavior of the Fletchers was solved. They confessed that their quiet weekend escapes while on Cape Cod were to join other friends, au natural. They delighted in telling me their location and urged me to try it but I never did. One visit to a retirement nudist camp was enough for one lifetime.

They had asked about changes in Orleans, how the new people liked their old house, but their main interest was the Savages. "How is crazy Vinal?"

When people asked, "How is your crazy neighbor," I knew who they were talking about. In his shrill, high pitched voice Vinal Savage relentlessly expounded his opinions about everything as absolute truths. Democrats were communists, all politicians are crooks, and anyone who didn't agree with his interpretation of the Bible was a heathen. He stood firmly against alcohol, cigarettes and wasn't sure that dancing wasn't the devil's workshop.

He did, however, do something we all wish we had done. He bought waterfront property when it was cheap and hung onto it until it was now worth millions. His sound investments did him little good, however because he refused to spend any of it. He drove an old car because he "didn't want to feed those crooks at General Motors." His compulsive work as a mason made his sinewy body more like a high school football player than a man in his 60s. He loaded bricks onto his battered truck well before dawn and didn't return home until after sun set. He had to work alone because no one could keep up with his tremendous work pace nor tolerate his constant prostylatizing.

His one diversion from work and church was boating. He could have afforded any boat in the yard but refused to spend the money for anything except an old plywood scow that should have been peacefully rotting in the marsh. It was made of heavy plywood, about 26 feet long, had no seats, an open deck, and only a faded compass for navigation. Exposed wires running off in every direction threatened to ignite a fire and send the whole rig to the bottom.

He was the original "Do it yourself" person. Only once did he ask a repairman to come aboard to fix something. The mechanic rowed his dingy alongside, took one look at the wiring and said, "Vinal, if you start that motor, I'm jumping into the water," and rowed away.

He constantly asked us out for a day's boating with him but I always searched for some excuse to save my family. "Not today Vinal, Marilyn is busy…Sorry Vinal, Rob has a cold….I'd like to but Heather is going to a birthday party… etc.

Then one day he caught me defenseless. "Charlie, on the Fourth of July and there's going to be a hot air balloon race from Plymouth to the Cape. We could take my boat out of Meeting House Pond, trail it across town to Rock Harbor, and then go out and watch the balloons fly over the bay." Even Marilyn, the protective mother of our two beautiful children, agreed that might be worth the risk.

A week before the event, we bought our first brand new car. Marilyn and I were so proud of our shiny, luxurious

Chevy Malibu station wagon with every fancy attachment available at the time. It was a real gem. We took turns behind the wheel, showing it off to all our friends, basking in pride. We expected it to last until our kids went away to college.

On the morning of the Fourth of July, Marilyn packed sandwiches and got the kids ready while I went with Vinal to haul his boat out of the water and onto his trailer. We planned to drive across town where we would meet my family and start our day of pure joy, boating and balloon watching on Cape Cod Bay. The first challenge came when Vinal couldn't start his old truck. He cranked, pleaded, and prayed but the old wreck wouldn't start. I said, "No problem Vinal, I've got a trailer hitch on my new car. We'll hitch your trailer and boat behind my car. No problem." I was glad for another opportunity to show off the spotless Malibu.

That sounded easy enough so he paddled out to the mooring, started the motor and steered to the landing while I backed the trailer down the ramp. The problem was that we couldn't get his cumbersome boat all the way up to the lip of his trailer. We pushed and pulled but the bow of his boat came only to within a foot of its proper resting place. It came no farther. I suggested that with the heavy weight of his boat, it wouldn't slide backwards, and we could safely drive it the few miles across town to the bay. He agreed.

I slowly drove the car up the sloped ramp to the level road. We moved ahead a few hundred yards when Vinal said, "Charlie I've got an idea. You keep the car going forward and then put on the brakes and the momentum will bring that boat the rest of the way forward to the lip of the trailer."

"Gee, that sounds like a good idea Vinal." I drove ahead, jammed on the brakes and a sudden CRASH, BANG, and the tinkle of glass brought us to a quick halt. The sliding boat had picked up its own momentum, passed by the trailer like it wasn't even there, crashed through the back of my new car, and continued on until it came to rest almost in the back seat.

Vinal was so shaken that he didn't react when I yelled, "Shit." We both had our mouths hanging open as we stared at each other in disbelief. "What will Marilyn say?"

"What will Vera say?" he responded.

We got out, looked at the damage, paced around the car, speechless, avoiding eye contact. The tailgate was smashed in beyond repair and what had been the back window was now just bits of glass on the street. His boat, the battering ram, seemed intact, but it was hard to tell because it was such a wreck before the accident. I surveyed the damage and suggested, "Vinal, there's nothing we can do now. Let's continue on, enjoy the day and I'll worry about the car tomorrow."

We returned to our car seats and I was able to drive on into the town center where people were gathering for the Fourth of July Parade. Vinal seemed to be deep in thought. "Charlie," he said, "I've got an idea. Why don't you back the trailer against that tree, I'll tie a line to the stern and you can pull forward and we'll get that boat out of your trunk and back on the trailer where it belongs."

"Gee, that's a good idea Vinal," I responded.

Trusting him as always, I backed the damaged car towards a tree, leaving enough room for him to tie the line from around the tree to the stern of the boat. The crowd assembling for the parade came over to inspect the strange sight of a ruined new car trailing an old boat, tied to a tree in the middle of the town's square. "Was this part of the holiday celebration?" someone asked.

All I wanted to do at that moment was to disappear. People laughed, pointed, and took our picture. In a few minutes, the town constable pushed his way through the crowd, looked at the car, the boat tied to the tree, and Vinal and said, "Vinal, I don't know what you're doing in this predicament. I don't even care. But just get it the hell off the town's square. NOW."

"Yes, Sir," answered Vinal. I pulled ahead and miraculously the boat did slide backwards, onto the trailer where it belonged and we drove away towards the bay.

When we met Marilyn at Rock Harbor, she looked at the now wrecked car, gasped, but couldn't speak. "Don't say a word," I whispered, "I'll explain later." She stared off into space and kept shaking her head. She had been forewarned to expect anything on a day spent with our crazy neighbor.

The sun shined, the sea was calm, and his boat held together long enough to watch the multi colored hot air balloons, loaded with happy people, passing over our heads on their journey from America's home town to Cape Cod.

At the end of the day, Vinal sat in the car, with his head down and pleaded, "Charlie, don't tell Vera about your new car."

I never did.

As time passed, we learned to love Vera and Vinal Savage but heeded Ben Franklin's advice and didn't "pull down the hedge."

A Suspicious Character

In the early days of my East Orleans dental practice, I had no hygienist, no assistant, and almost no patients. We were deeply in dept and it was only some money owed to me from Cobleskill that paid the mortgage. When a patient appeared, he was much appreciated and treated with utmost respect. Usually there were only two cars in the parking lot, mine and the receptionist. I started wondering if our impulsive move to this paradise by the sea might be a business mistake.

Within a month a well dressed man about 30 years old came in who needed a lot of dental work. He was missing teeth and wanted the spaces filled in the best way possible. I gave him some options but he wanted only the best. The best in this case, aesthetically and functionally, were fixed bridges whereby the teeth on each side of the gap are capped and the replacement tooth is connected to the two crowns. Besides being the best option for him, they required the most work on my part but brought in the most money. I needed money and he needed his spaces filled. He required three bridges and each one would help pay one month's mortgage. I wanted to get the work started quickly and so did he.

Because I was just beginning my business, I explained to him that I needed half the money down before beginning and the balance paid off when each bridge was completed. He agreed, pulled out a fist full of cash, peeled off enough for the down payment and said, "Let's go." I was shocked at his ready cash. That wad of twenty and fifty dollar bills that he carried so casually was my mortgage payment, my kid's clothes, and the family's food. I felt like hugging him but instead enthusiastically set up a long appointment to start the work. In two weeks he returned, sat in the chair for two and a half hours while I did the procedure then returned in another two weeks to complete the job. We both liked the bridge. After his thorough inspection, he said, "OK, Let's do this other one."

I said, "OK, but just like the first time, I need half the money now before we begin."

He said, "That's fair," and pulled his wad of money, peeled off enough to pay for the work and stuffed the rest back in his pocket. The bills he gave me hardly diminished his stash. Two more long appointments completed his second bridge. We did this a third time with the same wad of money and immediate payment. He mumbled something about an aunt dying and I assumed that he must have inherited a fortune.

My receptionist said, "What a nice man he is. I wish my sons were gentlemen like him." The day after the last work was completed and paid for, I opened the local paper and read about a drug raid the night before in a neighboring town. My ideal patient was arrested for drug dealing. It was the talk of the town and incredible news in my office. My receptionist and I were both shocked that such a nice guy was involved in that dirty business.

My life went on, my practice grew, and I forgot about the drug dealer until a year later when I was in a poker game with the police chief of that neighboring town. We became fast friends. One day we were having lunch together after a church service. He said, "Charlie, do you remember a drug raid a while ago where one of your patients was arrested?"

"Yes, I do remember and I was so surprised. He seemed like such a good guy. I assumed that he inherited that money. I had no idea…"

The chief continued, "We were working with the FBI on that case for a long time. We tailed him and watched him every place he went. We watched him go into your office. He'd be the only car in your parking lot and stay for hours. We checked you out and found you were new in town and had a lot of debt. You didn't have much business but seemed to pay your bills all right. We assumed you were in on their drug deals and we wanted to get you too. A new dentist with a lot of debt and no business can do crazy things. We watched every move you made. The FBI put a tail on you and your wife."

Now he was really stretching it. "Are you kidding? Do you mean that when my wife would load our two innocent, Sunday school going kids into the car and go to the grocery store, the FBI was following them??? Do you mean Marilyn, my Marilyn, was under investigation by the FBI?" That image made me laugh right there in church. "I could understand investigating me, maybe, but not her. You haven't met her yet but you'll see."

"I'm sure she's wonderful. But anyways, we raided them and found all kinds of evidence against them. We were ready to pick you up too but we found your receipt in his pocket when we brought him in. You were under suspicion but when we found the receipt, 'For Services Rendered,' signed by you we decided you were clean. He claimed you were just some weird dentist who had no idea what was going on. I guess he was right. At least about the weird part. That receipt is what cleared you."

I didn't know whether to get mad or indignant so I started laughing. He joked, "I still think you were in it too, up to your neck." We laughed again and still do thirty years later.

I went straight home to tell Marilyn who didn't think the FBI tailing her was all that funny. "Me, you, the kids, dealing drugs? They were tailing me? Me? I wonder what I was wearing. Early in the morning? No lipstick? No eye makeup? And, Oh that hair of mine in the morning. Maybe we should leave town, right now. How about Alaska? Or Canada? Canada is beautiful in the summer."

She eventually calmed down and began to see the humor in it but never left the house again without her lipstick. She kept her distance from my police chief friend and became almost compulsive about checking her rear view mirror.

Patients

I was a dentist for thirty great years, most of them in private practice in East Orleans on Cape Cod. I had a small intimate office, with a secretary, an assistant, and a hygienist. I never thought bigger was better, at least not for me.

Betty, the secretary, greeted everyone with a smile. She was usually pleasant, but her religious fanaticism was a challenge. One day, when she overheard me discussing Darwin's Theory of Evolutionary, she came out of her chair, shook her finger in my face and said, "You're in serious trouble, Buster. You're going to rot in hell if you believe that stuff." She regularly predicted the end of the world after reading some passage from the Book of Revelations. On a Friday night, I might say, "Bye, Betty, have a nice weekend." She'd come up to me with a serious expression and warn, "Charlie, It's going to be a terrible weekend for non-believers. The world is going to end Sunday morning at sunrise." Of course, she thought anybody who didn't agree with her was a "non believer." Neither of us said a word on Monday morning when it was back to work as usual.

I liked the profession, but it was the interaction with the patients that brought the biggest rewards. I often scheduled extra time just for conversation. If I knew a procedure took half an hour, I might make an appointment for forty five minutes so there would be talk time. "How is your life going? Do you still have that same boat? How about your kids?" That kept me going.

Jimmy Roth was a Scotsman with a heavy brogue. He could be hard to understand but it was worth the effort because he always brightened the day. His passion was fishing. He caught tons of fish but each one was a new adventure for him. When he reeled a big one, he leaned over the transom for his first glimpse of his catch, yelled, "Wow," opening his mouth wide, and popped his denture into the deep blue sea. It was gone, and had to be remade. Twice he came in, embarrassed to tell me, "I did it again, Doc."

Another favorite was a robust eighty five year old woman, named Eugenia. On her first appointment, when I asked what medications she took, she answered, "None."

Then I asked, "Who is your physician?"

She answered, "I don't have one. Never been to a doctor."

"Are you a Christian Scientist or something?"

"No," she answered, "I've just never been sick. I'm getting older though. Do you think I should go see one?"

I looked at her bright smile, her healthy body and answered, "Hell No, You're doing fine the way you are." The fact that she had never been to a physician nor taken a pill, maybe contributed to her perfect health.

Cape Cod had a large retirement population. Despite this, I didn't make many dentures but I made one for Sophie Simpson, who was one of my all time favorite people. She was ninety six years old, but looked and acted like she was sixty. She was almost six feet tall, with straight posture, and always cheerful. She told my wife once that if I wasn't married, she would go after me, even though she was fifty years older. When I asked her about her secret of longevity, she replied, "I eat one onion a day, pray a lot, and read poetry." She also enjoyed watching soap operas. We couldn't make her an appointment between 1:00 and 3:00 in the afternoon because she "couldn't miss her soaps." She lived alone and drove her own car.

The first step in making a denture is to take an impression. This involves loading a mouth sized tray with some gooey material that hardens in a few seconds, conforming to shape of the patient's mouth. She said she dreaded this part of the procedure but could tolerate it if I distracted her by reading poetry while the material set.

I agreed to her strategy but could only find the poem, "Casey at the Bat," from a Cape Cod Baseball League brochure. She liked it. I placed the impression material in her mouth, sat behind her, one hand holding up the impression tray, and the other holding the book while I read the poem. My mind was more taking an accurate impression than the poem so I spoke without much feeling or emotion.

I recited, "It looked extremely rocky for the Mudville nine that day," in a flat monotone. I didn't make it to, "Mighty Casey has struck out," before the material set and I freed her from her discomfort. She didn't pause for a breath, but immediately pushed my hand away, grabbed her old dentures, and said, "Charlie, you read that all wrong. You've got to put some feeling into it. Here, let me show you." She picked up the poem and read from:

"It looked extremely rocky for the Mudville nine that day:" to

"---- Mighty Casey has struck out," with such verve and passion that I felt like crying for the fans of Mudville and their fallen hero, Casey.

I also felt like kissing my ninety six year old girlfriend, right there in the dental office, so I did.

At ninety six, Sophie was not my oldest patient. That distinction belonged to Todd Owen, who lived until he was 106. He had been a driver for Lt. Dwight D Eisenhower in World War I. This Lieutenant Eisenhower later became the general of the Allied Forces in World War II and our thirty fourth president. Todd was a retired stock broker and liked to offer tips. He was 104 at the time and still buying stocks, long term. He had outlived three wives. His last marriage was to a younger woman, 87 years old.

Todd was healthy but looked like he was 104. He was slightly built, stoop shouldered, and his wrinkled skin struggled to stretch over his skeleton. He lived happily in his own home and still drove around town. People knew him and stayed out of his way. It took him five minutes to disentangle himself from his car at the post office.

I once extracted a tooth for him and offered to add it to his partial denture, to save money. I thought at his age, this would be sufficient treatment. When I proposed the plan, he asked, "Is that the best you can do?"

I answered, "No. We could remake your partial."

Without hesitation, he said, "Let's do it." Despite his age, he assumed he would live many more years and wanted the complete job.

These centogenarians shared an optimistic outlook, a love of people, and an enthusiasm for life. I hope I learned from them.

My dental office was also a good source of marital advice. One loving couple, with a long successful marriage, always came in together. They were inseparable. Once they were late for an appointment because they confessed that they had been down to the beach hugging and lost track of time. I was surprised one day when the wife came in alone. I asked, "Where's Russell? Is he sick/?"

"No," she answered, "he's fine. We have had some problems though." She sighed, took a deep breath then went on, "As you know, Russell is hard of hearing. We thought it would be a good idea for him to try a hearing aid so he bought one. It helped his hearing but we started arguing all the time, which is unusual for us. When I asked him what was wrong, he told me that all these years he couldn't hear me when I rambled on. Now he could hear every word I said and it was driving him crazy. He didn't realize I was such a nag. The next day we took back his hearing aid and now we're doing fine again. No more arguments. We couldn't be happier."

Another old couple, probably in their eighties, came in regularly in the same loving way. The wife was a small, delicate, sweet woman with a soft voice and gentile manner. Her husband was huge, broad shouldered but with her soft mannerisms. One day his wife came in, avoiding eye contact, like she was ashamed of something. She had one black eye and it was obvious that she wanted to hide it. I said, "Hi Mrs. Nichols. How are you? What happened to your eye?"

She looked around the room and saw no one. She came close and whispered, "Horace was asleep last night, had a dream, and he rolled over and poked me in the eye with his elbow. He's so ashamed and embarrassed that he wouldn't come in today." I assured her that I would tell no one about her most gentle husband's accidental fling with violence.

Some aspects of dentistry can be challenging. Results have to be perfect and you are confined to the same rooms day after day. I don't miss the constraints but do miss the people. Every day I had fun with somebody.

Car

Marilyn and I came from families where frugality and education were prime values. We were taught to sacrifice material pleasures today for our children's college expenses of tomorrow. We considered it a natural part of a parent's role. One of the easiest things for me to do without was a flashy car.

A car represents to me safe transportation and nothing more. I've always resisted advertisers' attempts to associate a luxury car with self worth, success, and sexuality. We probably took it to the extreme in our early Cape Cod years, when we nursed our green Ford Fairlane station wagon well beyond its life expectancy. It was ten years old and looked older, had well over 100,000 miles on the speedometer, and was an eyesore to everyone in town.

I needed help in wringing every last mile out of that old wreck. Bill, one of my dental patients, owned a combination gas station, auto repair shop. He vowed that he would keep our car going, on as little money as possible, if we didn't care what it looked like. Appearance didn't matter to me so we had a partnership.

Bill's problem was his mouth, not his car. He had a hole in his palate where another dentist had extracted a tooth and the area never healed. He therefore had a fistula, or hole, connecting his maxillary sinus to his mouth. I referred him to an oral surgeon but Bill didn't want it repaired. It caused him no obvious problems and he bargained with me that if I wouldn't harass him about the hole in his head, he wouldn't mock me about my car. We made a contract- he kept his fistula, I kept my car.

This car was rusted everywhere in every way. On a weekend excursion to Bar Harbor, the rear window fell out of the tailgate in a thunderstorm. To keep rain water out, we taped a garbage bag to the empty window casing and drove slowly on our way. When we returned home, Bill replaced the tailgate with one from the junk yard. It fit fine but the esthetically it was a disaster. Our car was of various shades faded green and orange rust, but this tail gate was of artificial wood paneling that was popular at the time on station wagons. I could now see out the back window and was happy to have the car almost rain proof again. I looked the body, now a combination of different cars and colors and said, "Thanks Bill, Looks fine."

When we transported neighborhood kids in the back seat, they asked Rob and Heather, "Why are you leaning back in your seat and raising your legs off the floor?"

Rob replied, "Because it rained last night. When we go over a puddle, the water splashes up through the holes in the floor. We get wet. If you raise your legs and lean back, you can stay pretty dry."

Those holes saved us one Saturday morning, when I took five friends fishing. We towed my boat behind the car and drove to Wellfleet. We were drinking breakfast beers on the way and I was anxious to get the boat off the trailer and into the water. We were laughing and having fun and

I wasn't concentrating on the road. I ran through a yellow traffic light. A policeman signaled for me to stop and parked in front of us. Our first concern was not the yellow light but what to do with the opened beer cans. If we opened the door and threw them out, the policeman would see it and ticket me for drinking and driving. Instead, we dropped the open cans through the holes in the floor boards, onto the ground. I could then look the policeman in the eye and ask with the innocence of a new born child, "What's the trouble officer?"

"It seems like you just ran through that red light back there. License and registration, Please." He put his arm out to lean against the door, but took a look at the rust and dirt and backed away. He wore a clean uniform and didn't want it soiled.

"I thought the light was yellow when I entered the intersection," I pleaded. "With this boat in tow, I was afraid of blocking the traffic, so I went through. I'm sorry, Sir."

He said nothing but ambled slowly around the car, smiled, and poked at some lose metal protruding from a fender. He paused for a moment at the two cases of beer in the back but continued walking. My prayers were answered when he didn't stoop to look underneath where the open beers lay in the dirt. "You know son, there's a rumor that this state is going to start car inspections this year. You may want to look into something Um, ah.. in better shape than this." He obviously pitied anyone driving such a wreck, "I'll let you go this time. Maybe the light was yellow. Just watch yourself OK? Good luck in your fishing." He must have assumed that with a car like this, we were fishing out of need, not sport.

"Thank you officer. I'll be more careful." I waited for him to leave and then slowly drove off to the landing

The climax for Marilyn, and our Ford, came the night we were dining out on some special occasion with three other couples. We were all dressed up and heading towards a fancy restaurant in the old car. Brian, a fastidious friend, was riding by the front window seat, beside Marilyn in the middle. The three other people were in the back, with their legs spread over the rusted out holes. Brian leaned too heavily on his arm rest and it fell off onto his lap. He picked up the broken piece and apologized, "Charlie I'm sorry. I just broke your arm rest." and waved it at me in front of Marilyn's face.

To make him feel better, I gave a strong tug and pulled the arm rest off the driver's door, "That's OK Brian. Here take mine." Marilyn didn't see the humor in two rusty armrests waving in front of her.

A few days before, a patient had come into the office requiring a lot of expensive dental work. She wanted me to do the work, but would only do it, if I bought a new car with the money. She was tired of explaining to her friends that it was her dentist who drove that wreck that was the subject of town gossip.

I agreed to do the work and use the money to buy a new car.

We sweated as our old Chevy struggled each one of its last twenty six miles to Hyannis. The tires had no tread, one door would not open, another rattled its warning that it was about to fall off. There was no paint, just rust, a windshield wiper slapped at the window like a bird with a broken wing, and the engine sputtered, warning us it was about to quit. We were that pitiful car that everyone scorns going thirty miles per hour on the sixty five miles per hour highway.

We struggled into the closest car dealership. The car would go no farther. A salesman strolled over and joked, "I guess you got your moneys worth out of this baby." He knew we were desperate and was ready for a sale. I didn't bargain with his offer of a hundred dollars in trade.

Seven Year Itch

Marilyn and I loved community theatre in Orleans. We seldom missed an opportunity to pay our five dollars and watch our ministers, lawyers, friends and acquaintances act in the small intimate theatres. We sat close enough to see the sweat on the forehead, watch them struggle to remember lines, and hear the singing off key. Often the plays were of high quality, matching professional theatre. Even when blunders prevailed and amateurism flourished, it was still a great evening.

I had such deep admiration for anyone who could recite lines in front of an audience that the quality of the performance was secondary to simply having the courage to try. I struggled all my life with shyness and acting in front of a crowd was the essence of conquered inhibitions. These local actors, who had careers during the day and then acted at night, were my heroes. I congratulated, praised, and encouraged them but never dreamed of joining them onstage. I was comfortable being a cowardly spectator.

Marilyn wasn't satisfied. She had never acted but was driven to try new things. One Sunday we were relaxing around the house, reading the newspaper, when she interrupted my peaceful day by saying, "Charlie, they're having tryouts this afternoon for a play at the Chatham Drama Guild. I'm going to try out. Why don't you come with me? You're always talking about community theatre. Here's your chance to try it. Come on. It'll be fun."

"Are you serious? I can't do that. No way can I do that."

"You can too. Come on. What do you have to lose?" she persisted.

I could not resist. "Okay. I'll go but I'm only going to watch…. I think." I had successfully avoided being trapped in front of an audience since those elementary school embarrassments and I wasn't going to change my timid behavior now. I was stuck in a rut, but it was my rut and I was comfortable in it. I would do anything for Marilyn but giving up this lifelong fear was not an option! Damn that "can do" attitude of hers anyway.

We filed in the back door of the Drama Guild and sat quickly in the back row. I looked around and saw many of those talented performers that we had been admiring all those years. I shrunk down in my seat and thought, "Charlie, you do not belong here. These people are in a different world and its not you're world. They're gifted. You're shy. Get out before you made a bigger ass of yourself." Marilyn sat poised and relaxed beside me. I just wanted to escape. The director came by, smiled, and asked us to fill out note cards:

Name: Charlie McOuat

Theatre Experience: None

Roll you are interested in: (I was tempted to put down "None" but wrote "Any.")

Marilyn filled out hers and I took them to the director, up front. I walked back to the safety of my seat and thought, "this thing is really snowballing. I'm stuck. I'm going to have to read for this part. How did this happen?" My protective skin was gone and I was soon to be exposed before the world.

The director had a long table set up on stage where he called people up to read a few lines. He made no comment as each took their turn. Everyone seemed confident except me.

I was sitting, fidgeting when I glanced across the aisle and saw the most beautiful pair of female legs I had ever seen. I followed the legs upwards past a perfect body to a gorgeous face. When I reached her face, two deep blue eyes looked right at me. My head snapped down. *What was that?* I wondered. I had lived in the area for seven years, been to almost every play and had never seen a woman as beautiful as that. I moved closer to Marilyn for comfort. She was concentrating on the people reading onstage.

The director was calling my name. I walked to the front, sat down, took a play book and started to read. I was reading for the part of Tom who was a writer and playboy. I did not identify with either of these characteristics. I was reading along in a flat, nervous manner, when I came to the lines:

"Oh Helen, Thy beauty is to me like those Nicean barks of yore,"

I felt so strange reading those words that I blurted out, "Do I really have to say that?" It was just an impulse but the director and the audience thought that I was trying to be funny and they laughed, "Yes, you do. You have to say those lines."

I finished reading in my emotionless, monotone manner, and then returned to my seat. I thought, *Well that's over now. I tried, failed, and now can go home, proud of my effort but determined never be trapped like that again.* I was day dreaming , congratulating myself for trying when I heard my name called again. "Charlie, would you read the part of Tom again and Bet, would you please read Helen's part?"

When they called Bet's name, the incredible beauty from across the aisle stood up. We smiled at each other and I followed her onstage. I looked at her and I was no longer Charlie McOuat, dentist, father, and happy husband. Now I was Richard Burton and she was Liz Taylor. Together we were going to show the world how to act. The adrenaline bubbled inside and I was going to show these petty local amateurs what theatre was all about. This time I read with emotion that I didn't know I possessed. I was using my hands, varying my voice, pausing, eye contacting Liz, I mean Bet. Was that electricity between us? I came to the lines:

"Oh Helen, thy beauty is to me like those Nicean barks of yore,"

But this time I read like they were my original lines. I was Edgar Allen Poe, Richard Burton, and Sir Lawrence Olivier, all in one great acting and writing package.

When we finished reading, the director looked at me like I was his long lost friend. He said nothing but stared at us as we descended the stairs to our seats. The audience was silent. I had cast off my anchor of shyness and was taking off to new heights. I was flying. I sat down next to Marilyn who said nothing but gave me that look of "Who do you think you are? What got into you and where is that predictable guy I've been married to all these years?"

I sat back as if nothing had happened but now I wanted that part. I wanted to be Tom and feel like that again. Tom and I, Bet and Helen were linked together like Siamese twins. I wasn't surprised when the director handed out the parts and I did get the part of Tom and Bet, my new partner, was Helen.

Inside, I felt like I had just won the lottery but for the sake of my precious marriage, I tried to downplay the situation as if it wasn't all that big a deal to me. Keeping my head out of the clouds on the drive home required better acting talent than I had just shown at the try outs. I wanted to shout," Did you see me? Did you see what I just did? And Wow! She sure is beautiful," but instead I reverted to my best monotone voice and remarked that "it might be sort of fun to be in a play after all."

Marilyn didn't respond but was busy reading the playbooks given to us on the way out the door. "Gee," she said, "you've got a big part, and me, I've only got a few lines in act one and that's it. You're in the whole play….. and look at this…. You've got to kiss that woman…. on stage…you've got to kiss her."

I noticed that she was already calling Bet, "that woman." I wondered where that came from all of a sudden, "that woman." I thought to myself, so what's the problem? Where was that shy dentist, father, husband who sat peacefully reading the Sunday paper so long ago? He was gone. At least he wasn't in this car, not for tonight anyway.

Marilyn broke an uncomfortable silence when she said, "Charlie, we're pretty busy. You've got your dental practice, I've got my career and then there are our two kids. Being in this play might be too much. Maybe we should just explain that we don't have time and go back to our normal lives."

I thought, absolutely not. The genie is out of the bottle and can't be stuffed back in. I replied in the nonchalant tone of a professional, "I think we'll be all right. The kids can come to some of the rehearsals. I think it'll be fine." Inside, I was thinking that this was my chance to break loose and nothing would come between me and "that woman."

I drove on past Pleasant Bay, past the sign, "Entering Orleans," awaiting a reply.

"That girl you're supposed to kiss is very, very pretty. She's beautiful."

"She's no more beautiful than you are, dear," I said with conviction. Marilyn was beautiful and the absolute love of my life.

"Well, I don't believe that but we can try…. If you want." I did love Marilyn and I knew that even that beautiful Bet would not alter anything between us.

"I want to do it. We've gone this far and this could be good for both of us." That was settled. The crisis was over. We would be in the play. I will kiss the glamorous actress then come home to my fantastic, understanding wife. Thank you God.

That night, she made a few calls to girl friends to find out about Bet. She ran into the bedroom, "Charlie, Bet, that woman, is a former Miss New York State and a runner up in The Miss America Contest. Are you sure you can handle this?"

"What do you mean by that dear? It's only a play. Of course I can handle it." I didn't sleep that night thinking about the pleasant challenge before me. Miss New York State, Miss America, Hmm. I was feeling guilty already and rehearsals hadn't started. Tomorrow I think I'll grow a mustache, maybe a little Grecian Formula to "wash away that gray." I could diet. Lose those five pounds. Miss New York State, Hmm. How am I going to downplay those passionate love scenes when Marilyn is lurking in the audience?

I lived this wild playboy fantasy for a few days until reality hit and we started rehearsals. This was going to be not only my first time on stage but also the first time kissing another woman since our marriage, ten years before. Even on New Years Eve or birthday celebrations, I always turned my cheek when a woman approached with puckered lips. I was absolutely monogamous and kissing another woman on the lips was too intimate for me. I loved parties but also loved my wife and valued our marriage.

Bet was not only incredibly beautiful, she was also a very nice person. She realized that I was nervous around her and did everything possible to put me at ease. I'm sure she was accustomed to her beauty intimidating men and knew how to help them relax. She was completely poised onstage and I was swept along by her confidence. When I told her about my fears, she dismissed them as normal stage fright and something shared by everyone. She was so relaxed and poised that I couldn't get nervous. We became friends and I couldn't let a friend down by messing up the play. It became a team effort and my inhibitions were secondary to the success of the play. If I embarrassed myself, I would drag my new friends down with me and that was impossible.

Still there was that doubt when I stood before the audience on opening night. The whole cast encouraged me and once I heard the sound of my own voice successfully reciting lines, it was fun.

The kiss? Like reciting lines or moving on stage, it simply became a part of the performance. I reserved my emotions for Marilyn but it was nice to have that interlude. And wow, was she pretty.

A Day Sail

Our 19 foot O'Day Daysailer was my first extravagant purchase ever. It was sleek and shiny, brand new, right out of the show room. All its lines seemed to be gently curved for a purpose. Its well polished hull perfectly engineered to skim over the top of the water, the sides curved from front to back to aerodynamically charge into the wind, the transom wide and sturdy for stabilization, to keep it from tipping in strong ocean winds.

The problem of me not knowing how to sail was solved by my friendship with Fred Johnson. I was new to the Cape, had moved in only a few months before, but he was born there and had sailed since he was a young boy. He taught me how to tie fisherman's knot onto a mooring, to keep the main sheet running free with no tangles, all lines had a purpose and were to be treated with respect. I felt like a sailor calling ropes sheets and lines like he did, The right side became the starboard, the left the port and always, "red right return" to keep channel markers on the correct side of the boat.

Maybe too soon after we started our lessons, he had me take control, "Come on Charlie, you can do it. It's your boat. Just make sure when you turn or tack you come into the wind, That way you do a nice controlled tack. If you turn away from the wind, that's a jibe. The wind gets behind the sail and the boom can knock you in the head or the force could capsize the boat."

Well, I didn't want to capsize my prize new boat so I tried to always come into the wind. "It's hard to remember which way the wind is coming from" I commented. "I guess I'll have to concentrate."

"If you feel yourself being knocked over, just let go of the mainsheet, the sails will luff and the boat will turn into the wind. You'll be in irons, but safe. "Don't worry," he assured mc. "it will become second nature. In a sailboat you automatically pay attention to the wind."

Okay I thought it's so simple: Turn only into the wind and keep the lines free to run, No tangles.

We sailed around for a few Saturdays and I was feeling confident. I liked Fred and was certainly grateful for his friendship and assistants but I really wanted to share this new exciting sport with my seven year old son, Rob. I had formed an inexplicable bond with Rob the minute he came out of Marilyn's womb. I vowed at the time to do anything for this beautiful son, to share everything, to have fun together. That feeling had only increased each day for the seven years of his life. At that time, Rob also loved being with me. He followed me, trusted me, looked up to me as his flawless father. I somehow convinced Marilyn that I was now capable of handling our new boat well enough to put our son in my hands. She trusted me too.

This Saturday I awoke early, the sun was shining, and more importantly the wind was mild. It was mid- April and I had already wasted precious Saturdays learning from Fred. Soon the water would warm up and then the kids would just want to go to the beach. We had to go now. The leaves at the top of the trees hardly moved and there was scarcely a ripple on the water. This was going to be a great day, father and son, sailing together on Pleasant Bay. Rob was equally eager to get going. He couldn't yet swim but we both felt safe with him in his life jacket.

We used the motor to get away from the mooring, steer through the river, and keep the boat into the wind while I raised the sails. We were alone sailing together in beautiful Pleasant Bay. Life doesn't get any better than this. The weather was perfect with sunny skies and friendly winds, but also this was Cape Cod where weather can change in a second. It did.

We sailed, we turned into the wind, laughed, joked, and bonded some more. I was concentrating on the joy of the day and didn't notice the dark cloud approaching from the south. By the time it was on us we had turned back and were headed up the river under sail towards our mooring. By the time we came to the second bend in the river the gentle wind turned vicious, white caps surrounded us and we were still under full sail. In the last bend, a sudden gust got behind the sail whipped the boom around as Fred had warned and suddenly the boat capsized and we were in the freezing water. He screamed, I yelled, we hugged and I assured all was well if he just hung onto the hull. He calmed down while I swam underneath and somehow got the sails down and stood on the centerboard. The boat popped upright. I helped him aboard and thank you God the motor started and I was able to steer us to our mooring, our dingy, the land, and home.

Rob rushed into the kitchen and told his Mom about our great adventure. We both downplayed our panic when we capsized. Marilyn had soup ready after we came out of the hot shower and I thought the incident was forgotten until the next night at the dinner table.

"How did school go today everybody?" I asked Rob and Heather.

"Not too well Dad." answered Rob.

"Really! Why what happened?"

"Well Dad, when the teacher asked everybody about their weekend, Sara Fuller spoke up and told the whole class, 'my Dad and I were watching this boat sail up the river in front of our house. This crazy guy and his son tipped over in the wind and my Dad said they did everything wrong. He said 'guys like that shouldn't sail with little kids until they know what they're doing.' We laughed at them but it really wasn't funny. The little boy was crying like a baby. They could've drownded."

I slunk down in my chair waiting for a response from Marilyn. All she said was, "What did you say Rob?"

"I didn't say anything. Not one word. I didn't want the class to know who it was."

Neither did I and my beautiful wife never brought up the subject again. She didn't want to add to my already excessive guilt. We didn't sail together again until the water warmed in the summer and I learned more about the wonderful world of sailing.

Cod Fishing the Cape

Dick's half hearted attempt at a backhand made it obvious he wasn't into tennis today. His third shot in a row clanged off the rim of his racquet and died into the net. Instead of hustling up to retrieve the balls, he sauntered, head down, moving slowly, sending the message that we needed to find something else to do. I knew what was on his mind. "It's not a bad day," I said as I approached him. "I know high winds were predicted but look at that flag. It's almost limp. Maybe we should give it a try."

"I hardly feel a breeze," he responded, "and this is Cape Cod. Nobody can predict weather around here. Too many variables. If we waited for good predictions, we'd never get out to the Cod grounds."

I had known Dick since I was an eight year old youngster, tagging after him when he dated my oldest sister Betty in their college years. He was more than a role model to me in those days. I envisioned him as six foot four, broad shouldered, muscles exploding from his oversized body. I was surprised thirty years later when he knocked at my door and I looked down at his slightly built frame, the top of his head at my chin level, wire glasses of an intellectual sliding off his nose, and bald head. By coincidence he owned a summer cottage in Orleans, only a few miles from my house. He used it as a sanctuary from his career as the head of the Art Department at Wellesley College. When he saw my name in the directory, he called, and we bonded immediately. Outwardly we were equals but I retained some of that boyhood hero worship of him. I was comfortable to fall in step behind.

One of the fondest memories of my youth was floating on an inner tube alongside Dick, each with snorkel and mask, peering down into the clear waters of Conesus Lake, dangling a worm in front of the yellow perch feeding below. We could pick our prey by tantalizing only the biggest fish, watch them swallow the worm, and then witness the struggle as they attempted to free themselves from our hooks. When we caught one, we stuffed it under our swim trunks, and proceeded to the next catch. He always had good inventive ideas and now, I thought he had another. "Come on Charlie. Let's get out of here. The season's short and I can't see passing up a day's fishing for a few half assed whacks at a tennis ball. Let's go."

An hour later we were launching my 22-foot Sea Ox into Chatham Harbor. My dependable 90 horse Evinrude responded after a few chokes on the engine, a squeeze or two on the gas line. We were off. Although it was my boat, he took control so I watched the shoreline go by as he steered through the harbor. "Look Dick. The small craft warning flag is up over Chatham Light." We smiled at each other too enthused about being on the water to heed the warning.

"I know," he answered, "but it's calm now. We don't get many days like this and the Cod are running. This is a nice sea worthy boat. Are you with me?" he asked.

"Sure, I'm fine. Let's go," glad we didn't let a silly flag stand between us and a boat full of Cod. He steered through the buoys, skillfully avoiding the lobster trap lines that could entangle in our propeller. He slowed when we hit the surf, keeping the bow pointing off a slight angle to their oncoming crests. "Heavy surf today," he shouted. I hung on the grab rail and spread my feet for maximum support. He once owned a 35 foot Newfoundland Trawler that he used to supplement his professor's income with catches from the sea. I felt secure with him at the helm. He pushed the hammer forward, speeding again as we reached the calmer waters beyond the breaking surf.

Although I'd been boating for years, I still felt that being on the open ocean in a small boat was my ultimate thrill. My early years in Upstate New York confined me to ponds and finger lakes so moving to Cape Cod was like reaching the major leagues after being in the minors. I had taken safety courses, knew the basics of navigation along with a respect for the ocean and its dangers, but I was still learning. Every trip brought new challenges. The weather, the tides, the shifting sands of Cape Cod made every trip an adventure.

And, I loved my Sea Ox. I don't get attached to material possessions but this boat was different. It was small enough, 22 feet long, that it could easily be moved to and from one of the many launch sites on the Lower Cape. Some days the kids and I spent the morning water skiing on the calm waters of Town Cove and then in the afternoon, trailer it through town to Rock Harbor where we fished the bay for bluefish and strippers. My ultimate thrill was fishing the deep waters of the Atlantic on the backside of the Cape for codfish.

I sometimes went by myself which was foolish because I knew nothing about outboard motors and if it failed at sea, the next stop could be Spain. It was equipped with only a center console, a compass, an unreliable depth gauge, and a short wave radio that no longer worked. If anything went wrong, we were at the ocean's mercy and that foolhardy risk made my heart race to the pace of the waves. Now I was headed out with an experienced fisherman, an honored professor, and a man I'd looked up to all my life. The small craft warning flag was far astern, and soon we were out of site of land, with open ocean in all directions.

After an hour ride, he slowed, read the depth gauge at 110 feet. The rhythmic ocean swells rocked us like a baby carriage as the sun peeked through the overcast clouds. I was doing one of my favorite things with a valued friend and life doesn't get much better than that. We grabbed our rods, baited the hooks with squid, sea worms, or clams and soon our stiff rods carried the baits down to the large fish feeding on the bottom. We waited and waited, caught a few midsized cod, maybe ten pounds each but the strong ocean currents made it hard to keep our baits down. If the bait is not on the bottom, fishing is hopeless.

A few more fish and a lot of waiting convinced Dick that we needed to change strategy. He said, "In my boat, I keep the motor running just enough to keep the bow in the direction of the waves. This will keep our lines straight, and we'll be on the bottom where we need to be."

"We've got plenty of gas, plus a spare tank. Sounds good." Just like he said, our lines straightened out, the baits stayed down and soon we were catching large cod with regularity. Again I admired his ingenuity. We fished and chuckled and told stories until the box was full. He let out his line one more time. "This is it Charlie. We can't hold any more…..Wow! What the hell is this?"His rod bent double, jerked him to the side of the boat. His reel screeched as line striped off. He let the fish run, he couldn't do anything else, until gradually it slowed. He pumped his rod, able to make a few turns with his reel, gaining a little with each pump.

I pulled my line up quickly. I didn't want to get tangled in whatever he had. "I don't know what the hell this is, but it's no ordinary cod." He kept pumping his rod, reeling when able. Sweat dripped off his chin. He took off his hat, threw it on the deck, and bit his lip. I grabbed the gaff, leaned over the side, and saw nothing. "He's coming but I don't know who's going to quit first, him or me. I'm tired."

"I love this place. You never know what you're going to hook into."

He leaned back to get more leverage and suddenly his line went slack. "Shit, I lost him. He now reeled the rest of the line until the broken end came over the side. "I think that sucker just played around with us until he saw the bottom of the boat and took off. We'll never know.

"Too bad Dick. I would've at least liked to have seen it. Maybe it was a halibut. That was forty pound test line."

"Too bad but that's it. We've had a great day. We'll never know. It's time to go."

"Yeah," I agreed, "It's getting' rough out here. Let's not push our luck."

We laid our rods in the rod holders, slapped each other's hands like the Boston Celtics after a victory, then he sat down to steer us home. He pointed us west, gave the engine a little gas and the bow of the boat popped up instead of leveling off. Instead of skimming over the water the sea Ox was almost at a right angle to the sea. I looked back and saw the motor was almost underwater. We had little power.

"Holy shit, Dick what's wrong?"

"Damned if I know. You've got floatation under this thing don't you?"

"Yeah, but look. it must be full of water. All the weight's in the stern. The bows up, the sterns down, I'll walk up front. It might help." I walked to the front but the bow still pointed skyward. "Hey man, are there other fishing boats out here. I haven't noticed any all day."

"Maybe we've just been too busy. We don't need a tow yet. We are making headway." We looked at each other and shuttered. We said nothing but both felt the power of the sea tossing our small vulnerable boat. I felt the wind streak through my hair. The sky darkened. Each wave showed various shades of gray, except at the crest, where the white foam hissed and crashed against the Sea Ox

"Stay up front, it help's a little. We are going west but just really slow." I looked in all directions, saw only water and endless sky. Neither of us thought when he suggested keeping the boat headed in the direction of the waves , that his 35 footer, with its higher transom provided more protection from the following sea than my much smaller Sea Ox. Waves had broken over the transom all the time we were fishing and some had splashed into the floatation. Now instead of being full of life saving air that would keep us afloat, it was at least partially weighted down with heavy sea water, putting all that extra weight in the stern.

We had little power, the wind was picking up and for the first time, I remembered the small craft warning flag. "Het Dick, are we skrewed? I haven't seen another boat all day and who knows how far we've drifted. I'd trade every fish in that box for a glimpse of land."

"Easy guy. We're not screwed yet. I think we've been drifting westward. It's an on shore breeze. That damn bow pointing up might be like a sail, blowing us landward." *I thought now there's a classic example of the glass being half full.* "Hopefully it's not that far. Hang on. We are making headway, just very slow." I admired his optimism, but the boat's slow progress was a direct challenge to my lack of patience. I wanted that bow down where it belonged, I wanted to see land. I wanted a passing fishing boat to throw us a line. Instead I watched the horizon rise and fall with each wave and the sky turn darker.

"You know Dick, I always wanted you to marry my sister. I don't know what happened but you both went off and married somebody else."

He laughed, "Ha. I don't remember what happened." He hesitated, looked off in the distance, and rep;ied. "We were young that's all. No big problems, we just went our separate ways. I've got no complaints. I'm sure she doesn't either."

"I hope not. Life is pretty short." I didn't mean to say that while being tossed around like this at the mercy of the building sea. "Let's just pray that the wind and currents stay in this direction. We've proved that we're not very smart so we'd better be lucky."

The Sea Ox rocked, slipped sideways, and bobbed up and down but its slow, steady movement was forward. Forward to our first sight of land, a small streak at first, and then close enough to see the outline of beach cottages and long sand beaches with white waves bathing the shore. "This thing is holding up despite our stupidity, we're going to make it."

"Did you ever have any doubts?" he said in jest. And then answered his own question. "I did. I sure did. I almost shit when that bow stood up like that but what else could we do?"

"What the hell else could we do? Hang on and that's it." And that's what we did, hung on, back through the building surf, past the warning flag to the launch area. The boat, loaded with heavy water, was hard to pull onto the trailer, but it came. We unscrewed the stopper from the floatation chamber and the water gushed out. It kept coming for an hour. That chamber was completely flooded, acting more like an anchor than life saving floatation.

We stepped back, smiled, praised the Sea Ox, and shook our heads. I controlled the urge to kiss the ground. Despite our foolishness we were home and very lucky.

Foot in Mouth Disease

Mark Twain said, "It's better to sit quietly and have people think you're a fool than to open your mouth and remove all doubt." Most of us have said the wrong thing to the wrong person and wished we could take the words back, but once they are spoken, it's too late.

Like the time in my dental office when I asked a slightly fat patient, "How far along are you in your pregnancy?" and she answered, "I'm not pregnant." Ouch. It hurt even more when two days later she requested her records sent to another dentist where she would be treated with more sensitivity. Now that is "sticking your foot in your mouth."

I discussed this experience one day with my son and he remembered, "Oh, that's like the time you were getting back to socializing after Mom's death and you were playing tennis with a bunch of people. You were playing mixed doubles and a guy in the next court was loud and obnoxious. I asked you 'Dad, who is that obnoxious old fat guy in the court next to you who keeps yelling and swearing at everybody.' Your partner who was that sweet Mrs. K said, 'Oh, that's my husband.' Once the words are out, there's no going back, no retraction possible.

One of my classic fopas, started when I was a little boy creeping around the floor while my mother listened to soap operas on the radio. This was in those pre-television days of radio when melodramatic soap operas were fifteen minutes long and sponsored by soap companies, hence called soap operas. My Mother's favorite was Helen Trent, who asked the question, "Can a woman over thirty five find happiness after life has knocked her hopes against the rocks of despair." The actress was a golden tongued woman named Julie Stevens. I learned much of the English language by listening to that beautiful voice.

Thirty years later, when I was a dentist on Cape Cod, I learned that Julie Stevens lived in a nearby town. I was thrilled one day when I looked at my scheduled patients and saw her name on the list.

The day progressed slowly until I heard that familiar melodic voice out in the waiting room. It was THE Julie Stevens in my dental office. When she came in, she was very nice and Hollywood like, calling me "Sweety" and "Darling." She not only had a great voice but the face and body of a beautiful mature woman. Her only challenge seemed to be that she was not growing old gracefully. She was probably sixty five years old and trying to look thirty five, like Helen Trent. She wore the tight jeans of a teenager, a lot of make up, high heels, with long hair streaming down her neck. I chuckled at the thought of this pseudo acquaintance standing before me in my office. I said, "Oh, I remember you, I used to listen to you when I was in my crib." Now that's not what a woman who is challenged by age wants to hear from her dentist but it was too late, the words were spoken. My face turned red and she did her best to allay my embarrassment. Eventually she became a treasured friend, even referred her family and friends to me. We never again discussed her role in my infancy.

Young children regularly put their foot in their mouth and thankfully do not yet have the social sophistication to suffer embarrassment. Like my three year old grandson. One of my favorite people is Tiger Woods and anytime he was golfing on TV, Aidan and I would sit on the couch and cheer, "Come on Tiger. Come on Tiger." After we watched him win another tournament, we walked over to the local golf course where a young Afro American man was peacefully practicing his putting. Most of the golfers were white but when Aidan saw the young black man he yelled, "Hey Charlie, there's Tiger Woods." I tried to ignore the comment and the golfer chuckled but said nothing. Aidan would not be ignored however so repeated, "Charlie, Charlie, don't you see? That's Tiger Woods over there."

By now all the golfers in the area were standing uneasily when the man said with a laugh, "I wish I was Tiger Woods."

And I said, "I wish I was too." The tension was broken and Aidan to this day thinks he saw Tiger Woods on the local golf course.

Mark Twain's gives good advice but if we always sat quietly, we'd miss a lot of fun.

Gus Yearing

Gus and Betty Yearing were a contented couple, happily enjoying their retirement together. She did most of the talking but he was always warm and friendly. He smiled with ease and spread his positive attitude to everyone. They were faithful patients, valued friends, and lived nearby in a Cape Cod Style house overlooking the ocean. We often talked about our families and how lucky we were to be living on Cape Cod.

One day, Gus came into the office shortly before Rob, Heather, and I were going to leave for a dream trip to Italy. I was gushing with excitement and assumed that he would share my enthusiasm. He was polite but uncharacteristically silent. I was confused, so as he was leaving, I asked, "Gus, Have you ever been to Europe?"

"Yes, I have," was his short answer.

"Wouldn't you like to go back?" I persisted in a not very sensitive way.

Tears came to his eyes when he answered, "No, Charlie, I wouldn't," and he walked slowly out of the office.

I felt bad that I had upset such a gentile good man by asking what I thought was an innocent question.

A few nights later we happened to be at a party together and I related the incident to his wife. She said, "Oh Charlie, don't feel bad. That's just Gus. You see in the Second World War, he was a conscientious objector. He never could hurt anybody. They made him a medic. He was in Italy and all over Europe from 1943 to 1945. He saw his friends suffering and dying, and lived with things he's never been able to talk about. He got out of the army and has never spoken one word about it. Even to me."

I think of the agony of that gentile man and what he lived through and I cry today. I want to thank each one of those from "The Greatest Generation."

Lies

Like most families, the McOuat children were taught never to lie.

"George Washington never told a lie," we heard from our kindergarten teachers. infering that we should follow his example.

Yeh," I thought, "but who wants to be a famous president. I just want to play shortstop for the Rochester Red Wings. Nothing more. Shortstops lie when they do the hidden ball trick. Deception is part of the game." I was confused.

On Sunday, our Baptist minister shook his fist and warned from the pulpit about the eternal damnation awaiting sinners who lied, cheated, or committed something called adultery, which I couldn't understand at the time. It was scary.

At home, when I asked about hell, both parents shuffled their feet and mumbled vaguely as if it was something just too horrible to understand. Despite exposing me to Baptist theology, my parents did their best to shield me from the horrors of this world and whatever lies beyond.

Soon after our pseudo-discussion, my Mom found a glass broken on the front sidewalk and asked, "Did you break that bottle, Charles?"

"No Mom. I didn't do it. It must've been Jay Wilson across the street," I lied. When I spoke these words, I noticed that the sky didn't fall and I actually slept well that night despite the guilt implanted by ministers and parents.

As an adult, I was once publicly shamed when I was caught telling a lie.

My daughter Heather and I had just finished running a 10K road race on Cape Cod. We joined hundreds of other exhausted runners enjoying post race beers in a large field behind a tavern. Race officials stood high on a stage awarding prizes to male and female, first, second and third place finishers. After these real winners received their awards, categories were contrived to give away the remaining prizes. For example, prizes were awarded to all teachers, or pregnant mothers, or anyone from more than one hundred miles away. I had won nothing and they were nearing the bottom of the prize barrel.

The last call was for anyone who had played a college sport. I shared my disappointment with Heather because I wasn't eligible and they were giving away a nice "Brew Run" baseball cap. She looked at my disappointed face, patted me on the shoulder, and said, "Dad, just go up and tell them you played baseball for Tufts. No one knows. No one cares. Who will ever know?"

"But I never played baseball when I was at Tufts. I'm not sure we even had a baseball team.

"Dad, so what? The prize is only a stupid baseball hat. Go on. Tufts is so small no one will know. That was a long time ago. Go on."

"Well, I'm sure this is my last chance," I replied.

I walked up the stairs and stood on the stage, high above the crowd. A tall man with a booming voice asked, "Did you play a college sport?"

I answered in a softly, "Yes I did,"

I hoped that was the end of the questioning and I could quickly pull the hat over my head and slink down the stairs, but he persisted, "What sport did you play and at what school?"

I answered again even more meekly than to the first question, "I played baseball for Tufts."

He bellowed out to the crowd, "Wow, what a coincidence. I played baseball for Tufts too. What year did you play?"

Through the haze of my beery bloodshot eyes, the loudmouthed MC was starting to look familiar to me. I wanted to disappear at that moment. I said, "1963."

Big mouth persisted, "That's when I graduated. I don't remember you playing. What's your name?"

I now recognized him as an old college friend, much grayer and paunchier than when I last saw him, 25 years ago. I whispered, "Freddy, give me the damn hat. It's me. Charlie McOuat."

He pushed the microphone aside and said, "Oh shit Charlie, Why didn't you just say it was you. I would've given you two hats."

We both laughed at my embarrassment. I took the cap and ran off the stage, red faced and humbled. I descended into the crowd and didn't stop running until I reached the beer tent. That hat hangs in my room today to as a reminder of the consequences of lying.

If I said that I learned my lesson and never lied after that embarrassing incident that would be a lie.

Louie Eldridge

I was a new dentist on Cape Cod with a lot of debt and few patients to help pay expenses. I appreciated every patient but some more than others. One day an old man with a prominent New England accent, bad teeth, and a constant smile came into my office. He wanted to know everything about me and was more concerned about my adjustment to my adopted town than with his own dental problems. "Hey Doc, you're goin' to love it herah. This is a wonderful town, full of great people. You did your wife and kids a big favah by comin'' heeyah." His eyes widened and his whole face lit up when he described the treasures of Cape Cod that were so important to him.

We became quick friends. I was enchanted by his stories. One day I complained to him, "Louie, we've got skunks under our old house. The smell is embarrassing when we want to invite friends over. What can we do?"

He looked up at me with the most sincere caring look of a wise old man instructing the young unenlightened, "Doc, you don't have to do anything. You're lucky. With skunks under your house, their smell will clean out everybody's sinuses. Your kids will nevah catch a cold. Leave 'em theyah.

You don't want to hurt one of those beautiful creatures anyway. When I was a boy," he continued, "there used to be a bounty on skunks. I used to hunt 'em on my bicycle. We'd sneak up behind 'em, grab 'em by the tail so they couldn't let go, then I'd take 'em to town hall and get paid for each dead skunk. Now, .I couldn't kill one of those beautiful creatures for all the money in the world."

Louie loved all of God's creatures, including most humans. I scheduled his appointments only at the end of the day so when his dental work was finished, we sat back and talked without interruption. I told Marilyn about this loveable story teller and he became a regular guest in our kitchen. She too enjoyed his tales.

He told her that he had only been off the Cape only once in 52 years. He had to go to Providence for something, and he couldn't wait to get back home. She asked, "Louie, don't you want to see Paris or New York City?"

He said, "No. I can see everything I want right heeyah in Town Cove. I don't have to see anything mowah than that." I learned later that his nickname was "King of the Cove." He lived in a small house a few feet from the shore and daily raked its clear waters for clams, dug in the mud flats for sea worms which he'd sell to fishermen, or troll in the deep channel for strippers.

He educated us about our unwanted skunks. "They can't climb. When they fall in a pit under your house, they can't climb out like most animals. You're lucky, they'll probably stay with you." Marilyn didn't agree that a family of skunks living under our new home was "good luck." She was skeptical about his medical opinion that their aroma prevented sickness, but she fell in love with the "King of the Cove," like I did.

He promised to take me eeling with him if the winter was cold enough to freeze Meeting House Pond. He described making a hole through the ice and then spearing them as they sulked in the sandy bottom. He went into graphic detail about the catching, cleaning, and eating. He died before the Cove froze over so I never did go with him.

Flounder fishing in one of the salt water ponds in Orleans was a special family treat. We fished from an old wooden rowboat that had been abandoned in a forgotten fishing shed. It hadn't been in the water for years, leaked from both bow and stern but it was all we could afford. We had more fun in that old wreck than any of the fancier boats that came later. We used it only in small ponds and kept it close to shore in case the leaks ran faster than the bailing. When we caught an eel instead of a flounder, it was exciting to see Marilyn, Rob, and Heather recoil, like there was some escape from their slime in a small boat in the middle of a pond. I admit that I didn't enjoy an eel winding up and down my arm while I tried desperately to get it off the hook. More to honor Louie than from hunger we took some home and prepared them as he had instructed.

I carefully cut a ring behind its gills with a sharp knife and then grabbed a loose piece of the skin with pliers and pulled it off, over the body and tail, like a shirt over a child's head. Then we cut the body into three inch pieces, fried them and ate the meat off the bones like chicken wings. Marilyn and I toasted our wine glass to Louie before we ate the eels. We enjoyed the chicken like taste but not the strong smell in the house that lingered for days after our feast. No air freshener known at the time even touched the smell.

One day I mentioned Louie to another elderly patient who came into my office. Louie took up golfing later in his life and the patient, Charlie Clough, was one of his partners. Charlie said, "Yes I loved Louie too, but he was crazy you know?"

I said, "No, I didn't know he was crazy. What do you mean?"

He said, "I'll give you an example. One day we were in the middle of a golf game when this wounded duck walked by. It was limping and had a broken wing. Louie picked up this dying duck, carried it in his two hands to this pond that was hundreds of yards away. All the time he was carrying it the duck kept pecking at him, biting his hands and all up and down his arm. Louie held on and carried the thing to a pond and gently laid him in the water. When he came back his arm was all bleeding and sore from this stupid duck. I don't know who was in worse shape, the duck or Louie. Now isn't that crazy?"

I don't know," I said. "I'm not sure."

"Another time," he continued like he had to prove to me that there was indeed something wrong with Louie, "we were waiting on this tee when this ugly, slimy bug slithered across right where I wanted to tee up my ball. I reached down to shoe it away, when Louie grabbed my hand. He picked up a big leaf and enticed this ugly thing unto it and then carried it over and laid it in the bushes. He interrupted our golf game to save an ugly, slithering bug. Now I ask you. Isn't that crazy?"

I didn't answer but have spent the rest of my life trying to be crazy like Louie.

Captain Mike

Years ago I was spearing flounder at Pricilla Landing with Rob and Heather. They were probably four and five years old and sat in our old wooden rowboat, anchored in the shallow water. I snorkeled nearby trying to spear enough flounder for dinner. I swam along the top of the water, looking for the telltale shape of the fish, outlined in the sand. When I saw one large enough, I speared it and then dropped it in the boat with the two kids. They were amused but not frightened by a flounder flopping towards them. The boat was anchored in only a few feet of water so if they fell in, I was confident they could walk to shore. I stayed within easy swimming distance in case there was a problem.

I speared a large one and was swimming towards them to unload the catch when I looked up and saw Rob leaning over the stern of the boat. He was looking at something swimming underneath and became so engrossed in whatever it was, that he fell headfirst into the cold water and the muck and mire below. He came up without a problem and stood in the waist deep water with seaweed and mud covering his face and little body. I quickened my pace in case he needed help but was relieved to see him calmly walking ashore.

Heather, unfortunately took one look at his predicament and started laughing. That made him mad enough to take out his misfortune on her. He yelled and cursed which made her laugh even harder. This vicious circle continued until I was able to disentangle my catch from the end of my spear, drop it in the boat, and intercede in their squabble.

Three fat flounder and two squabbling children is quite a load for one tired twelve foot rowboat so I decided to call it a day. I pulled the boat up on the sand and carried the fish and spear towards the car, followed by the two kids still yelling at each other. Rob was wiping pond muck from his face and pulling sea weed out of his hair. His face was bright red with anger aimed at his sister. Our gruesome threesome was walking towards our car, when I saw a young man, bent over his pickup truck, which was stuck in the sand. The man, about thirty years old, his body bursting with its own anger, was trying to hammer a four wheel drive adjustment into place. He was making no progress. Without the four wheel drive, he couldn't free his truck from the sand. He hammered, cursed, stomped, and screamed, then stood back and threw his hammer at his reluctant vehicle. His hair was blond, his face a bright red, and his mouth was spewing forth cuss words that were making me blush. Clearly, the truck was getting the best of him. The kids continued walking towards our car and asked me what was wrong that guy. "Dad, is he crazy?"

I had no answer but walked over and asked, "Can I help you?"

He retrieved his hammer, looked up at me without embarrassment, and said, "I don't think so. I just can't get this damn lever over here to shift it into four wheel drive. I've gotta get these lobsters to the market before it closes and this f-n truck won't move."

I said, "Well I don't know anything about trucks, but I could take my kids home, get us a couple of beers, and maybe we can figure something out."

He didn't say much but was not in a position to refuse help. He gave a friendly nod of his head as I put flounder, kids and spear in my old car and drove off.

I came back in a few minutes, minus the kids who were safely home with their Mom. The truck was now free of the sand and the lobsterman stood leaning against the cab, smoking a cigar. He reached out his hand, smiled, and said, "Hi, I'm Mike Kartazewitz."

I thrust a cold beer into his outstretched hand and that was my introduction to Captain Mike, lobsterman and legend in EastOrleans.

He seemed to be impressed that I could spear flounder near his boat mooring and I wanted to learn everything about the lobster business. He spoke with a thick New England accent, mixed with a unique enunciation at the end of certain words that reflected his Polish heritage. He never did address his verbal and physical assault on his truck as if that was a normal behavior for him. His deep blue eyes lit up when he talked about anything but his favorite subjects were women and lobstering. After one beer together, we parted company but I was hopeful to learn more about this man.

Days later, I recognized his truck in town parked outside the general store. He was in the driver's seat, wearing an old sailor's hat, one arm out the window, the other draped around a beautiful girl. Another girl sat beside her, both smiling, enjoying his company. I said, "Hi Mike, I'm Charlie, I met you down by the shore a few nights ago."

"Oh sure, I remember, thanks again for the beer."

"No problem," I replied, "but who are these beautiful women beside you?"

"Oh Yeh, These are my mates. This is Julie and her friend is…Sorry…What was your name again? Oh sorry… This is her friend Marge." Julie hooked her arm around Mike's like she didn't want to let go and Marge snickered at Mike's inability to remember her name.

"Pleased to meet you both," I said. "But Mike, did you say they're your mates? I saw your boat that night. It's a beauty. But do you need two mates for a thirty five foot lobster boat?"

He looked up at me and spoke like a man addressing a boy. "Charlie, I only use one at a time but you've always gotta have a spare." He said spare with the dropped "r," like "spa-yah."

I laughed, the women giggled, and Mike smiled like he was educating the unenlightened. When he said he always needed a spare, I wasn't sure whether he meant as a lobster boat mate or as a bed partner but it didn't seem to matter to anyone. I didn't ask.

Julie, the mate with the long black hair said, "Charlie, we've… er I mean Mike has a new pet. It's a crow that flew into the side of his boat and hurt its wing. He brought it home and now he lives with us."

"Gee, that's great Mike I never heard of a pet crow before. How's it going?"

Mike answered, "It's going great. When I go offshore, he perches on the bow of my boat. He faces into the wind. He loves it. I go home, he sits across from me at the table. We have dinner together. He even watches TV with me."

Now I sensed that Mike was exaggerating. "TV? Really," I thought I was being mocked so I asked, "What's his favorite channel?"

Without hesitation, he answered, "The Weather Channel, of course."

Of course I was the stupid one because any intelligent person would realize that a TV watching bird would prefer The Weather Channel. The two beauties kept their adoring eyes on their hero, believing everything, and I just wanted him to keep talking.

"Mike, you seem to have everything right here. Do you ever go off Cape?"

"Sure I do. Last weekend I went to Providence to get a boat engine repaired. My dad lives in nearby so I stayed with him. I parked the truck along side his house and then went out to see some friends. I had the broken engine in the back and I was afraid it was going to get wet if it rained so I asked him to throw a tarp over it in case of rain. I went out and didn't think much of it. The next morning I left early but when I tried to stop the truck, the motor made this cracking, wacking, ugly noise. I turned off the motor, raised the hood, and I see the tarp over the truck's engine.

The broken engine was still in the back of the truck uncovered. I thought for a minute, then went into the house to my dad. I told him, 'Dad, when I told you to cover the motor with the tarp, I meant the motor in back, not the truck's motor. I don't believe it.... Now I know why they make jokes about us.'"

Now Mike is almost sixty years old, still lobstering, just as handsome, still unmarried, completely independent but everybody's friend. His blond hair has turned gray, but he maintains the body of that thirty year old from his hard work at sea and the constant care it gets from his adoring women.

Graham Coveyduck

On our traumatic first day in the dental clinic I was glad to have Graham Coveyduck set up next to me. Most dental students were very serious but he was one of the few with a sense of humor. He was brought up in an orphanage and learned along the way that life was not to be taken too seriously. He had been a gifted student who started at a community college, graduated from a four year college, and ultimately on to dental school.

Our class had been through the basic sciences with the medical students but now we were going into our first day in the dental clinic. This was our initial exposure to our chosen profession. We had practiced on plastic teeth but had never before worked on live patients. I was nervous like everyone else except Graham who just kept talking to his patient like they were old friends. She was a short, sweet gray haired lady, with a broad smile, and a maternal demeanor that suggested that she spent most of her time in the kitchen baking apple pies for her grandchildren.

The instructor checked what Graham intended to do, then stepped away to allow him to give his first injection of novacaine. He was working on an upper molar so the needle had to go above the roots of the teeth. Somehow he went too high, too deep, and injected into the trigeminal nerve that innervated the face. He injected, the old lady jumped, and Graham let go. Immediately the old lady's face drooped and her eye on that side closed. Graham stood back and looked at her half paralyzed face, ran over to me and asked, "Charlie, I don't know what happened but look at her. Something's wrong. What the hell do I do now?"

I looked at her closed eye, her face drawn to one side and shrugged my shoulders, "I don't know Graham. Call the instructor, I guess." I was glad it didn't happen to me.

Graham returned to his patient, trying to reassure her everything was all right but wasn't very convincing. The old lady felt her face, looked around the room through her one good eye, put her hand on Graham's arm, and said, in a sugary sweet way, "Sonny, you better do what you have to do today because I ain't ever comin" back to this dental school again."

He had to dismiss the patient and I'm sure she never did return to the school or maybe even to a dentist.

Years later, I had an established practice on Cape Cod and was glad when Graham visited my house for a night. He brought his two teen aged kids who were about the same age as Rob and Heather. My father was also spending a few days with us so I decided to cook a nice dinner and serve it in our dining room. My father had a good sense of humor but he was the straightest person on Earth. He didn't drink, smoke or swear and couldn't tolerate even slightly tainted joke. The dinner was progressing well until Graham decided to liven things up with a joke.

He started, "Did you hear the one about Tarzan and Jane meeting in the jungle? Tarzan said, 'Me Tarzan. What your name?'"

Jane answered, "Me Jane."

Tarzan then asked, "What your whole name?"

Jane said, "Cunt."

I burst out laughing, not because the joke was funny but because of the interplay between the insensitive Graham and my straight laced father. My Dad cleared his throat, said nothing, but immediately bolted from the table. Graham saw me howling with laughter but thought my father didn't understand the joke so followed him into the kitchen to explain it to him. "You see Mr McOuat, he said 'What is your hole name like first and second name but Jane thought he meant whole name. w-h-o-l-e name like vagina." To further clarify the confusion, Graham made a round whole with his thumb and forefinger to represent a woman's vagina. My father kept walking away with Graham in hot persuit explaining the stupid joke over and over again. I was doubled over in laughter at the contrast between them but regained composure long enough to grab Graham, shut him up, and lead him away from my very uncomfortable father.

I explained that my Dad hates dirty jokes and Graham responded in all innocence, "Why didn't you tell me?"

I said, "Graham I kicked you under the table, waved my arms, did everything but tackle you but you wouldn't stop."

After everyone regained their composure, we returned to the table, enjoyed our ice cream dessert and confined our conversation to fishing.

Bad News

I was glad to be home from the dental office. I knew Marilyn had an appointment after work and would be home late but I was still anxious to see her. We usually sat in the kitchen, let the kids play in the back room while we talked about today or planned for tomorrow. We had been married for 14 years but my spirits continued to soar during our quiet times together.

Our kitchen was long and narrow, with a bay window on one side overlooking fruit trees; on the other side a smaller window looked out over an open field to the neighbor's distant house. We ate our meals at either a breakfast bar or an antique kitchen table. Besides being our primary eating place, it was the center of our family life and the popular gathering place at parties.

Most nights when our work days ended, I would sit across the table from Marilyn and admire how her long black hair formed a curl as it flowed below her shoulders, how her brown eyes would flash when she became excited, and how her full red lips turned upwards at the corners to form a natural smile. Only a dentist could appreciate the beauty of her big sparkling, white teeth. She was tall, straight backed, with a regal posture that others tried to copy. She was gentile, never raised her voice, but all would listen when she spoke because her words had value. She was 35 years old but maintained a childish excitement towards the world and its people. Strangers would meet her and ask me, "Where did you find that beautiful woman?" I knew I was a lucky man.

I was about to start preparing dinner when our 11 year old son Rob approached and asked, "Dad, Eric said that his parents are thinking of moving away from Cape Cod."

"Really, I wonder why?" I loved talking to Rob. Although he was only 11, he was nearly my height, handsome, with an athletic body. He daydreamed often, slightly shy, a friend to everyone, and was very sensitive. He seldom needed discipline and always tried to please.

"I think Mrs. Knowles doesn't like it here and Mr. Knowles wants a better job. Do you like it here Dad? Are we going to move?"

"No Rob. We aren't going anywhere. Your Mom likes her career. I like mine. We've got the two best kids in the world and we couldn't be happier. We're so lucky to have a beach so near and a marina right across the street. I can't imagine living anywhere else. This is our home."

"That's good Dad. I don't want to move either." His smile was a gift from his mother.

"Life couldn't be any better than this, Rob. Don't worry." After a pause, I added, "Come on. I'll play you a game of ping-pong. Heather is upstairs showering. Mom won't be home for a while. Let's go." Heather was a year younger than Rob and almost a foot shorter. She hated her freckles but loved everything else. She too was sensitive but much more emotional. I admired the comfortable way she expressed her emotions, from anger to joy, often separated by only a few seconds. Rob would use his size to get what he wanted but Heather would yell, cry, or persist until her soft hearted brother would give in. Both were almost always at peace with each other and the world. Marilyn and I seldom had to intervene in any childish squabbles.

I could hear the shower running so I knew that Heather wouldn't be ready to eat for half an hour. "C'mon Rob. I'll play you a full game to 21 and then we'll cook some spaghetti."

Rob spread out at the far end of the table and tried usual his power game to wear down his slower father. He was able to beat me occasionally but if I could be patient his power shots would get wild. The score was 3-2 when a knock at the door interrupted our game. I hurried because I knew that whoever was there would be freezing on this cold December night. I peered through the darkness to see the town police chief standing on the entranceway with a serious look on his face. Chet was everyone's friend, about fifty years old, with a muscular build that suggested regular exercise. He and I had become friends when I rescued him from a toothache one weekend. He remained grateful that I had persisted for an hour to extract a broken bicuspid from his jaw on a Saturday afternoon.

I was surprised when he didn't smile or shake my hand but pushed past me, into the kitchen. "Hi Chet, How ya' doin?'" was all I could manage to say.

He wiped his feet on the welcome mat, handed me a slip of paper, and, in a scary professional manner, said, "Charlie, Please call this number."

It seemed like a strange request but I immediately dialed the phone. I was puzzled by his formality and noticed that he avoided looking at me. "Cold, isn't it?" I said to him while waiting for someone to answer the phone. He was pacing the floor and looking around like he wanted to escape. I took a deep breath and realized my heart was racing. Something horrible was happening and I couldn't stop it.

A man answered and after I identified myself to him, he said, "Dr. McOuat, I'm afraid I have some bad news. Your wife was in a car accident on the Mid-Cape Highway. She was killed instantly. She never made it to the hospital."

I yelled into the phone, "Who hit her? Some drunk?" The man never got a chance to answer. I threw the phone against the wall and approached the chief.

Chet grabbed the phone, hung up the receiver, put his hands on my shoulders, and cried. He said, "Charlie, I'm sorry. I couldn't tell you. She was hit by a wrong way driver. He was on the wrong side of the highway. He was killed too. She never knew what hit her."

I don't recall what happened next. I was furious and there was no outlet for my rage. I think Chet tried to wrap his arms around me but I pushed him aside like he wasn't there and hugged Rob while yelling, "Rob, Mom is dead. She was in a car accident. She won't be coming home." I could feel Rob's arms tighten around my neck and his tears rolled down my cheek.

Both of us were yelling and hugging when Heather ran into the kitchen. She wore a pink bathrobe and a towel wrapped around her wet hair. She had a confused look on her face that I remember today as clearly as that night, 25 years ago. "Mom is dead, Heather. A car accident. I'm sorry."

Rob and I continued cursing and screaming. Heather, the emotional one, hugged hard but said little. She was too hurt and shocked to utter a sound. She could not understand that her mother, her best friend, was gone, forever. The three of us huddled together in triangle of shock, misery, and fear. "What are we going to do Dad?" one of them asked. I had no answer. Chet's attempts to comfort were ignored.

Within minutes, it seemed like half the town was in our kitchen, hugging, crying, trying to comfort each other, but nothing could stop the disbelief and the despair. The kitchen, which had always been our peaceful place, was now just a room of horror, full of tears, curses, and prayers, but nothing could dull the reality that Marilyn was not there.

One woman, who I hardly knew, said that it was part of God's plan. I now had someone to focus my anger on, and I did. I screamed at her to leave the house, immediately. I could not tolerate such nonsense. Not now. Not ever. Everyone else exuded love that still warms me today.

Crowds gathered in our kitchen, all shocked and feeling helpless but I was strengthened by their efforts. It was almost midnight when the last person left. Rob and Heather were in bed, dealing with their own agony. Although the adrenaline was still pumping feverishly through my body, I climbed the dark stairs and went to bed. I wrapped my arms around her pillow and laid there wide awake listening to cars drive slowly by the house all night long. The entire town was awake and having trouble accepting the tragedy. They wanted to help.

I was comforted by Chet's words that "She never knew what hit her." Maybe she didn't suffer. I hoped that she died before she realized what was happening. Alone in bed, I thought about those two beautiful kids growing up without their mother, and the tears did not stop.

Twenty five years have passed since that horrible night. I have gone on with my life, the kids with theirs. We've done well, but nothing had prepared us for the shock, the emptiness, the anger, the pain of going on without Marilyn, our wife and mother.

Art Gives Permission

Art drove over the Sagamore Bridge, across the Cape Cod Canal, and headed north to Boston. We were on our way to the weekend dental conference. This was my first venture from Orleans and the kids since Marilyn's death, two months before.

"Art, I can't believe how good everyone has been to us since her accident. I've hardly cooked a meal. The casseroles, the diner invitations keep coming. It's unbelievable."

"I'm sure of that Charlie. We can't do enough. Everyone wants to help but don't know what to do." I had sometimes mistakenly thought of Art as a clown, someone who needed to be partying or joking all the time. He, his wife Susie, Marilyn, and I had been constant friends for years. Whether it was for a casual cup of coffee, a weekend getaway, or throwing a party, they were always there laughing and having fun. He was the first one to our house after her fatal accident. There were no jokes this time, only tears and hugs.

"You two especially have been great, Art. I don't know what I would've done…. Others too have surprised me. Like Gordon Ames. I always thought he was a snob. He and Debby came over and told me about his brother's early death. It helps. A crisis like this can bring out the best in people."

"I'm sure of that," he answered.

I thought for a minute. A sick feeling came into my stomach. "Art, I know that Marilyn's been dead only two months, but this girl came into my office…" I hesitated. "She's been a patient…. A young lawyer from Chatham. She's beautiful." He leaned towards me trying not to miss a word. "I had a cancellation yesterday. I told Betty, 'Get in that young lawyer from Chatham.' She immediately knew that I meant Sue Perkins."

We drove past a sign for Plymouth. I knew we had plenty of driving time remaining. I continued. "At the end of her appointment, she said, 'I know you like community theatre. Maybe we could be in a play together sometime.' I drooled and answered, 'That would be great.' I think she likes me, Art," I added like a schoolboy.

Talkative Art remained silent. I wanted his approval so I continued, "I feel like I'm cheating on someone I love, but I've thought of nothing else since then…Maybe it's too early. I don't know."

Finally he said, "Charlie, only you can tell if it's too early. No one else. Obviously you're going to date sometime. If you try and screw up, your friends will stick by you. When someone judges you at a time like this, they're not much of a friend anyway. What do you care what they think. When you feel up to it, give her a call."

I interpreted this as an unqualified endorsement. I also thought that this was pretty good advice, coming from someone who I had once branded as a clown. I tried to switch the conversation to something else, dentistry perhaps. Nothing worked. I kept thinking of that beautiful woman and her smile. We drove on towards Boston where the crowded convention and empty bed awaited.

....

After daydreaming all the way to Boston about the "beautiful lawyer from Chatham," I was able to relax, focus on the convention, and bring home some helpful ideas for the office. It was great to be home. My two children's smiling faces reminded me again what is really important in my life. Heather's freckled face looked up and said, "Hi Dad," and I melted. Rob stood behind her waiting patiently for his hug. I wrapped my arms around them both, laughing and crying at the same time. I was away for only two days, but their welcome made it seem like I had just returned from the war.

We played penny poker after a spaghetti dinner, and then they went upstairs to bed. The loneliness of that big old house struck deep into me and wouldn't let go. I had been with Art all weekend, enjoying the constant adult companionship. Now I was alone. I dreaded going upstairs to that empty bed. I could read myself to sleep, but knew that I would wake up in two hours feeling the hollowness within, and be alone with my anxiety for the rest of the night. That had been my pattern for two months and was getting worse instead of better.

As I washed the dishes, the internal debate between my emotional and rational selves began:

Emotion: She's unbelievably cute. Sooo friendly. I'll bet she's waiting for my call

Rational: She's too young. She'll laugh at you. Last summer she talked about her boyfriend. Grow up.

Emotion: Why would she suggest a play together if she wasn't interested? What a great smile.

Rational: She just graduated from law school. You can't trust lawyers.

She's probably 26. You're 39. She's in a different league.

Emotional: She's obviously smart. And wow! Is she's beautiful.

Rational: She'll be busy. Be responsible. You don't have a chance. Don't come crying to me to bail you out of another jam when you get hurt.

Emotional: She's cute. She's beautiful. She's friendly. Life is short. Go on, do it.

Rational: I quit. You're hopeless.

Emotional: You never had a chance, you old fart.

I walked quickly into the dental office, fumbled through some records, and found her phone number. My heart pounded. I paced the floor, sat, stood up, blew my nose, paced some more, sat, dialed the first three numbers, hung up, then dialed again. "Hello Susan. This is Charlie Mc…. Oh. Sorry. This isn't Susan. Oh. Can I talk to her? Please. Thank you." Charlie, calm down. She's only human.

"Hi Susan. This is Charlie McOuat Your dentist…"

"Oh Hi," she answered with enthusiasm, "How ya doin'?"

"Fine…I just got back from a dental convention in Boston….With a friend.."

"Oh. I love Boston."

"Yeh. Me too. It's nice to be back on the Cape though. We have to keep taking courses to maintain our license. Do you?"

"Yes. But I just graduated so I don't have to worry for a while."

I could picture that beautiful face on the other end of the phone. This is fun. People are wonderful. "How's your job?"

"I like it. It's a lot of work though. I work ten hours, five days a week. Mom says I need to go out and have some fun"

Now I was flying. She was making this so easy, like we were a team. "Your Mom sounds very wise….Would you like to go out Saturday night…?" I was going on but she interrupted.

"That would be great. I'd love to."

Now I interrupted her. "Good. Let's go to dinner, then a show. Mary Tyler Moore is out with a new movie…"

"I love Mary Tyler Moore. It sounds wonderful."

"Okay, I assume the movie starts about nine. Could I pick you up around six? I don't care where we eat. We'll find someplace nice."

"That's terrific." Was that electricity I could hear in her voice? I sat up straighter. "Where do you live?" She described her location, gave some directions, but I was confused. "Was that two rights after you turn off route 28 or one?"

"Two. But why don't you buy one of those maps if you're confused?" I didn't like the way she was already spending money for me but I was too euphoric to care.

"Okay, See you about six on Saturday night." I hung up the phone, danced into the bathroom and looked in the mirror. You did it. Your life isn't over. I noticed a touch of gray around my temples and those worry lines on my forehead.

First Date

I put the kids' favorite dinner of spaghetti and meatballs on the table, told them to help themselves to some ice cream for dessert, and kissed them goodbye. I just couldn't tell them that I was going on a date with a beautiful woman, two months after their mother was killed in a tragic car accident. I felt like I was abandoning my first love, my family, to pursue my own pleasure.

My guilt drifted away when I sat behind the wheel of the station wagon and drove towards Susan's house. I couldn't wait to see her. I practiced a smile into the mirror while I was waiting at a STOP sign on route 28. Despite the cold, I was careful not to wear a hat. I didn't want to sit across the table from her with cowlicks sticking up in all directions. Chatham, her town, in February is dark and deserted. There wasn't a traffic light working, motel signs were turned off, and no one walked the streets. I passed few cars on the trip over. I drove by her house 45 minutes early.

I turned around and saw a dimly lit general store on the corner. A blue ice chest and red Coke machine, both empty, guarded the entranceway. A hand painted sign advertised, "Fish Bait, Hot Dogs, and Souvenirs." Inside, a slim teenaged boy, teeth blackened with nicotine, greeted me with a blank stare. "Cold tonight, isn't it?" I commented.

I paced up and down the aisles of the dingy store, glancing at cans of tuna fish, Cape Cod potato chips, Cape Cod candles, Ocean Spray cranberry juice, Chatham salt water taffy. My teen aged friend put down his newspaper and followed me like I was a criminal. I kept my hands in my pockets to allay any suspicions. "Do you have any Certs?" I asked. I had brushed my teeth three times before leaving the house, but I needed to say something just to break the silence.

"No Certs," he answered. "Got some peppermint Life Savers. They might help."

Were my insecurities that obvious, I wondered. If this acne scarred teenager realizes I'm nervous, Susan will see it in no time. I've got to relax.

I picked up the life savers. "Fifty cents please." I could see my hand shaking as I handed him a $10 bill. "Is that the smallest you've got?" He asked.

"Sorry." He stared at my trembling hands and chuckled.

He reluctantly counted out the $9.50 change and handed it to me. "You'll be fine, Romeo." I wanted to reach across the counter, grab him by the shirt, and smack his grinning face, but instead I put the change in my pocket, lowered my head, and walked quickly from the store.

The dashboard clock read 5:55, Perfect. I threw the life savers in the back seat. I had seen enough of them and I didn't want to greet Susan with a hard candy stuck to my dry tongue. I looked at myself in the rear view mirror and thought, *What is wrong with you? You've got two kids, a career, tons of friends but you're acting like a frightened teenager. Relax. This isn't you're first dinner date with a woman. I* scraped the frost from the window and slowly drove down the hill to her house.

I was relieved to find Susan alone in the house when she answered the door. I didn't want to make small talk with her mother. Not tonight. She looked even more beautiful than I remembered. She wore a dark brown skirt with contrasting white blouse; a small gold locket sparkled around her neck. She wore little lipstick and not much eye makeup. She didn't need any. Her eyes danced as she greeted me. "Hi Charlie. Did you have any trouble finding the house?"

"No. Your directions were perfect. I'm glad you told me about that peacock in the front yard. I couldn't read your house number but that sculptured peacock led the way."

"I'm so embarrassed. Mummy thought we needed some color out there so we hung that horrible peacock," she said without real signs of embarrassment.

"I kind of like it. A colorful decoration for a colorful woman." As soon as the words were out of my mouth, I regretted their casual tone, but I was already under her spell. She seemed happy, probably because I was taking her mother's side in the peacock debate.

"It's cold," I added. "I made reservations at Brax Landing so we wouldn't have to drive too far. The roads are icy."

"I know where it is but I've never been there. I've been too busy with school and now my job for fine dining. This is a real treat."

"Well it certainly is a treat for me. You look great." I couldn't stifle the compliments and she didn't seem to mind. "Maybe we should go because our reservation is for 6:30."

She deftly handed me her coat like she was more accustomed to a fancy night out than she was admitting to. I was breathing again and caught a tantalizing hint of perfume. We smiled at each other as I helped with her coat. Her charm was putting me at ease and allowing me to concentrate on the joy of the evening instead of my own anxieties. It seemed natural when she held my arm and we walked carefully together, down the icy sidewalk leading to my car.

Brax Landing is a popular upscale restaurant on the main road through Harwich Center. I chose it because of its seaside location, excellent reputation, and distance from Orleans. I didn't want to run into familiar faces on this first entry into the dating world after a long marriage. This is an area of small towns, full of friendly people, but I didn't want to start rumors flying before I did anything worthy of rumor. I recognized no one as we entered.

I had called the restaurant three times to make sure we would have a table for two in a quiet corner. The hostess seated us at a perfect table. A single candle danced in a hurricane lamp sitting on a linen table cloth. Behind me, a blazing fire from the stone fireplace warmed my back. Susan placed her napkin on her lap and together we marveled at the miracle of flood lights reflecting off the water. Waves broke around pilings, standing strong against the winter wind. Sea gulls, standing on wooden bulkheads, tucked their heads beneath their wings and braced themselves on one leg. Spray from onrushing waves rhythmically painted our window with ocean frost. We could barely hear the piano player above the crackling of the fire. The smell of burning locust wood gave an outdoor feel to our cozy table. Susan was transfixed by the scene but I couldn't take my eyes off her. She leaned forward in her chair and warmed me with a silent smile. When our eyes met for the second time, I had to look down at the menu.

"With a background like this, I'm definitely ordering seafood," was my best attempt at conversation.

"I agree," she said. "Who would think of perverting a scene like this with a steak? One of the bonuses of living here is the fresh seafood. I eat it all the time." We studied the menu together. A waiter wearing a white shirt and black bow tie patiently awaited our drink order. Susan asked if I would order the wine. I chose my favorite Pino Gregio. "Don't you just love the Cape in the winter? No crowds. No traffic. Its so pretty here."

"It's beautiful. It's like living in two separate places. In the summer, the tourists, the beaches and swimming and now, its like small town America. I'm not sure which I prefer. I just feel very lucky to be able to live here and feed my family."

The waiter presented the bottle of wine and poured a taste before filling our glasses. We clicked our glasses and I proposed a toast to the joy of life on Cape Cod.

"I can't imagine living anywhere else." Her lips curled up in a smile with every word, putting me at ease. "I've had sand in my shoes so I guess I'm hooked."

The waiter returned and asked if we were ready to order our dinners. "Are you ready, Susan?" I asked.

"Sure. I'll have the haddock with a baked potato, no butter and a salad with Italian dressing."

I liked the self assured way she made her decision. "I'll have the same except for rice instead of the baked potato." The waiter thanked us. I wondered if his gratitude was because we gave our orders so simply or was it just that the whole world was in a good mood that night. I couldn't stop smiling.

Our eyes met as she asked, "Does your practice slow down in the winter?"

"Not at all. The year around residents want their work done in the winter when they're not so busy. In the summer we're loaded with tourists. I'm as busy as I want to be. I'm so lucky to be able to live here. No cities . No commuting." Her sincere interest in my life was making this easy and I was on a roll. "How about you? You say you're always working."

"I am. There's so much real estate work. Everybody wants to come here. Yesterday I did three closings. I had to go in this morning, Saturday, just to catch up." When she became excited about something, like her new career or life on Cape Cod, she would lean forward and her face and entire body would tense up with enthusiasm. Her eyes sparkled like the light reflecting off the ocean. "The guys I work for are nice. They treat me well."

"I'm sure you do a good job for them." I was also sure that her good looks and enthusiasm about everything would brighten up even a law office. I was enthralled by her exuberance, her looks, the seaside setting; tonight, everything was beautiful, even the practice of law. She kept talking, I kept staring. Neither of us noticed when the waiter brought our salads. "I know they're lucky to have you. You can't miss."

"Thanks. That's a really nice thing to say." She paused and looked away for a second. "I'm pretty green but they have a lot of patience with me. It's easy to make mistakes when you're so busy. I have to get used to the fast pace. It's not like school."

Maybe she's not as self assured after all, I thought. I saw this as a strength, not a weakness. She kept on talking, a model of happiness; I didn't want to miss a word. I almost interrupted her when I said, "I was in a play once with your Mom. She had a big part, I just had a walk on but I was impressed with her in every way. I remember there was a guy in this play who made me laugh no matter what he said. Opening night, when I walked on stage to deliver my few lines, he did something and I broke into hysterical laughter. I couldn't speak. I was out of control and totally embarrassed. Luckily, it was at the end of the first act so they dropped the curtain and most of the audience wasn't aware of what happened. Your mother would have known. She must think I'm a complete jerk."

Susan's head snapped backwards and her mouth opened wide when she laughed. "My Mom has a great sense of humor. She would have thought it was funny. She's had so much fun in community theatre."

"I hope so. How is your Mom?"

"She's great. She works so hard though. She's a nurse and hardly ever gets a night off. Those plays are her only breaks. She's always lecturing me about working so hard and she does it all the time. If I ever make enough money as a lawyer, I'd like to be able to help her." The waiter was bringing our haddock, although neither of us had touched our salads.

We continued talking about her mother, the theatre, scuba diving, Cape Cod life. I was fascinated by the way she cut her fish with a knife instead of a fork as I always do, or how she peeked over her glass when sipping her wine, or turned to the side when reapplying her lipstick. Every mannerism suggested that she was having fun and wanted me to like her.

The night was flying by, and I didn't want it to end. The waiter returned in two hours to remove our empty plates. I looked at my watch and realized that we would miss the movie if we didn't leave soon.

"I'm having a great time but would you like to see the movie?" It's with Mary Tyler Moore? I don't know what it's about."

"I love Mary Tyler Moore, but it's up to you. You're driving."

"Let's go," I said, then paid the bill and put my arm around her. As we left the dining room I could feel her slender waist and the warmth of her body. We both smiled when her sideways glance caught me staring at her again.

Months later she confided to me that she was glad I talked so much that night because she was a bit nervous and my constant chatter put her at ease. That surprised me because I thought that she did most of the talking. I'm sure my adrenaline was flowing but any success I had was due to her charm, not my personality.

When I parked outside her house after the movie, I was beguiled by her but confused. I still felt married to Marilyn even though she was dead. In our fourteen years of marriage, I had never kissed another woman, not even on New Years Eve or a birthday. I had always turned my cheek to meet their lips to avoid any real intimacy. Now, I felt that a kiss would be an appropriate ending to a perfect evening, but that I would somehow be cheating on my wife's memory. I turned to Susan and said, "I really had a great time tonight. The dinner, the movie, you…. I'd like to see you again…soon"

"OH, Me too," she answered. "What a thoroughly enjoyable evening."

"I don't want to wait for next weekend. Can I see you Wednesday night for dinner? After work?"

"That would be great. Let's do it." I slid over in the car next to her and we hugged. I could feel the softness of her cheek against mine, the lightness of her hair, and smell of her perfume. I pulled away and retreated to the safety of my side of the car.

I escorted her to the door, hugged her again, then drove away smiling. On the way home, I caught myself humming, "What a day this has been, What a rare mood I'm in…." I had done it, called her up and we had spent a magical evening together. My new life was beginning.

It was almost midnight when I arrived home. I entered the darkened house, climbed the stairs two at a time, and went immediately to Heather's room. She stirred in her sleep when I kissed her. "Did you have fun tonight, Dad?" she murmured, more asleep than awake.

"Yes Heather, I did. I'll tell you about it in the morning. I love you very much" She was already asleep again and didn't reply. Rob was asleep and didn't move when I said, "I love you." His face was smooth, round, flawless and as innocent as the day I first held him, 11 years before.

I brushed my teeth, changed into my pajamas and climbed into the cold bed. I could hear the furnace humming downstairs. Moonlight outlined the bare tree branches slapping against the window. I thought of those two beautiful children, snuggled in their beds, their whole future looming with no mother. Tears flooded my face. My body shook, out of control, in spasms of anguish. When I raised my hand to wipe my face, I smelled Susan's perfume. My new life was beckoning to me but I hadn't said goodbye to the old one. Marilyn, was still my wife and mother to my children. My body tightened and I couldn't stop crying. "God help me," I prayed over and over again, but the pain didn't stop.

Living Rooms

We sit in Slusky's living room, smiling at each other, trying to be friendly with the other guests, but I keep thinking of her. She has that natural smile and beauty that make her look comfortable in a crowded party but I wonder. She's ten years younger than everyone else, probably the only one without kids, and is thinking more of establishing a career than comparing diaper brands. She's only four years out of college, closer to frat parties than problems of children in school, but still her face lights up when she answers Bruce, "Yes, Charlie and I have been going out for a month now. We're having a ball."

"How can you stand it? You think he's fun? I thought a sharp woman like you would have better taste than that." jokes Bruce, nodding towards me, hinting that he can't imagine me being fun. She balances her meat balls on the paper plate with one hand, puts the other to her face as if to stifle a laugh but her mouth flies open, emitting a loud guffaw from way down in her belly.

"From the way you guys tease each other, I sometimes think you're serious."

Bruce continues, but can't hold back a broad grin, "We are serious. You're way too good for him."

"Well I think he's great. But he does complain a lot about having weird friends."

I stand up, wipe the red sauce off my chin, and show my appreciation of her defending me, "Susan, let me rescue you from this guy. As you can see, Bruce has trouble relating to people in a civilized manner. He's from Ohio. You know, Midwest and all that. He's not use to high class people like you and me. Plus, people do question his sanity."

"Oh yeh," she responds, "you warned me about him." She turns away goes to the safety of the three women standing nearby. She stands on the periphery of the group and listens as they continue their conversation. Bruce and I stare at her back, admiring her erect posture, the shape of her bottom, the erotic curves of her whole body. She shifts her weight from side to side, strokes her hair, and waits for a convenient entrance into the threesome. Bruce interrupts our silent gawking.

"Charlie, have a ball. You deserve it. She is excellent," he adds in a serious tone.

I hear him talking but I'm more focused on Susan's back than his words. Her flowered dress clings tightly to the prominence of her bottom, which is perfectly sculpture by years of dancing. Besides a law degree, a passion for Shakespeare, she has the body of a "Playboy" centerfold model. I'm in awe of her youth, beauty, and charm. I suppress the impulse to go over, wrap my arms around her, and tell her how much I am under her spell.

She uses her whole body when she talks; her arms and hands in motion, her eyes get bigger, and she raises her forehead in a show of enthusiasm. She stands tall, straight back, appearing confident but she hasn't yet entered into the threesome of women. Despite her beautiful appearance, she almost looks out of place among all the mothers who are used to each other and share common interests.

Is she more comfortable around men than women? Is she having fun? I want to rescue her. I don't want her to feel uncomfortable for one minute. I want her to like me and my friends. Bruce continues to talk but I'm thinking only of her. We have progressed to heavy necking in the last weeks and I think of her comment as we parted on our last date. "I get so steamed up when we kiss like this, but we always part. I get frustrated." I interpreted that as an invitation to go the next step and enjoy each other's bodies. She seems to need me tonight. I wonder if underneath that beauty, the obvious charm, and poise, she might have some of the same insecurities as everyone else.

I circulate around the room, try to enjoy my friends, listen to their witty conversations but I really want to be alone with her. Even in a crowd of friends like this, my mind wanders to her. She takes me to levels of happiness that I can reach in no other way. Our conversations are easy, I like to look at her, be with her, and when we're apart, I reminisce about our last date and fantasize about the next one. I'm used to being married, to have someone there, and I don't like being alone. This fantastic woman has entered my life, filled a huge void, and put joy back into it. It's much easier to look forward to a future with her, laughing and frolicking together, than to look backwards at tragedy, loss, and despair. We're in this crowded living room, amongst close friends, all doing their best to include her, but when she looks at me out of the corner of her eye, I think that she too wants to leave.

She is talking with our hosts, the Sluskys, complementing them on the prints of famous paintings adorning their walls. I walk towards her, put my arm around her slender waist, draw her towards me and say, "Susan, it looks like you're having fun, but I've got to get up early tomorrow. Are you ready to leave?" Richard gives me a strange look that makes me wonder if my blatant show of affection to her might make them wonder if I'm going too fast. They're accustomed to seeing me with Marilyn. They loved her and now, I'm introducing this new face to old friends, and we're already hugging and flirting in their living room.

"Whatever you say, Charlie. I've got a lot of work to do tomorrow too," she says. " I make excuses to our hosts, try to say goodbye to the crowd without drawing too much attention, but everyone is interested. Despite the conflict, I'm feeling great. I have introduced her to my friends, they have accepted her and my new life, and now we can be alone. I help her with her coat, more goodbyes, then we walk arm in arm through the snow to my car.

It's dark but the light from the house, reflecting off the snow onto her radiant face, brightens the night. I open the car door for her then go around and sit behind the wheel. I turn to her, she puts her head down, feigning shyness. I touch her chin and draw her face towards mine. When I kiss her lips, she throws her arms around my neck, and thrusts her tongue into my mouth. My body tenses. Her hot breath warms my cold face. We're breathing as one. I think of her beauty, charm, and her inviting statement about being frustrated when we neck like this. I'm breathing hard and my fully erected penis rubs against the constriction of my pants.

"Susan you were terrific. You mixed so well with my friends. I don't want this evening to end. I don't want to take you home."

"I don't want you to Charlie. Your friends are nice, but I want to be with you. We have so much fun together,"

"Let's go to my house. The kids are at the OHaras for the night. We can be alone."

She smiles. Kisses my neck, my cheek, my mouth, my nose. "That would be fine," she says. I start the car and turn on the heater for her comfort. I'm already steaming in the cold air. The window is fogged up but it's a short ride to my house. We hold hands all the way.

The house is dark when we arrive. I switch on the kitchen light, the furnace is going, we kiss again. I turn off the light. I take her coat and guide her towards the living room. Everything seems so easy, like a natural progression. The Franklin stove sits along one side wall. I light one of those quick flame logs which I had set in the stove before I left the house. It flames up as quickly as advertised. I throw in some newspapers and then some small logs and once they've started, I add larger logs and we watch them burn. Soon the living room is warm. I think about my empty bed upstairs but I'm not yet ready to share that with her yet. Marilyn's memory lingers there. I say, "This is a great room, with a warm fire, I'm going to pull those cushions off the couches and we can lie here and enjoy the fire."

She smiles but says nothing. She's lying on the cushions, stretched out on her stomach, propped up by her elbows, gazing into the fire. I lie along side, see the fireplace fire light up her face. I kiss her and she responds warmly. She lies on her back, I try to unbutton her blouse, but fumble with the buttons. She offers to help. I sit up, take off my shirt, pants, shoes, struggle with my socks and turn towards her.

She is already sitting naked before me."Wow!" is all I can say. I'm staring at the largest set of breasts that I've ever seen or could imagine seeing. "Wow, Susan, I know you are beautiful but I had no idea."

She chuckles, "Haven't you noticed? I try to keep them hidden but I thought you could tell."

"Susan, you are absolutely the most beautiful woman in the world. You are beyond beauty."

"Thank you Charlie," she responds without hesitation.

I run my fingers along her soft breast, stopping to kiss each nipple, both erected, signaling they want attention. I suck one and bury my head in the softness behind. I move to the smooth skin of her stomach, admiring the precious hair below. I return to her face, kiss behind her neck and her left ear. When I reach her mouth, her tongue enters my mine like it belongs there. It's quickly at the back of my throat, messaging my tonsils. I'm on top of her in a second. She doesn't have to guide my penis into her warmth. I'm hard and inside her immediately. She responds like a deep hunger is being met but she wants more. I respond to her excitement. Her legs open wider to allow me in deeper. I scream and everything inside me explodes into her body. All the frustration and romance leading up to this moment explode into her willing body. My orgasm is powerful, total, like being set free. Every inhibition, every conflict, every frustration explodes from me. I empty myself into her. We hold each other. I roll off, we cling to her each other. I feel her softness, smell her perfume, and hear the rhythmical sound of her breathing. I lie alongside, put my arm around her, and draw her close. I don't remember feeling so relaxed and so content with the world. "Susan, that was unbelievably fantastic. You are wonderful but I'm sorry I came so fast. That's usually not a problem with me but it's been a while, and you are an incredibly sexy woman. It's been a long time for me,"

She smiled, rested her head on my chest. "That's okay, you were great. I hope this is only the beginning." I appreciated her encouragement. We lied there, clinging to each other, warmed by the fire and the interlocking of our naked bodies, stroking each other, trading smiles, knowing that we had entered a new period of our lives, together.

Haiti

Years ago, a friend called to ask if I would go to Haiti with a small group. I enjoy foreign travel and different cultures so I accepted with enthusiasm. Peter, the caller, was a friend of Marilyn. She liked him, introduced us, we became friends and he was supportive to me after her death. He was a clinical psychologist who seemed to look through me when I talked. When conversing, his silent, penetrating stare made me want to scream, "Say something, Please, Anything," but I soon adjusted to it and it no longer bothered me.

Peter was going to help the Haitians with a chicken raising project with a man named Jim, who was a teacher at the local community college. A nurse was going to help set up a medical clinic and a social worker was going to help me with tooth extractions. Dentistry was limited to extractions, no fancy stuff here.

My dental supply house was generous in donating needles, sutures, anesthetic cartridges, cold sterilizing solutions, gloves, masks, and even some outdated antibiotics. I brought all of my own extraction paraphernalia like forceps, scalpels, retractors, my experience and youthful exuberance for the project.

Our neighbors, the O'Hara's agreed to have Rob and Heather stay at their house for the two weeks. The O'Hara's were like second parents and this gave the kids their own adventure and a welcomed break from their Dad. At twelve and thirteen years old, their first choice was to stay home by themselves but that was not an option.

I left the house before daybreak one Spring morning and drove to Sandwich to pick up Catherine, the social worker. She was an attractive blond, about thirty five, with two children. One of her first comments was that her husband did not want her to go but it was such a rare opportunity that she was going anyway. I had never met her before and she only knew Jim, the college professor. Peter was my only contact with the group and we both admitted our fears about going to a foreign country for two weeks with strangers. Our easy conversation on the one hour drive to Boston, convinced me that this would be a friendly trip.

We met Peter and Sheila, the nurse, at the parking lot at Logan Airport. We stood with our baggage and made small talk together while waiting for Jim. I wondered what kind of people I was traveling with. Were they religious fanatics, cultists, boring do gooders or what? And where was Jim?

It was approaching time for departure and Peter was getting nervous. "I think he knows the time," he said rechecking his watch. Peter breathed easier when a pickup truck approached with dents on all sides, rusted fenders, a faded paint job, and an engine that roared like a jet plane in the underground garage. The truck bed was littered with old newspapers, lumber, rakes, saws, empty bottles of water, a weeks worth of garbage and a suitcase. A young Black boy sat in the front between a young man and woman. The woman hugged the boy as Jim hopped out of the car.

"Peter, what the hell time is that plane leaving. You told me nine. I helped Jane get the three kids off to school.

Now you're standing around fidgeting like I did something wrong. Relax. What kind of bull shit is this, anyway? You're acting like an old lady. Get over it. We've got plenty of time." Jim was tall and broad shouldered like a linebacker. His booming voice had people turning to see the source of all this noise. Everything about him, from his oversized hands to his flashing eyes, dominated the area and his self assured entrance indicated a man who was comfortable with having people fall in line behind him. His gutteral speech allayed my fears of him being a religious fanatic.

He shook my hand, "Hi, I'm Jim," and then turned around to kiss his wife. Tears formed on his cheek when he lifted the young boy for a special good bye. They cried and hugged together, neither wanted to let go. There was an obvious soft underbelly to this big man with the intimidating personality.

His wife wished us all well and told Jim in a forceful, almost desperate, tone, "Do not bring anymore kids home from the orphanage. Please. Remember, you promised. No more kids."

Jim looked off in the distance and agreed, "I know. I know. You've told me that every day for a month."

His wife strapped the young boy into the front seat, gave Jim another kiss, and a final warning, "Remember no more kids." Her forefinger drummed on his chest for emphasis.

"Okay, Okay. I know. Don't worry. Bye Darlin'." His wife sped away in the pick up with a worried look on her face. The little boy waved until the truck turned the corner, out of sight.

Jim and Peter led the way past the porters, through the automatic doors, and into the airport. Catherine, Sheila and I fell in line behind. I thought our hierarchy was already forming and I was comfortable following. The odd quintet was on its way.

The Flight

I sat behind Jim and Peter on the flight to Port-au-Prince. I listened as Jim talked most of the time about his son who we just said good bye to in the parking garage. When he was in Haiti on a previous trip, he learned that a child would be born and then abandoned by the mother. He thought of his own three kids, his crowded house, his busy schedule but then remembered the conditions in Haiti and the abundance of everything in the United States. With his wife's permission, they agreed to adopt the child. The legal papers were set but the boy was born with brain damage that would affect his ability to learn. The Haitian authorities called and offered to let them adopt another child, but Jim said, "No," They wanted this one, my son. Catherine, Jim's wife, agreed but was afraid now that her soft hearted husband would find another abandoned child on this trip and therefore gave the stern warning at the airport, "No more kids." I had spoken few words to Jim but as I listened, I became more impressed.

In less than an hour from Miami, we approached the Island of Hispanola. I strained to get first glimpse of the high mountains of Haiti through the small plane window. A

Haitian man, named Jacques, sitting next to me gave a quick lesson in Haitian history and culture. His French accented Creole was hard to understand but worth the effort. Haiti means "High Mountain," in the Arawak language. Arawaks were the Indian inhabitants of Haiti before Europeans came. Haiti is the poorest country in the western hemisphere and one of the poorest in the world.

Jacques speculated that when Columbus landed, he first thanked God for safe deliverance and then asked "where's the gold." Many of Haiti's riches were stolen to satisfy the excesses of French royalty. Black slaves were brought from Africa to operate French sugar cane fields. In 1804, while Napoleon was preoccupied with European expansion, the slaves staged the world's only successful slave revolt and threw out their French oppressors. The United States, the land of the free, could not help this young nation because we still had slaves of our own and would continue to have them for another sixty one years. Allowing Black ambassadors into the U.S. from a country that had just had a successful revolt would set a bad example for our own slaves.

Even from the air, I could see that trees and vegetation were thin on these high mountains. Tree branches held no leaves, the soil was brown, devoid of green grass, few roads connected villages; this was Haiti. Nevertheless, Jacques's eyes widened and his speech became rapid and excited as we approached his homeland. I thanked him for the Haitian history lesson and his friendship. We shook hands and he warned me that I would be a different person when I flew back home in two weeks. He was right.

Tonton Macoutes and the trip to Plaisance

Young men with big guns eyed us as we walked though the airport gates and onto Haitian soil. This was my first look at the Tontons Macoute, the henchmen for Baby Doc Duvalier, the latest in their long line of dictators. Jacques had warned me of their reputation for intimidation and torture. Jim lead us past their hostile stares and loaded rifles slung loosely over their shoulders, to intimidate newcomers. This was their country and they were in charge. We hurriedly found our baggage and I was relieved when we passed through a cursory inspection without incident.

We were anxious to get on our way but had to wait for two hours for the delivery of our rental car. The sun was setting over the distant mountains before we began the drive to Plaisaince. Jim drove with Peter in the front seat to help navigate while I sat between the two women in back. As soon as we left the airport area, everything became dark. There were no street lights, no neon signs advertising businesses, and only a few headlights from the scattered cars that we passed driving out of Port-au-Prince. I stared straight ahead where headlights penetrated the darkness, showing that large crowds of people were bustling around in the darkness, carrying on their lives, without electricity.

Jim and Peter found our way out of town and onto even darker roads leading to Plaisance. We were speeding along, heading towards the mountains, when our casual conversation in the backseat was interrupted by Peter's shout, "Watch out. There's something in the road." Jim hit the brakes and the car swerved sharply to the left. We avoided whatever it was and drove ahead slowly.

"What the hell was that?" asked Jim.

"I don't know. It must have been a dead cow or bull or something," answered Peter.

"Jesus, I thought it was a dead person, at first. It was some kind of animal, I guess." I was glad that I wasn't driving and relieved when Jim slowed down. He looked in his rear view mirror and saw a crowd gathering so we continued on. "We'll be late for dinner at the clinic. They don't need us here." he added.

We soon had to go even slower because of the winding trail through the mountains. Jim said, "There are no guard rails. I wonder what's off to the sides of these roads, anyway."

I said, "I know what's off to the side. A big nothing. A long drop to the bottom. That's what's there." We were getting comfortable with each other despite the hard driving over strange roads.

Three hours later we arrived in the hillside village of Plaisance and drove right to the clinic. The clinic had been built by missionaries and was the only source of health care for miles around. As soon as we parked the car, a smiling black woman wearing a nun's head covering, ran out and threw her arms around Jim's neck. "Oh Jimbo, It so good to see you. Thank you for coming." She squealed when he picked her up and gave her a big kiss on the cheek. The two of them were laughing and hugging and dancing in a circle, when she remembered that there were four more of us standing around watching. She excused herself and extended her exuberant welcome to us all. "Hello, everyone. I'm Sister Antoine. Thank you for coming. I thank God for each of you." She glowed, she hugged, she danced around and then led us into the clinic.

I struggled through my first taste of goat at dinner along with local vegetables, bottled water and home baked bread. We then went to straight to bed. It had been a long day and we were worlds away from Cape Cod where my day began. Jim, Peter, and I slept in a back room on small cots. The clinic must have had its own generator because a single hanging light bulb lit up our small room. We could hear the women talking next door, through the thin walls. I thanked God for safe delivery and went to sleep.

I awoke the next morning before dawn to the sound of human voices outside. Through the window, I looked down at a busy town preparing for its day. I dressed quickly and walked to the street. Already, beautiful Haitian women were hurrying to market with baskets balancing on their heads. They wore bright colored clothes, had straight backed posture that would be the envy of any model in the United States and all were slender. I walked outside and saw no old people but children running everywhere. The language barrier prevented conversation but their smiles made my feel welcome. A huge Catholic Church across the street dwarfed every other structure in town.

I returned to my new friends, we had breakfast and then Sister Antoine escorted Catherine, Sheila, and me into the clinic. Sister Antoine, being a nun and a nurse, administered to the people's spiritual and physical needs. The courtyard was already full of patients waiting to see the dentist.

A storeroom had been cleared out to make a dental office. We spread out my instruments on a long table and filled three pans with cold sterilizing solution. There was no real sterilization, no X rays, no dental chair or any other equipment that I had thought essential for extracting teeth. We did what we could with the equipment provided plus what we brought with us.

A Young Haitian man and woman, who had been extracting teeth in the town, came to help and to learn. The language problem prevented real conversation but I was happy to have some help and proud to share my knowledge with them. They would be the town dentists when I left and I thought my real mission was to teach them as much as possible in the short time we would b together..

When a patient filed in, we sat him down in a straight backed chair and leaned him back against the window sill. Either Catherine or an awaiting patient held a flashlight so I could see into the patient's mouth. The two Haitian assistants appeared to have some knowledge of extraction techniques but knew nothing about anesthesia. Their extractions had been done with little anesthesia. They were eager to learn.

Some cases were simple extraction of abscessed teeth but others came with acute infections affecting not only their mouths but causing serious health problems throughout their bodies. I had never before seen fistulas, or infection tracts, draining through cheeks to the outside. Some faces were so swollen, their bodies so weakened that they could barely open their mouths for treatment. This was a shock to me but a way of life for them.

Cases of severe infection like this would be hospitalized in the USA but here I offered the only treatment. I extracted as many infected teeth as possible, put some on antibiotics, and asked them to return in the morning to be checked. Most had never taken an antibiotic so often the results were dramatic. I had no instances of penicillin allergy.

I didn't count the patients, but we worked every day from 8 AM until the evening hours. I worked harder here than in my office, on people I could not converse with, but I felt needed. I loved the work and the people. I felt the direct connection between tooth problem and general health. In some instances, my services might be essential for them to stay alive. I never had that feeling in the United States. I understood when they said "merci," but their real gratitude showed on their faces. They stimulated something in me that made me comfortable with them and myself. They made me feel at home in their country and with their culture.

After a week, I was accustomed to the clinic routine so I was unconcerned when a healthy looking, broad shouldered man came in with a toothache. As usual we were all busy. The female Haitian assistant injected him with a local anesthetic as I had shown her and after a few seconds, the man slumped to the floor. I stopped what I was doing, came over, raised the man's feet and applied cold towels to his forehead. I got no response from this and he appeared to be getting weaker. An ammonia capsule broken under his nose did not help. Sheila, the nervous nurse from Boston, came by and took his pulse. She said, "Charlie, I hate to say this but I don't feel a pulse on this guy." I refused to believe that.

I looked at her worried face and asked the Haitian assistant to get Sister Antoine. I thought if this guy dies, I could go to a Haitian jail and never see my kids again. My heart was racing. Sister Antoine came in smiling, took a look at the patient and said, "He be Okay. No problem."

She tried to get the man to swallow some sugar water but he couldn't .We carried him into the nearby medical clinic where Sister Antoine administered an IV solution of glucose. Again she assured me that, "He be Okay." I wasn't as confident as her but I went back to work while she went on and treated someone else.

I checked him in a few minutes and he seemed to be reviving. I felt good but panicked again when I returned in two hours and found him gone. The bed was empty. I asked Sister Antoine what happened and she said. "He gone home. He back to his village. No problem."

She explained that he was malnourished. He probably had the toothache for a while, couldn't eat, and became more malnourished. He walked a mile or two in the hot sun to see the dentist from America, weakened more while waiting outside, and then passed out when he was injected. Treating starving people was a new experience for me. I was surprised to see him the next morning, waiting patiently in the back of the line. We motioned for him to come in, I injected him, and extracted his tooth. He got up, smiled, shook my hand and went on his way. I was impressed by him and other Haitians like him. No complaints, just gratitude. I was lucky to be able to offer some small relief from their hard lives.

On our last day in Plaisance, Sister Antoine treated us to an afternoon at a nearby beach. I'm sure that she rarely took a day off and was glad to share it with her new friends. While we were wading in the water together, she took a string of beads from her pocket. She stopped, put the beads around my neck and said, "Thank You." Those beads and those words mean so much to me today, twenty years later.

…………………..

When we packed the car to return to Port-au-Prince, I noticed that Jim and Peter were fussing with something under the hood. Sister Antoine brought out an odd assortment of nails and screws. They took one and debated for a while. "I think it will be Okay," said Peter without much confidence.

"We don't have any choice. There's no repairman in town. We've got to go." They asked me if I knew anything about cars and I confessed that I didn't. They said that something was loose in the steering mechanism but they thought they had repaired sufficiently to get us back to Port-au-Prince. I thought of those narrow, bumpy roads on the mountain ledges we had encountered on our way, but agreed that we had no choice. Jim drove slowly back to the city, joking all the time about, "wheel lock." When we encountered one of the many hairpin turns, without guard rails, he would say, "Hope we don't get wheel lock," and laugh. I didn't want to know what he meant by this but assumed that our steering mechanism was being held in place by one of those small nails donated by Sister Antoine. By this time, I had such faith in everybody that I knew we would make it to the city safely.

We did arrive safely and checked into a guest house before night fall. Our guest house sat high on a hill overlooking the big city. Jim pointed out a huge slum, called Brooklyn, where hundreds of thousands, maybe millions of Haitians lived crowded together in unbelievable poverty. We could see the tops of tin, card board, or scrap wood rubble that were homes to our fellow human beings. Occasionally, we saw people moving about but these shacks were so thick that they blocked out the humanity living within. They stretched on for miles and miles. Gradually, night fell and where we saw this slum in the daytime, we saw nothing at night. There was not one light or candle to signify life. It was like this huge city and all its inhabitants disappeared at sundown and only existed in the light of day. I went to bed wondering what happened to all those people.

I worked the next few days at an inner city clinic where conditions were much like they had been in Plaisance. There were too few hours to treat too many patients but I felt honored to have the chance to do what I could. It was worth all of the sweat of dental school to be here at this time. I was exhausted at night, but couldn't wait for the next day to come.

One afternoon we took off to visit one of Mother Teresa's homes for the dying. I was able to see firsthand the incredible work of these dedicated nuns. They radiated a childlike enthusiasm when they talked about their work and their faith. They all agreed that the poverty in Haiti was worse than in Calcutta or elsewhere in India. They thought that the percentage of people struggling with nothing was much higher here.

Each day began with two hours of prayer and meditation asking for God's help in their work. They spent their day tending to the needs of these homeless, penniless, dying people. Two mid day hours were devoted to more prayer, and then more work until sundown when they closed their day with more hours of prayer and meditation. They did that day after day without break. Their obvious inner peace had to come from feeling they were close to God. I have never seen such joy in people doing any type of work. Their day was full of cleaning toilets, changing contaminated dressings, always kind and caring, praying, touching, stroking, whatever they thought necessary to usher their patients into the next world. A typical patient was a man whose posterior was completely eroded by bed sores. Flies crawled around his face and open sores. His bones were exposed by an absence of skin, muscle or soft tissue. He would die soon but in the meantime was treated with the respect that is too often reserved only for royalty.

Jim arranged for us all to spend our last morning at the orphanage. I had never been to an orphanage before and was unprepared for the emotional pull of the children. A friendly nurse led us to a large room full of baby cribs. Inside each of them were one or two Haitian babies. She encouraged us to pick up any child we wanted to, which we did. The problem was putting them down. I picked up a little girl in diapers who immediately snuggled to my shoulder. We walked around the room. I talked to her, sang a little, jostled her some but when I tried to put her back into her crib, she rubbed her cheek against my chest. She was enjoying the rare feeling of human contact and she didn't want to return to her lonesome crib. When I rolled her off my shoulder to lay her down, she became agitated, like this was her last desperate hope for connection.

Jim held a hydrocephalic baby, with a huge head and he would not put him down. He walked, he talked, and he stared into the doomed youngster's face. The boy could not respond in any way but Jim was entranced. Eventually he must have remembered his wife's warnings because he returned the baby to his crib. He stared down at the boy, held his hand, and stroked his enlarged head, before reluctantly moving on. He later confided to us that he felt like he was looking into the face of Jesus Christ.

Peter and I spent the afternoon walking through the Brooklyn slum area that we had viewed from our hill side guest house the night before. It was daylight now and we could see that each tin shack that we had seen from the hill represented five or six of our brothers and sisters. We were the only white faces amongst the millions of Blacks but we both felt at ease and safe. The dominant mode was apathy, not hostility. Children played in the streams of human waste that flowed alongside the streets. More waste material lay stagnant close to the dwellings. Small fish and not too fresh vegetables, rotting in the hot sun, were sold as food. Flies swarmed everywhere and there was no refrigeration, no electricity. Thousands of people were milling about trying to scratch another day's sustenance from this hostile world.

Unemployment and starvation were rampant. There was no stimulation from books, TV, or even radio. Many of these people had moved to the city from rural areas like Plaisance to find work but instead found a life of unimaginable horror. This completely different world exists only a short plane ride away from our land of plenty. The few schools were run by missionaries. We were unaware of government funded education. Did no one care?

One man invited us into his house. He was proud of it, because, unlike the others, it was made of some solid structure, like concrete. Inside the one room dwelling was a chair, a few blankets scattered on the floor, which was probably their bed. There were no lights or windows. It was so dark that we had to strain to see his wife, huddled in the corner. When he introduced us, we stooped to avoid hitting our heads on the tin roof ceiling. The whole family lived in this structure that couldn't have measured more than six feet by eight. Our eyes hurt from the blinding mid day sun when we left the darkness of his house.

Another man, realizing we were from the United States seemed to be offering us a child, maybe his own, to take back with us so that the child could have a better life. Somehow they knew that something better existed elsewhere.

We left Haiti the next day and flew back home. Just as Jacques warned me when we landed, I was a different person. We all were transformed by our short exposure to life in these conditions. Just as it was a shock to see the poverty of Haiti, it was an almost equal shock to return to the affluence of our home. The grocery stores loaded with produce and huge department stores offering every toy imaginable now were superfluous. The acquisition of more trinkets from our endless list of desires was exposed as a waste of effort. Are we ever thankful for what we have?

Despite the Haitian's poverty, they have something that we have difficulty finding in our land of affluence. We search for our happiness in department stores and then are disappointed when our emptiness persists. The Haitians don't have the shopping option so they search for more spiritual answers. Their prison is poverty; we are often shackled by compulsive consuming and striving. Our handicap is less obvious but may be just as cruel as theirs.

Any contribution one dentist could make in that world was insignificant. The demand for services was infinite and the inability to deliver made the effort meaningless. I went back to school at Boston University and earned a master's degree in public health, taking as many courses as possible in international health. My ambition was to promote health programs in developing countries. Programs in immunization, family planning, oral rehydration, nutrition are helpful. Instead of treating one patient at a time, I wanted to help large groups through public health policies. I earned my degree fifteen years ago but have not used it and it looks like I never will. There is a strong pull to the familiar, the comfortable, and the known world. I envy people who cast off from their moorings when given the opportunity and devote their lives to this type of work. I had a short glimpse of it and its tremendous rewards.

I thank my two kids, the people of Haiti and my four friends for making this trip possible.

Worst Date

I had many laughs while dating as an adult but also a few disasters. None of the disasters compared to my worst date ever.

One evening my two teen aged kids and I were eating at a local sea food restaurant. I began flirting with our pretty waitress. Each time she came to our table, I made some light hearted comment, she laughed and eventually we began joking back and forth. Heather said, "Dad, I think she likes you. Why don't you ask her out?"

When she brought our bill, I asked her for her name and phone number which she carefully wrote on a piece of paper. I waited a few days, called her, and she agreed to a dinner date. She also said that lived with friends of mine, the Gregorys. I knew immediately who she meant. The Gregorys were a free spirited young couple who made no secret of their fondness for recreational drugs. Their eight year old daughter disclosed one day that her schoolmates teased her about the garden in their front yard because they cultivated not only flowers and vegetables but also marijuana. I don't know if that was true or not but it made good small town gossip.

Paula Gregory greeted me at the door when I went to pick up Lois, my date. Paula and I chatted for a few minutes about her daughter, the weather and how wonderful it was that Lois and I were dating. She assured me that we would have fun together and "maybe the four of us could get together some time." I agreed that it would be a fun evening but clarified that one date was not "dating."

In a few minutes, Lois came bouncing down the stairs like a loaded spring. She looked beautiful, with her hair flowing to her shoulders and tasteful facial makeup, but she talked incessantly. She wouldn't stop. This wasn't the quietly seductive young woman I met in the restaurant, but an incoherent noise in a pretty package. Her speech was loud, senseless, with thoughts running together without reason. I thanked Paula for her hospitality and quickly escorted Lois to the car.

Lois's only became more irrational when we sat together in the front seat. I watched her staring straight ahead, glassy eyed, yakking away, and decided that this was a night for Hyannis. Hyannis is a small city twenty six miles away from the peering eyes of our small town. Tourists flocked to its tee-shirt shops, malls, fast food restaurants but natives avoided it like a contagious disease.

I planned on having a quick dinner there, away from familiar faces, being polite but escaping the evening without incident or insult. I drove around the city, looking for a isolated bar, hopefully with a back room, where she could relax and try to resurrect something positive about the date.

I found one. Tucked away on a side street, a restaurant I'd never heard of before, advertised a tavern downstairs and quiet dining above. Quiet dining up the stairs, away from people was perfect for tonight. "This looks good. Is Vic's Tavern OK with you?" I asked.

179

"Sure. Sounds fine," She slurred. She was now concentrating on each word so her sentences were drawn out and labored. I wondered if we should head for the hospital instead of continuing to pretend that this was normal behavior. In a few moments, her rapid, meaningless speech was replaced by almost complete silence.

I parked the car in front. She waited for me to open her door and then leaned heavily on me as we staggered up the stairs. She was almost dead weight in my arms when we reached the top. I eased her down into the first available booth and took a seat across from her. Her eyes were almost closed and her head swiveled around her neck in an effort to maintain her balance. She seemed bewildered about where she was and who she was with. "Are you OK?" I asked.

"Yesh. I'm fine." She was incoherent and struggling to stay awake.

The waitress brought the menus and asked if everything was all right. She glared down at Lois as if she too couldn't decide how to react to this woman in distress. When she asked, "Can I help you?" I wasn't sure if she wanted to take our order or call 911. I assured her that we were fine and that my friend was just recovering from a long day at work. Lois propped the menu on the table and tried to act like she was reading but it was obvious that she was puzzled. She wasn't making a sound. When the waitress returned, I ordered two hamburgers for us and, "No, we don't want anything to drink." I requested rare burgers thinking they required less cooking time and allow us to be on our way home.

The waitress left and Lois slurred something about being tired. She squinted at me like she wanted to ask, "Who the hell are you?" but said nothing. The next sounds I heard was a thud from her head hitting the table followed by a distinct snore. She was sound asleep. Her head turned to the side, her cheek flattened against the wooden table top, and her arms hung lifeless with hands resting on the floor. My date had turned into a rag doll and it was only 6:30.

I had never seen anyone suffering from a drug overdose but assumed that she was accustomed to it. I was more comfortable with her asleep than awake. I contemplated my next move when I looked around the room and saw the familiar face of a dentist friend. My heart sunk at the sight of Rob Wells. We had been close friends at one time but I hadn't seen him in over a year, only because our lives had taken different directions. This chance meeting was what I had driven to Hyannis to avoid. I was trapped in an embarrassing position, without an excuse.

He came to the table with his lovely wife Pam. "Hey Charlie, its good to see you. How have you been?" His smile turned to a look of concern when he looked down at my sleeping companion who was now sprawled out over table. Pam shuttered, probably contemplating how far I had fallen in a year.

I stood up and Pam stiffened when I hugged her. "Oh. I've been fine. Never better," I said. I thought that this must look to her like I had resorted to getting young women drunk in seedy bars and then taking advantage of them. "I'd introduce you to my date, but she…. She Ah.. She must've gotten her medical doses confused… Actually… She's .. Well OK… She's asleep….Nice to see you again…. We'll have to do lunch sometime."

"Yeh," said Rob. "I'll call you." That was one call I never received. They politely said good bye and retreated to their table, whispering to each other, shaking their heads.

I sat back down, looked at the back of Lois's head, listened to her snore, and decided that there was no possible way to resurrect this evening. It was beyond hope and the sooner it ended, the better. I summoned the waitress and paid the check before receiving our burgers. I refused her offer to call for an ambulance. "No. She just had a long day. She'll be fine. We'll see you another night when she feels better." Now I felt like a liar as well as a dirty old man.

My lifesaver training and a fervent determination to end the evening allowed me to pick up Lois and firemen carry her down the stairs and out to the car. Spectators wished me well and opened the car door. I drove back to her house with the windows wide open hoping to revive her. She rallied a bit before we arrived so with only a little directional help, was able to stagger onto her living room couch. The Gregorys were home and said they understood what happened and promised to tend to Lois. I thanked them all for an interesting evening and excused myself.

I was glad to be alone again in my car.

Heather greeted me when I arrived home, "Dad, You're home early. Its only 7:30. I thought you had a date."

"I did Heather. I did have a date. I've driven all the way to Hyannis and back. Come on. I've got a story to tell you."

PART IV

Hilton Head

Around the World
on Hilton Head

Across the parking lot from the town offices in Wexford sits an old wooden building nestled among tall pine trees. A welcome sign in the yard reads, "Literacy Volunteers of the Lowcountry." This is where I teach English as a second language to some of our island's newcomers. These students are fluent in their native tongue but now need to learn English as their second language to better adapt to their new home.

I have no formal education as a teacher. I am a retired dentist who was adequately trained by a devoted staff to teach these students who are eager to learn I have been teaching now for two years and have never done anything more rewarding or enjoyable. These students are my good friends, but it goes beyond friendship, to respect and admiration for these people who have greatly enriched my life.

I sit around a long table with six or eight students from all over the world. There is no "head of the table" because we learn from each other. I try to teach them English while I receive from them lessons in humor, adaptation, determination, and wisdom.

I have always been interested in foreign travel but this is better. I don't have to deal with arrogant taxi drivers, airport security or a ten hour flight on a crowded airplane. All I have to do is sit back, listen to my friends, occasionally correct their English, and enjoy the trip. This is not a trip limited to museums and cathedrals, but takes me into their living rooms, enjoying the food and family traditions of these wonderful people.

As they talk about their native cultures, I am immediately transported to the souks of Marrakech, a 4,000 year old palace in Korea, or family life in rural Mexico. Just as a glass of Merlot tastes better while sipped in a sidewalk café on the Champs-Elysees than in my own dining room; a description of Maracaibo, Cartagena, or Timbuktu sounds richer when told with a native accent.

Across the table from me sits beautiful young women from Korea with a unique talent for looking at the world and expressing her perceptions on paper. She reaches deep into her heart for emotions that most of us are not aware of and she can state them clearly in her writing. I hope that she will continue her English so that her incisive perceptions are not confined to the Korean language. She is gentile, intelligent, articulate and firmly rooted in the customs and traditions of her culture. I have learned so much from her.

Next to her sits an affable ex-college professor from Venezuela. She laughs at her own frustration when she tries to express deep thoughts from her quick mind. She began her sentence in English then regresses to her familiar Spanish when trying to explain an abstract concept. She leans forward in her chair to listen to every word as I explain the choice of "has" rather than "have" while describing her fear from the recent hurricane.

A Mexican lady sits next to her. She expresses her devotion to her beautiful daughter who is in second grade at Hilton Head Elementary school. Her daughter learns faster than she does, because she is younger and surrounded by English speakers in school. Her mother is determined to keep up.

On the coldest day last winter, she rode the four miles to class on her bicycle without gloves or a proper winter coat. After an hour of trying to thaw out in the warm classroom, she said, "I no feel my fingers." We all learned that day the true meaning of the word "numb."

Another day that same woman taught me the derivation of the word "gringo." When U.S. soldiers came to Mexico in the Mexican War, they wore green uniforms. The Mexicans would look at the invaders and say "Go home green, go." Later that was shortened to "Go, green, go" and finally to just "Green, go" of "Gringo." She tried to assure that this is not a term for resentment, but I wonder.

Another student is a twenty five year old man from Venezuela. Each morning he greets me with a warm smile and a handshake. "Glad to see you, Charlie." He talks easily in class, showing wisdom beyond his years. As he leaves, I receive another handshake and a "Thank you, Charlie." I once asked him how he remains so friendly each day. He responded, "People have taught me to always be positive, always think 'I can,' ever 'I can't.'" I constantly thank him for the lessons he teaches me.

We have discussed ethnocentricity in our class. That is viewing your own culture, history or language from your own experience and looking down on any other group. We don't have a problem with ethnocentricity in our class. These people are all proud of their homelands, customs, and traditions. I am proud of mine. I help them with their

English; they help me with my life. We share experiences. I cannot wait for class next Monday.

Dancin' in My Sixties

I had never even been to a ballet and now I was in the middle of this mirrored room in The Arts Center, taking a lesson. The *Island Packet* ran their ad for a week, showing three beautiful girls in classic ballet poses, inviting people of all ages and abilities to join them on Saturday morning. They encouraged all to come for this one time opportunity to dance with the Harlem Ballet Company. I tried to entice a teenage friend to join me but when she declined, I decided to go alone.

I stood off to the side with maybe forty other people waiting for class to begin. Almost all of them were teen aged girls, scantily clad in tutus, tights, and ballet shoes. I watched them stretch their soft flexible muscles, resting a foot on a bar that was above my eye level. They stretched, pirouetted, and plied while I strained to bend over to untie my shoes. My back ached with the effort and I thought, *What the hell am I intruding on these good people's class and putting my aged body in positions it doesn't want to go?* The dancers around me balanced on one foot while effortlessly holding the other in their dainty little fingers. It seemed like they could hold position forever.

I stood up, rubbed my back and neck, and looked around. I recognized a tall man approaching as part of the Art Center staff. He greeted me, "Hi, Welcome to our class. Nice to see you, again."

He remembered me. I had tried out for at least six plays at his theatre, feeling secure that I would never get a part. I was right. I was always politely rejected. I don't think he or anyone else understood that I enjoyed the tryouts but really didn't want to commit to all that time and energy in rehearsals.

I said, "I remember you. You're always so kind in your rejections."

He smiled and said, "Keep trying. We'll get you on stage sometime. In the meantime, enjoy the class today."

I stood mesmerized by the arabesques and plieing going on around me. I was tempted to touch my toes but it was early in the morning. I didn't want to force anything. Instead, I turned away and saw a slightly fat, gray haired woman, about my age, standing nearby. She stepped towards me and came right to the point, "What are you doing here?"

"Damned if I know. I was trying to interest a teen aged friend but when she dropped out, I thought I'd give it a try. I'm here and, I must say, I am glad to see you." I felt an immediate bond with this woman whose wrinkled face showed as much character as mine.

This magic moment together was interrupted, when in the front of the room, a handsome perfectly proportioned man in a tank top clapped his hands and shouted for everyone's attention. "Hello, I'm Ralph. I will be your teacher today and I'm thrilled that so many of you showed up." He seemed to look at me and continued. "It looks like we have people here of all abilities. Let me ask, how many of you have taken at least three years of ballet?"

Most hands shot towards the ceiling. "And then, how many of you have never taken a class?" The gray haired lady, a man with a limp, and I raised our hands. "Well, that's fine. We have something for everyone." In every direction I looked, a mirror reflected my pot belly, sagging skin, and thinning hair. I couldn't get away from my own image. "All you experienced dancers, move to the left side of the room, and you people," pointing to the neophytes, "will be there, close to the piano." Maybe he wanted to keep a special eye on us. His insurance might not cover aging, arthritic prima donnas.

In about two minutes, he demonstrated the five basic techniques of feet and arms always with grace and balance. He explained that by mastering these simple poses one can make difficult steps seem effortless. I stumbled with each "simple pose," lunging each time for the bar to break my fall. I tried to look away from the young well trained girls. It was too discouraging. Their waists were about the circumference of my wrist.

The instructor had the real dancers go through eight steps of taping, extending, and balancing while standing on toes. He asked, "Can everyone feel their weight supported by big toe and second toe?" I certainly didn't because I remained flat footed and felt no social pressure to keep up with the class. I expected to be awkward and flat footed throughout my entire ballet career.

Another pose for us to master is standing on one leg, bringing the other toe up to the knee, holding position, and hardest of all, breathe. I bent and balanced to the best of my ability which I realized, was at ground zero. My goal was not to fit in but to avoid injury. A pulled muscle here could curtail normal activities for a month.

I observed, admired, and made a reasonable attempt to follow along until the very last exercise. This involved movement. He chastised one of the real dancers for taking steps that were too short. He said, "I want you to MOVE like this," and he seemed to fly from one end of the room to the other. I watched, smiled and thought, "to hell with that."

I saw that the hour and a half was mercifully coming to an end. I'd had enough and wouldn't attempt to imitate his airborne grace.

A young girl stepped aside and asked, "Do you want to get through here? You can still get in that group."

"No," I answered, "I've had enough. I'm going home. It's been fun though and I've learned so much," I lied. My ballet career was now over, one hour and thirty six minutes after it began.

Bill Bligen

I first saw Bill years ago when he was speaking to a large group at the dedication of a Literacy Volunteers building. He was in his seventies but moved around the stage like a college athlete. He was tall, thin, black, and smiled at each individual in the audience like they were his best friend. He talked about how he had to leave school as a child, spent his life unable to read and write, and was now learning as a seventy year old man. He held no grudges and wasn't at all ashamed when disclosing his difficulties. Instead, he was thankful for the help he was getting and willing to speak as a literacy advocate.

After his speech, we talked and I was impressed by how he gave me his complete attention, like there was no one else around. We were friends within minutes and he invited me to his annual Labor Day party. He was warmth personified.

I went home and circled Labor Day on our calendar for his party. Lorrie and I knew how friendly people are on Hilton Head but his deck party raised amiability to a new level. People were joking, laughing, scurrying about preparing food or eating together in small groups. "Hi

Charlie. I'm glad you came. Come on in. We've got too much food; you've got to help us eat it."

He introduced his girl friend Janey, who was younger, pretty and equally friendly. "Hi Charlie, I'm glad to meet you. Bill is so happy you're here. Here, take a plate and have fun," she said.

Bill built his oversized deck just to accommodate crowds like this. There were at least seventy people milling around but we socialized in comfort. He saved beautiful live oak trees to allow the deck and environment to flow together and blend with people. Tables were loaded with trays overflowing with beans, rice, fried chicken, spare ribs, ochre, mashed potatoes, baked macaroni, and fish. Children scurried to claim their share of a huge basket of fresh crabs. A colorful display of irresistible cakes, fruit pies, and cookies overflowed their trays and ice chests were packed with soft drinks. The aroma from a cooking shed told us that more food on its way.

We sat next to a well fed woman who put her fork down to introduce herself, "Hello, I'm Emma. Welcome to the party. Do you have enough room there?"

"Got lots of room and more food than I need. This is unbelievable." I answered.

"The unbelievable part is that he does this every year, just so his friends can get together." People ran out of superlatives to describe their love for him. He coached youth baseball, boxing, and football, emphasizing stretching and conditioning.

He walked towards us beaming with joy. "Hey Charlie, are you getting enough to eat?"

I put down a chicken leg, and said. "Bill this party is fantastic. So much food and such nice people."

"That's why I have it, Charlie. I just want people to have fun together."

He ushered me into his house to show me a gym that he built so neighborhood kids could keep "their little bodies in shape." It was equipped with treadmill, punching bag, speed bag, jump ropes, Stairmaster. Physical conditioning held a high priority in his active life. He still jogged regularly and urged friends to start their own running programs. Around the walls were photographs of Bill in his boxing days, or recent ones of him crossing the finish line in a road race, and countless pictures of him with little kids glowing in his presence.

Another wall displayed framed letters from Hilary Clinton and Strom Thurmond, praising him for his passion in promoting literacy. Whenever anyone voted to slash the education budget, he sent them a scolding letter, preaching the importance of a good education. He was proud of his letters and honored by their responses.

We returned to the party where he introduced me to more friends. One was a nursery school teacher who said that he comes to her school at least once a week just to hug the children. "When the kids know he's coming, they press their noses against the window anticipating his arrival, 'Here comes Uncle Bill,' they shout. He's everybody's uncle, including me."

He urges high schoolers to stay in school. His spends his time helping other people. When I left, I asked, "Bill, how can you always be so nice to so many people? Are you religious? Do you go to church?"

He answered, "No, I don't go to church much, but I do ask God to help me to love everybody."

God answered Bill's prayer because he does love everybody and in turn, everyone loves him. I thought at the time that if I can live like he does, I too will have led a successful life.

One day we went to lunch at a local restaurant. After studying the menu together, he put it down and said, "Charlie, order me some oysters." His high level of intelligence made me forget that he had trouble reading and needed help with the menu. I admired him so much, and he compensated so well that I never thought of his handicap. In different circumstances, he could have been a college professor, a doctor, or anything else he chose, but here he was limited by his inability to read.

Years later, a friend called to tell me that Bill was dying in the Intensive Care Unit. I rushed to the hospital where Janey met me with tears running down her face. "Charlie, thank you for coming. He's in there. You can see him but he won't respond. We all know this is the end."

I didn't get an opportunity to say goodbye. All I wanted to say was "Thank you." I looked down at him and thought of all the people he had influenced and how he would be missed. He spent every day of his eighty years brightening other people's lives.

He was not in the hospital long before he died of cancer. Possibly his training as a boxer, marathon runner, and his lifelong struggle with literacy had taught him to ignore pain. His diagnoses came late. He met his final challenge with the same grace and class as he did with everything else.

He had almost no formal education and was categorized as an illiterate but he was one of the wisest people I have known. His picture sits in a prominent place in my living room as a constant reminder of how to live successfully.

Rosario

Everyone in our English as a Second Language Class was drawn to this middle age black women woman with the strange accent. She was always positive, constantly smiling, and interested in everyone. When she was absent, we all missed her. "Where's Rosario. I hope she's all right. I miss her." Her eyes flashed when she became excited and she was enthusiastic about everything. She laughed loud and often and we all laughed with her. She cleaned houses for a living. I asked her, "How can you always be so happy? Have you always been like this?" She smiled and said nothing.

One day we were alone after class and she told me her story.

Rosario was born among the poorest of the poor in Nicaragua. She attended school for a few years but soon had to quit because she had no money. She worked at any job available to feed herself and help her family. She went to Panama where she thought she could improve her life. She cleaned houses. From one of her employers, she heard about a great country to the north where she would find better opportunities. Someone offered to guide her to the United States for two thousand dollars. She worked, she cleaned, she sweated, and she scrubbed until, years later, she saved the money needed to get her to this land of better lives.

The guide took her to Guatemala and put her on a train that was going through Mexico to the United States. One night, a Mexican railroad official shined a light in her eyes and asked her for proper papers, which she didn't have. She was taken off the train and put in a Mexican jail and then returned to Guatemala where she was jailed again. Three times this happened. She was a woman alone, in strange countries, with no one to help. One night she was alone in a field, starving, freezing, and near death. She begged a man for help. He took her in, fed her, gave her some clothes and one hundred dollars. What did she do with the one hundred dollars? She went back on the train. She had to get to the United States.

Finally she made it to the border and was told to lie on an inner tube that would float her across the Rio Grande to her land of hope. She couldn't do it. She was deathly afraid of water. One man held his hand over her mouth so she wouldn't scream, while another man kicked the tube across the river. She made her way from the border to Washington, D.C., where she had a sister. Again she cleaned houses. One of her employers noticed the same magnetic personality that we did in our class. The woman sponsored her and she became legal.

Years later she entered our class to improve her English. She raved about how happy she is in her new country. She told us how proud she is of her niece, who recently received a president's medal. This medal is given to only five high school students in the United States who excel in citizenship, scholarship, and community service. Tears streamed down Rosario's cheeks and she had to whisper the words when describing how proud she was when she witnessed the President of the United States pinning a medal on her niece.

When our class ended and she was returning to Washington, she gave me a T-shirt. I felt guilty accepting a gift from this beautiful woman with little money. The shirt had a picture of the Statue of Liberty with the inscription, "Let Freedom Ring." I have never worn that shirt and never will. I don't even know if it fits. It is too precious to wear. It reminds me of Rosario.

Two Swims

The sky was clear on Saturday morning when I went out to get the newspaper. I smiled up at the star filled sky, raised my hand and felt no wind, both good indications that we could row. I hadn't been for two weeks because of the Christmas holiday, poor weather conditions, and my own inertia. I was falling into the habit of rolling over in bed rather than jumping up to row on the river.

Now was the time to fight off that laziness and renew the habit of early rising and being on the water to see the sunrise. I picked up the newspaper from the frosted grass and climbed the stairs into the warm house. After a quick read of the paper and a few stretches in my room, I drove off to meet my friends on the banks of Broad Creek.

John and Bob were already there when I parked in front of the Oyster Factory. I could see their frosted breath rise in the clear air and watched them jumping around to keep warm. I put on my rubber soled beach shoes and walked towards them. "Hey, I've missed you guys. It's been weeks. It's great to see you on a beautiful morning like this." They looked at me funny, as if to say, "what's he talking about?".

"Beautiful Morning?" questioned Bob. "Cholly, it's 37 degrees. It's cold."

"Yeh, but look, no wind," I said. We walked together towards the water.

John, a retired marine colonel and a natural leader, said, "We're here. Let's at least take a look."

There wasn't a ripple on the water as it flowed past the dock. The beach grass on the far shore stood straight up, not a sign of a breeze.

"Let's go," said Bob with enthusiasm. We all wanted to go despite the freezing temperature. I helped Bob launch his favorite boat- the blue Peinert,. It is 26 feet long, about as wide as a thin man's posterior, with a rounded bottom to skim over the water, and sliding seat for greater speed. It weighs less than thirty pounds. While Bob rigged his oars and carefully seated himself, John helped me carry the red Peinert from its perch to the water. John urged me to go ahead while he launched his racing boat.

"Man this current is strong today. It's like somebody pulled a plug. I'm movin,'" said Bob who was rowing in the middle of the creek, streaking by the dock. He was hardly rowing but the current from the receding tide was carrying him out towards the channel.

I pushed off and made sure John was okay before rowing away. I flew passed each channel marker and reached the main part of Broad Creek in minutes. Bob was a small figure far down the creek by the time I turned the corner to follow him.

John, the fastest rower with the sleekest boat passed me easily. We remarked about the beautiful morning and how lucky we were to be rowing again.

By the time I reached Broad Creek Marina, about three miles away, they were already turning back, into the current, to return to our dock. "It's so nice out here. I wish I could take off this heavy shirt. I'm sweating," said John, not believing we could be so warm on this cold day.

"I am so thankful for this morning row," was my only comment.

I carefully turned my boat, started back, enjoying the smoothness of the water, the bright sunshine, and the incredible views in every direction. The channel markers that I passed so easily coming down, now passed slowly and took a lot of effort. Easy rowing and gentile exercise on the trip down with the current now became drudgery and exhausting going back. The skin on my right hand was red and starting to hurt. By the time I left the main channel and reached our little creek leading to the dock, I was tired. I wiped sweat from my face to clear my eyes. My t-shirt was soaked with perspiration and my body ached with exhaustion. I was glad to be almost home. The current continued its powerful force against me, draining the creek, exposing oyster beds on both sides. I kept meditating on the view, the dolphins, how lucky I am to live on Hilton Head, and to be healthy enough to row on its waters. Sometimes when things are going so well, I'm reminded of the Biblical phrase, "Pride goeth before the fall." I ignored those words of warning and struggled past the first and second channel markers.

I made an easy turn towards the last one when suddenly my right oar buried under the water, waking me from my daydream. I swerved, couldn't free the oar, and felt that sinking feeling that tipping over was inevitable. I leaned, the boat kept tipping. I yelled, "Oh Shit," and was in the water. Splash!

As I hit the water, my sweaty body and heavy winter clothes took the chill out of the dunking. The current was carrying me fast away from the dock back out towards the channel. *This isn't cold now but I've got to get out fast. The water and air are freezing, even though I don't yet feel it.* I couldn't touch bottom. I decided to swim the boat into the shore and use the sandy bottom to help me get back in. I knew from previous experiences that unless your weight is completely balanced when getting back in the boat, it will just flip over and throw you back into the water. *I don't want to waste energy, trying to get back in the boat in deep water; I'll swim it into the shore.* The current pushed me away from the dock. After a few minutes, the coldness of the water hit me and I realized I needed to get back in and home quickly. My legs ached from kicking myself and the boat towards shore against the rushing current. I was gasping for breath. The shore line didn't look much closer but after a few more determined kicks and some strokes with my free hand, I put my foot down and felt bottom. But the bottom wasn't hard and supportive; it was soft pluff mud and my feet sunk deeply into it.

Pluff mud is sticky, gooey like quick sand and it was pulling me down, sucking me under, acting like a suction cup, entrapping me. I tried to take a few steps towards the oyster beds but my feet and legs kept sinking into the mud. I held onto the floating boat and used its buoyancy to steady me. I lifted my leg with my free hand to free it from the mud, then let go of the boat, making sure it would catch on an oyster bed rather than flow out to sea. I grabbed at it and pulled myself out of the mud and onto the tippy boat. I sat backwards onto the sliding seat and tried to row back to shore. "Oh, shit. I'm going nowhere," I was high and dry on the oyster flats. The tide had receded so fast I was left in the boat but with no water underneath to support me. I struggled to turn in every direction to free myself but couldn't. I was hung up in the oyster beds. My weight was too much for the boat in this shallow water. I had no choice. Out of the boat and Splash, into the water again. I was hoping I would hit hard sand this time but I didn't. I was back into the same entrapping pluff mud sinking up to my crotch. One shoe was pulled off and that foot was bleeding. I got serious quickly. I remembered reading that oyster shells are full of bacteria and can cause bad infections. *Is this it? Is this how I'm going to die? In the water, stuck in the mud, freezing in the marsh? I'd better get it right this time.* I pushed the boat off the oyster beds and luckily was still in water shallow enough to help free myself from the mud. I heard John yelling, "Charlie, Are you all right?" He had relaunched his boat and came back to help.

"Yes, I am, I just have to get out of this mud and back in the boat." He yelled some advice to me but by this time, I felt pretty sure what I needed to do and was in a hurry to get it done immediately. I had to use the razor sharp oyster shells to gain leverage to get back in the boat. It was no choice. I grabbed onto the knife like shells which were at least firmly rooted and pulled myself up to get hold of the boat. I braced myself on both sides of the hull, pulled up, sat back, grabbed both oars, and was relieved when I didn't flip over. I was in the boat, oars in hand, the sliding seat was behind me but I didn't want to risk getting back into it. I sat on the hull and rowed towards the dock.

The boat was full of water and blood but I was no longer stuck in the mud fighting the current and fatigue. I felt safe. John rowed alongside and probably thought I was hallucinating when I started singing. I don't remember the tune but I was relieved to be still alive with my legs free of the mud. I was filthy, freezing, fatigued but happy to be heading home.

Relief was mixed with embarrassment because there was no excuse for tipping over on a calm day like this. Only extreme carelessness and my habitual daydreaming made me tip. Bob greeted me with a worried look on his face, grabbed my oar, and pulled me to the dock. I rolled out of the boat onto that lovely floating rubber surface. "Charlie, what can I do?" he asked.

"I'd ask for a hug but I'm soaked and filthy. I'll take one later. I'm okay though, just embarrassed." The adrenaline rush was over and now I was exposed to the freezing air. "I'm colder on this dock than I was in the water. I've got to get out of here. I lost my rubber shoe. I'll have to walk over the oyster shells to the car."

"No you don't. Take mine. Look you're bleeding."

"I know but it's okay. I'm more humbled than anything." I suddenly felt the cold air hit all my bones at once. "I've got to get home. I haven't been cold until now but I think I should get my butt in a hot shower." Bob's boat was already washed and put away which made me think that I was struggling in that frigid water for a minimum of half an hour.

John yelled, "Charlie, get home. I'll wash your boat. "

I accepted his offer.

My old Toyota never looked so good. I turned the heater up full but the shivering increased. My jaw clenched tight to stop my teeth from chattering.

Lorrie was there to greet me when I arrived home. "Charlie, are you OK? John already called and told me what happened. He wants me to clean those cuts."

"That's fine," I answered, "but first I'm getting in that hot shower, then we can look at cuts." I ignored my trail of bloody foot prints on the floor and headed directly to the shower. I turned the lever to the far left, the red side, and jumped in. Its healing heat flowed over my head, down my neck, over my whole body. I started singing again, enjoying the heat and cleansing waters. Steam filled the room. I didn't want to leave. After half an hour, I began feeling my legs again. I hadn't realized that they were numbed by the cold until feeling returned. After an half an hour of steaming water, I got out of the shower, looked in the mirror and thought, "Wow, Charlie, you're a lucky man."

I kissed my wife, hugged the towel, laughed in the mirror, and inhaled. I started singing and couldn't stop. My body ached, my cuts bled on the towel, but I was alive.

The Plate

Carmen looked over the edge of her coffee cup, into the sparkling brown eyes of her son, "I proud of you. You speak this new language like you born here. I trying but it hard. I no fit in like you do. I try but need practice more. I no speak English while I cleaning houses. I glad to have a job though. I love Mrs. Frankel so much. She so nice."

"I know you love her Mom. You talk about her all the time. How long has it been now?" Gerardo scooped the last of his scrambled eggs into his mouth, sipped his orange juice, and leaned forward to listen.

"It been five years now. Every Tuesday for five years. I cleaned every room in house. It hard but I glad to do it. She so nice. Last week we sat with coke. I tell her about my God. It the first time we talk together. She listen. I happy to tell her about my faith. How I put everything in His hands. She understand."

"I hope so Mom. Some of these people are strange, but she sounds OK.

I know she's your friend. I just wish you didn't have to work so hard. When I grow up, I'm going to be a teacher, then I'll be rich and you won't have to work at all."

"You sweet Gerardo, but no worry, I fine. You study in school. That your job. I thank God I able to clean houses. I do anything for Mrs. Frankel. The money she pay, put this food on table. I thank God for her y our lives here."

Carmen stood up, took her empty coffee cup to the sink, rinsed it thoroughly and said, "Come. We need to move. You catch bus. I no want to be late."

Within minutes she was at The Plantation gate, showed her pass to the security guard, and drove on. She passed the huge mansions on each side of the street, admired the Spanish Moss hanging from the live oak trees that spread out over the road to make a canopy for her to drive under. She looked down at the dashboard to check the oil gauge that usually registered "Oil Low." in her old car. She noticed a security car following close behind. She was careful to make a complete stop at the sign on her right. She drove ahead slowly and the policeman followed. She slowed down, he slowed. She turned right, he did the same. Finally she pulled into Mrs. Frankel's driveway and watched the police car pull up behind. When she got out of the car, two uniformed security men got out of theirs and stood before her. She asked the closest one, a tall man, with a bushy gray mustache pointed down at the corners, "Excuse me officer. I did something wrong? I think I go speed limit only." Her voice crackled, emitting a high tone that comes from tension. Her hand shook.

She looked up into his face but could see only her own reflection in his mirrored sunglasses. The bouncing of his droopy mustache seemed to dramatize each syllable, "I don't know, I just want to talk to the lady of the house."

Carmen breathed easier when he said this but still tripped on the first step leading to the front door. She rang the bell and Mrs. Frankel answered immediately, like she had been expecting everyone. Mrs. Frankel's gray hair was tied tightly behind her head in a bun, her stooped shoulders made her head protrude as she stood aside to allow them all to enter. She stared at Carmen and said, "Come in everyone."

Carmen attempted a smile but could only say, "What wrong, Mrs. Frankel? What happen. You OK?" The four of them eased into the large foyer and stood in an awkward square under the large golden chandelier. "What wrong here? I scared."

"What's wrong?" Mrs. Frankel repeated, moving towards Carmen. "Something is very wrong and it concerns you. Last night, I was looking over my dishes. Those beautiful gold rimmed 12 piece set that I have, and I found one plate missing. You know the ones. I mean, they're hand painted. There is one plate missing. I'm so disappointed. Those were a gift from my dead husband. Oh Carmen," she wiped a fake tear from her face and moved closer. "How could you?"

Carmen jumped back in disbelief, "Wait a minute. Is that what this about? You think I steal one plate from you? One plate? What I do with one plate? I can go to BargainBox. Buy one for dollar. Please Mrs. Frankel, what I do with one plate?"

"I don't know what you'd do with it. All I know is that it's missing and you are the only one that cleans my house."

Carmen's face turned red and she came closer to the old woman. "Mrs Frankel, you have guests in house all days. Maybe one take by mistake. I no know. I know I not take your plate. I a Christian. We no steal. I witness for my God. I never steal something from nobody. Not you, not nobody."

"My plate is missing and you clean my house. My beautiful set of dishes is ruined. Ruined. What am I going to do?" She again dabbed at her cheek with her lace handkerchief.

"Mrs. Frankel, You have people in this house every day. Maybe they steal. Just because I poor and no speak English well, you think I steal ? I never steal anything from anybody. You think I, Me, steal your plate. I no do it. Never would. I no take anything ever from this house, anybody house, any time. I no could do that."

Carmen stood shaking, with her hands over her face, crying, her body shaking, her voice hardly able to utter a sound. She said to no one in particular, "I love that woman. Five years I clean her house, I care for her, I do everything for her. I no understand."

The younger policeman moved towards her, reached out his arm like he wanted to touch her shoulder but his partner intervened, "Mrs. Frankel, I don't know what to do. Do you want to press charges?"

She ground her dentures together, making a scraping sound like gears grinding, and shrieked, "Charges. Charges? I've made my charges. Just take her away. I never want to see her again…ever… get her out of here … now!"

The mustached policeman put his hand on Carmen's back. She was still shaking, trembling, and crying. He led her out the door. The other guard thanked Mrs. Frankel for her understanding and shut the door behind him. He hurried ahead to open Carmen's car door.

His mustached partner removed his arm from the shaking Carmen and asked, "Why are you here? Why are you here Carmen? In this country?"

Carmen looked up, wrinkled up her nose and asked, "What? What you say? I no think I hear you right."

The policeman repeated, "Why are you here, in this country?"

She stiffened. "I here because I need work. I have eleven year old son. I single mother. My father at home, he no can work, He paralyzed. I need feed my son, help my father. At home I a teacher, here I clean houses. I have to work. I work hard, every day."

Ignoring her pleas, the policeman asked again, "Are you here legally? Do you have a social security card? Let me see your driver's license."

She felt her heart pulsating, her neck stiffened, her face flushed with anger. She took a deep breath, stepped back and remembered last Sunday's sermon about love, faith, and trusting God.

She reached in her purse and pulled out a well worn piece of paper, showing she was a legal driver only in her home country. "Here. Here, that all I have." She stopped shaking and was now resigned to whatever God had in His plan.

The older policeman took a pad from his pocket, copied her name and asked, "Where do you live?" While she gave her address, he wrote it carefully in his pad, "Carmen, I've got your name, address, all we need to know. It is recorded right here. Do not ever come back to this plantation again, ever, or you will be arrested. That's all. Good bye."

Carmen said nothing but squeezed into her car, looked straight ahead, and waited. The policemen drove off and she followed slowly behind. She drove carefully past the gate, turned unto the highway, and headed home. The pleas of her prayer competed with the knocking of her car's oil hungry motor.

The Man from Plains

I never heard of Plains, Georgia before he became president. My image of it was distorted by a Northeastern upbringing where everything the rural south was considered behind the times, made up of neglected farms, inhabited by poor blacks, and uneducated whites. Now we are driving to Plains, through picturesque, rich farmland, with slopping hills, and large well kept houses. There are no abandoned tractors or decaying barns like I had imagined. "This land is beautiful," I said to Lorrie. "This is like those rich farms in your state of Iowa."

She continued fusing with the GPS, looking up occasionally to enjoy the scenery. I wondered if she was getting bored with all this driving. I was glad when she said, "I like it too. It's so much better than traveling the interstate. We're going just about as fast anyway. All those highways look the same"

"I agree, I'm so glad we came. It's a long drive, though. Are you okay?"

"I'm fine. This is something you always wanted to do, so let's keep going."

I liked this togetherness feeling. Recently I thought we had grown apart; me busy with volunteering and exercise, her with volunteering and bridge. It seemed like we were spending less time together, maybe even avoiding each other. "It's great to be doing this with you. I get bored driving long distances. Not today though. It's nice being together."

"Oh, look, there's the sign, 'Entering Plains, Georgia.'" Her rapid speech showed her excitement.

"Good, we made it. Over there, an information booth. Let's stop."

"Yes, Maybe they can direct us to his church. It is Sunday morning, you know. Don't suppose we could actually attend a service, do you."

"Never can tell. Maybe this is our lucky day. It would be worth it just to drive by, take a picture." I parked in a large parking lot, empty except for one car. "Maybe it's open. Who knows?"

The information booth was well kept, with a fresh coat of paint, and manicured lawn. We followed the litter free sidewalk into a quiet building, which was more like a home than a place of business. I pushed on the door. "Hey, Lorrie. It's open."

A well dressed, gray haired lady, smiled, and extended her hand to greet us. "Hi y'all. Welcome to Plains, Georgia."

"This is too much. I didn't know if you'd be open," I added. "What beautiful country this is. I'm impressed."

"Well thank you, Sir. We're so glad you came."

"Now," I asked, trying not to be too abrupt, "are you allowed to tell us where Jimmy Carter's church is?"

"Why sure I can. Here's a map. You're here, and right there," she said drawing a circle around a figure, "is his church. It's just down the road. And by the way, he's here today. Right now he's teaching a Sunday school class. Would you like to go?" she teased.

"Like to go?" I interrupted. "Is it possible?" My thoughts and words were running together, like a child on Christmas morning. "I can't believe he's here. This is unbelievable."

"Sure, you can go. They don't want you to interrupt his lesson though, but you can go to the service and get your picture taken with him afterwards. You'll have to go through a little security check. It's not much."

I looked at Lorrie and saw her beaming, her broad smile exposing her white teeth back to first molars. "Do you mean we can just go in, and he'll be there?" She paused, "May I see that map again?"

"Sure, here it is. You just go out of the lot, turn left, and take a right at the Stop Sign. It's about a mile up the road. It's easy."

I didn't want to be impolite but we couldn't wait to leave this kindly woman and get to the church. I had thought about this ever since we moved to Hilton Head eleven years ago. We had even arranged a tour in the past but it was cancelled because we had to evacuate for a hurricane.

The town was small so after we left the Information booth and turned at the Stop Sign, we arrived at Manathama Baptist Church. We turned into the driveway where a young serious looking man, forcing a faint grin, motioned for us to pull up. He managed a quick "good morning" and got right to business. A large, leashed dog sniffed every inch of the Toyota. In less than a minute, the man motioned us on to the parking area.

We got out of the car and walked past three or four other military type men dressed in suits and ties. A slightly built woman, with short cropped hair greeted us with a handshake, a smile, and led us across the lawn to the church entrance, "Thanks for joining us today. We've been expecting you." Her comment made me think that sweet lady at the

Information booth was part of the Secret Service. "Isn't this a beautiful day?"

"It sure is." We both answered in unison. At the entrance two more security guards, searched us up and down like at an airport and then directed us into the church. This beautiful, idyllic sanctuary was maybe half full with seventy five people spread out in the pews. Up front, leading the service, with his characteristic smile was Jimmy Carter, thirty ninth president of the United States. "Oh my God," I thought to myself, "It's actually him. Jimmy Carter right here, giving a Sunday school class just like any other citizen of this great country might do." Lorrie and I filed into a vacant pew towards the back so as not to disturb anyone. We sat, held hands, and gushed.

Lorrie checked her watch and whispered that Sunday school was almost over. He was talking about some Old Testament character who I hardly recognized and then focused on his ending. He described how Jesus brought a new message to the world, different than the Old Testament. He asked the congregation, "What lessons can we learn from the life of Jesus?"

Various people gave the standard answers of Love, Forgiveness, Charity, Compassion, and Giving. He responded, "Yes, these are all good answers, all things we can learn from Jesus but there is one more. One more that no one has mentioned." He waited to allow us time to think. "He also taught us Peace. Peace both within ourselves and in the world." He paused again, "In our wonderful country where we have so much, it is easy for us to become arrogant, to think we are actually better than someone else. This allows us to look down on people, to drop bombs on them like in Kosovo or Iraq or in who knows where else without giving thought to the families and people below and how it affects their lives. We call ourselves Christians, and yet we do this. We support it. By our silence, we condone it. Either we are Christians or we're not. We can either accept the lessons of Jesus, or reject them. Each one of us must decide on that." He turned abruptly and exited the church with Secret Service men in front, behind, and alongside.

Lorrie and I squeezed each other's hands. A man of his stature, in this small town church, driving this basic Christian message deep into our hearts, made me tingle, and left both of us speechless. All I could say was, "Wow" and press closer to her. We didn't try to talk. His words and life said everything.

A church service followed with a lot of hymn singing and an uninspiring message from the minister. As he spoke, I was more interested in watching Jimmy and Roslyn Carter, sitting like any one of us, except they were surrounded on all sides by the Secret Service. After the last hymn, most of the congregation formed a line outside on the sidewalk waiting for a picture with the Carters.

"He really does live a Christian life," I said to Lorrie. "My mind was wandering during the service. I was wondering, whether it is possible for an authentic Christian like him to be a politician, especially President of the United States? A lot of bad things happened in his four years, the economy was bad with twelve percent interest rates. The worst thing was the Iran Hostage crisis where they held over 400 people from our embassy hostage for more than a year. A lot of people wanted to bomb Iran. I don't know what he could have done. He tried an abortive attack in the desert. It failed but all the hostages did get out. His push for human rights in China and Russia was consistent with his Christian viewpoint. He confronted the Shah of Iran about his use of torture. The Shah was toppled, the Iyatolla took over, Iran has been fervently anti- American ever since. Maybe a true Christian can't make a good president. I don't know."

"Most historians don't rate him very highly as a president, do they," asked Lorrie.

Before I could answer, we realized we were now next in line to have our picture taken. A friendly lady offered to use our camera to take our picture, "Is this all I have to do? Push this button?" she asked.

"Yes," Lorrie answered, "that's all."

She told us to step forward, stand on each side of the Carters, don't touch them, or say anything. I was speechless anyway. As we stepped forward, I controlled my urge to put my arm around him, but did whisper, "I enjoyed your message."

He may have said "Thank you," I couldn't tell. I was enjoying the moment. Our treasured picture shows four smiling faces, Lorrie and I gushing like teenagers on prom night.

PART V

Africa

Hilton Head to Africa

This African trip was a lifelong dream that became a compulsion. I had to see Africa now. Lorrie didn't share my enthusiasm so I invited my adult daughter, Heather. Her excitement matched mine so I'm on the plane to New York to meet her and then together we will fly on to Tanzania. We'll have almost a month to enjoy the people, safaris, and charm of Africa. This non-stop flight from Savannah to JFK will give us five to six hours in New York before we fly to Amsterdam and then to our destination. Non-stop flights to anywhere are as rare as the white Rhino, but I was fortunate to find this one to New York.

I put down my worn copy of "Out of Africa," to watch the plane descend into New York airspace. I wonder, How can Heather be so comfortable living amongst all those tall buildings crowded together to make up this impersonal city? She was brought up in a small Cape Cod village where everybody not only knew her but cared about every aspect of her life. The town's people followed her from Sue McNutt's nursery school, through the Orleans school system and watched her return from college as a young woman. Her graduate school at Columbia University introduced her to the big city life and now she is a part of it. I'm proud of her, but New York City? I'm overwhelmed by this mass of people and cement, but she thrives on it. Spending a month with her in Africa is a gift from God.

After Marilyn was killed in a car accident, we traveled often in a threesome together with Rob. Our trips to Hawaii, Brazil, Italy, Spain, and Morocco helped dull some of the excruciating pain we faced together. We had fun and got along well but at that time, I was the unquestioned leader, the father, and resolved conflicts as I chose. Now Heather and I are equals, two adults traveling together in a strange country. How would we get along now in the intimacy of this vacation? I wasn't worried about her, because her adult self has only drawn me closer to her. The problem is me. They used to be amused by antics like me losing my temper at a dishonest taxi driver, but now that amusement could easily turn to embarrassment. Would I measure up? When she saw me as an adult would she be titillated or embarrassed? The easiest way to avoid the dilemma is for me to behave myself. That's a good idea but less fun. AH. That's the solution- have fun.

As our plane landed smoothly, I contorted my body to catch a glimpse of the city through the miniscule plane window. I saw only paved runways, confusing signs pointing in every direction, and more airplanes. This isn't the small Hilton Head Airport that I am used to, with two small runways. This is JFK, home to practically every airline in the world and my introduction to the big city. My first surprise as I enter the terminal is that there is no one here. It's 8AM in this huge airport, in one of the world's biggest cities and there is almost no one around. My impression is that there are so many people in New York competing for space that privacy does not exist, yet this morning it's more like a library than a bustling airport. I could read a book and not be disturbed. Is this some kind of a joke? Did I do something wrong?

I'm getting the sinking feeling that I had once when Rob and I boarded the wrong plane on a flight to San Francisco. We crammed our luggage into the overhead compartment and settled comfortably in our seat before a loudspeaker announced, "Mr. McOuat, you're on the wrong plane." We had to run to the correct flight and then just made it as the door was closing. My tendency to daydream often complicates my life.

All the clothes I brought for the month of rugged travel are jammed into the canvass luggage provided by our tour group, Overseas Adventure Travel. The strap digs deeply into my sore shoulder. I can check that, I hope, and keep with me only a backpack loaded with essentials for the 18 hour trip to Kilimanjaro Airport. Backpacks are carried daily by almost every elementary school student in the country, but mine feels strange. I can't remember ever carrying one before. My shoulders and arms feel like they're pinned back, leaving me nearly helpless. I can't easily turn my head or move my arms. I look for a bathroom where I can brush my teeth, shave, and rearrange my books, notebooks, and pens that I will carry with me. Maybe I can loosen a strap on this contraption. Right now it is suitable only for a child.

I wind my way through the mazelike entry into the men's room, lay the backpack down on the sink, and look up at the worried face starring back at me in the mirror. The bags under my eyes reflect my lack of sleep the night before. My brain waves have been firing off in every direction because of the excitement of the trip. Some cool water will revive me. I want to look respectable when I meet Heather. There aren't any hot or cold water knobs to start the water. I hear water flowing but can't tell the source. Now there is plenty of water flowing in the next sink where I've laid my things.

Oh NO! These are automatic water faucets that are activated by putting your hands underneath. Instead of hands, it is my backpack that starts the powerful flow. The backpack, with all its precious contents are now soaked. I reach for faucet handles that aren't there. Am I an alien in the 21st century? I rally enough to pick it up and the water flow stops, but too late. The notebooks, papers, my cherished copy of "Out of Africa," are all drenched.

"Damn," I yell to the empty bathroom. I unzip the backpack and empty a gallon of water onto the floor. The Serengeti itinerary and my notebook are saturated. The KLM airline tickets are water spotted but not ruined. I empty everything into a nearby sink and carry the opened backpack to the air dryer. Air dryers are not meant to dry canvas bags filled with water. I laugh at my own stupidity. Toothbrush, shaver, airline tickets go back into the wet backpack and I leave the bathroom to find KLM. Everything seems heavier now, or am I getting older and weaker? My first mission is to check my luggage and find the bus to Grand Central Station.

I don't see any signs that mean anything to me. "Excuse me mam." I ask a well dressed fellow traveler who appears like she may know her way around this confusing city. "Could you please tell me how to get to the KLM terminal?"

She looks at me and smiles like city slicker taking pity on a country bumpkin. "Yes, You cross this aisle, go upstairs, take the Airtram to # 4 terminal, follow the moving sidewalk to the escalator, then go upstairs to KLM." She looks at the furrows forming on my forehead. "Don't worry, It's easy. Upstairs to Airtram, to terminal #4, sidewalk to escalator, then upstairs to KLM."

I wonder what someone would do who couldn't speak English. I wrestle my luggage across the aisle, go upstairs and see a sign, "AIRTRAIN." That's what she meant, I guess. AIRTRAIN, of course. Now her directions make sense.

I see the reassuring sign of other people waiting in line. I ask a bearded man with holes in his sweatshirt, "Is this the train to …ah…number 4 terminal?"

"It sure is, Jack. You're doin' fine." I think I must look as much out of place here as I feel. I don't bother telling him my name is Charlie, not Jack. I'm too busy faking sophistication to bother correcting him.

I board the bullet train; go two stops until I see the Terminal #4 sign, get off, climb the stairs to the KLM counters. This is getting easier. A lady wearing a powder blue KLM uniform points to the E-Ticket sign. She smiles but says nothing. Oh no. More machines without people. I stand in line and wait patiently while more confident passengers push ahead like kids in a grade school cafeteria line. I'm going nowhere until someone takes pity and says, "That one's free." I thank God for people who sympathize with confused travelers. I find my itinerary in the bottom of my backpack then try to read the directions on the E-Ticket machine. It's difficult for me to think when impatient people are scowling at me from behind.

Step 1- put in credit card. I do. Nothing happens so I look around for a friendly face. A man behind me says, "Push that, then how many in the party?"

"One," I answer. He pushes the buttons for me. Then, he pulls a strip of paper from a dispenser, points to a name "Is that you?" he asks with a condescending tone.

"Yes, That's me."

"Good, here's your boarding pass." My shoulders droop when I realize how simple it is. Lorrie is always encouraging me to follow directions. Maybe I should listen to her.

I drag my luggage to the check in counter.

"Can I check my luggage with you for a few hours while I meet someone in the city?"

A blond woman with polished nails, wearing a light blue KLM uniform smiles and asks to see my ticket. "Why don't you just check your luggage now to Arusha?"

"Arusha? What's that?"

"Arusha is your destination in Africa. See on your ticket, right here. You can check your baggage now and be done with it. Kilimanjaro Airport is in Arusha."

"Really," I ask in disbelief. "I can do that? I want to meet my daughter and have some fun in New York before we take a trip together. We're going to Africa." I may be getting paranoid but I notice the corners of her mouth turn up in a smile of derision, or is it sympathy?

"I know, Mr. McOuat. Arusha, I'll bet. You just relax and have fun in the city. KLM is going to take care of everything."

I think this woman is my guardian angel. "Oh thank you, mam. You're so kind. And how is it outside. Will I need my sweat shirt?" I ask like she is my mother.

"No, it's warm. Your t-shirt will be fine. You go on and find your daughter. KLM will handle everything here. You just have to be back here by 6:30. Ah.. 6:30 this evening, I mean."

I think New York is OK after all; it's so friendly. "Thank you. Could you tell me how to find a pay phone?"

"It's right behind you. See the sign. It says pay phone. Follow the directions on the wall. It's easy." Now her mocking smile is obvious.

The wall directions say; #1- Deposit six cents. Six cents. What do they mean by that? Six cents. Is that some New York City humor? Why is everything so different here? I hope the Red Sox beat them this year. Finally. I drop a quarter into the slot. A machine voice asks me for 25 cents more. Another quarter into the slot then I dial Heather's number. I hear her voice. I'm saved. "Yes, I'm OK. I'll meet you at the clock at Grand Central Station. And Heather, I've already checked my bags all the way to Africa. We're on our way... Yes Heather. I can find the bus to the city... Yes... OK...I know, don't act like a tourist. Yes..OK... See you in about an hour. Stop worrying about me. I'll be there."

I follow the signs to Ground Transportation, which is another huge area without many people. I ask a man in a bus driver's uniform how to get to Grand Central Station. He points to a line of empty seats and says in a foreign accent, "Sit there. Lady come, sell you ticket, no problem," and walks away.

I sit down, afraid to deviate from his instructions. In a few minutes a uniformed lady approaches and asks, "One way or round trip?"

Her directness catches me by surprise. "Oh, to New York? Round trip please."

"That will be twenty seven dollars. Cash please. No, we don't take credit cards. The bus leaves at 9:45." She takes my two twenty dollar bills and disappears without a word. I sit back down and think. That was stupid. I just gave forty dollars in cash to a stranger in a big city and watched her disappear without a receipt.

I fidget for half an hour, afraid to leave and thinking that I've had my first lesson in big city con games. Its 9:43 by that clock and nothing is happening. No money, no change, no ticket. Oh. Here comes a lady in a uniform. What a great smile she has. I stand up and ask, "Do I look lost?"

The robust black woman answers, "Darlin' you look like you need me."

"I do. Oh, I do. I do need you."

She hands me a bus ticket, my change and says, "Now you go out side this door. The bus stop is right there. See it?

The bus will be here in a minute. The bus driver will take care of you."

Everyone seems so paternalistic here. I guess I look like I need help.

The bus is almost empty when I board. After the driver assures me for the second time that we are indeed going to Grand Central Station, I quietly take a window seat where I expect to view the sights. After a few minutes delay, the doors whoosh shut and were on our way. From my wet backpack, I pick out my dampened paper back, "Out of Africa." The man and woman in the book are composing a silly poem together, "Turn your mournful ditty to a merry measure, I came not for pity, but I came for pleasure." I think that will make a good mantra for this trip to Africa. When our traveling companions complain, I'll recite this poem. Only good spirits are permitted.

JFK Airport is like a city in itself. I wonder if this bus will ever run out of terminals. We go ahead a few feet, pick up some speed, then the brakes and another stop. Whoosh, he stops, the door opens, people board loaded down with suitcases, they sit, we proceed, then another whoosh, more people, more whooshing. He stops at every airline within each terminal. The bus is almost full when a very fat man chooses to sit next to me. He crushes me against the side of the bus when he sits. He says nothing. I can no longer read or write in my journal because I am wedged between the fat man and the bus. What was that poem, "Turn your mournful ditty to a merry measure???"

We are finally at terminal one. I boarded at terminal 4 so are we now ready to head towards the city or do we just keep going in an endless circle, 4-3-2-1-4-3-2-1? Across the aisle, I hear a man talking loudly into a cell phone in Spanish. This is my first time hearing Spanish with a New York accent. My book mark from the Hilton Head library drops to the floor, lost forever. With my fat friend pinning me against the side of the bus, I'm helpless. My last contact with home may as well have flown out the window as be on the floor. I'd like to put my return bus ticket in my pocket but he's now asleep and I'm immobilized. More airbrakes, more stops and then a freeway, jammed up, but at least we're free of JFK. Our next stop will be the Grand Central Station, or was that the Port Authority, I forgot.

Out the window, I see more regular cars and less SUVS than in Hilton Head. The houses line up like Archie Bunker's in, "All in the Family." Maybe the guy crunching me is Archie, twenty years later. Is that Edith and Meathead walking their dog? People wear T-shirts and shorts like normal folks, but where is the space? There are few lawns, just cars, stores, and cemeteries. Humanity condensed, right here, on a doorstep. A man with a long beard rides a motorized bicycle with a dog on a leash scurrying behind. We pass normal businesses like Fish and Chips, Kitchen and Bath, the ubiquitous cemetery, a chiropractor, a bakery, pharmacy, another funeral home, martial arts, and restaurants. Our little town has all those businesses but here they look out of place crowded together like this. Traffic is light today, Saturday, so we're making good time. We've gone four miles in forty minutes.

The beautiful Manhattan sky line welcomes me and leads to my daughter. Bronx houses give way to apartments the size of small cities. Small lawns are replaced by plants and trees surrounded by grill work, cars by taxis, door steps by door men, and parks by the wide boulevard in the middle of Park Ave. In a few minutes, the driver announces that we have arrived.

I get off the bus and try to fit in. Heather warned me to look confident, to walk briskly and not look like a tourist. "Excuse me please. How do I get to Grand Central Station?"

"You're there Mister. That's it right in front of you. Congratulations. You made it." I think he may have been sarcastic, but I'm not sure. I don't care. I made it and Heather will be here to meet me. Now she can lead, all the way to Africa.

....

Heather's smile is as big as mine when we meet under the clock in the middle of Grand Central. "Dad, you made it. You look great."

"So do you Heather. Of course I made it. What a crazy city. Are you hungry?"

"A little. Have you eaten anything today?"

"Two bananas and lots of water. There was no food on the airplane." She has her backpack and huge canvass bag like mine. I offer to help her but she refuses. "Let's find someplace close."

We find a delicatessen nearby and sit at a round table with high stools. I buy a bottle of water, take a drink, and put the cap on the table. She is maternal. She absent mindedly picks up the cap, puts it on top of the bottle and gives it a quarter turn. I pick up the bottle to take a drink, the cap pops off and the water pours out all over the front of me. This time, my T-shirt and shorts are soaked. We both laugh. She says, "Dad, I think we've got to have better teamwork than that."

"I agree Heather, I agree."

An early hint that this is going to be a great trip and that we are going to be compatible comes when we leave the deli. I take my empty water bottle and look for a trash can. She says, "Dad, don't throw it away. We can fill the bottle on the plane. We'll keep drinking without buying." I wonder if her frugality comes from inheritance or her upbringing. Either way, I welcome it.

It is an eight hour plane ride from Amsterdam to Kilimanjaro Airport in Tanzania. My aching back has already been "broken in," by the six hour ride from JFK to Amsterdam. KLM seems to have a company policy to avoid serving any food on the Atkins Diet. We are saturated with carbohydrate rich delights like pasta, bread, ice cream, and cake. "Would you like another Danish?" asks the pretty, red headed flight attendant.

"No thank you. I get a little crazy when I have too much sugar."

The first thing she offered was a glass of orange juice, which I immediately poured down my shirt. Ever since then, I've been drinking water because it wears better on my clothes. I drink white wine instead of red for the same reason.

I treat myself to a break from the crowded seats by going to the men's room. Ah, Privacy. This is my little room away from home. Unfortunately, I forgot to lock the door and a fat lady barges in while I'm sitting on the toilet. "Oh, I'm sorry," she says, "I didn't know it was occupied."

"That's Okay," I respond, "I forgot to lock the door." Each of us is apologizing while silently blaming the other person. What ever happened to "say what you mean and mean what you say?"

My room (this bathroom) has so many mirrors that I feel crowded by my own reflection. I can tell this is a Dutch airline because everything has been cleaned and cleaned again. Anything brass or metal is super shined so that it too becomes a mirror. I can't avoid seeing the bald spot forming in the back of my head. I pat it with my hand. Nothing is hidden in this house of mirrors.

I imagine that the whole plane is waiting in line to share "my room." I come out and a woman asks, "Where are you going?"

I think this is a strange question because we're all going to Tanzania. There are no intermediate stops. "Tanzania," I answer. "We're traveling with Overseas Adventure Travel," I add to keep the conversation going. Also, there are twelve people aboard this flight who will be with us for the next fourteen days and I'm anxious to meet them.

"We've been traveling for two days already," she adds to be sociable. "We're going to a small town to do mission work."

I hear something familiar in the tone of her voice. "Where are you from?" I ask.

"Iowa."

I knew it. My wife is from Iowa. She has the same smile, the love of work, especially missionary work as this woman. Without knowing any more than her state of origin, I know that toilet that she just came out of is wiped free of water droplets and cleaned thoroughly like it has never been used. That's the way our house is, all the time. Lorrie's family came from Holland and settled in Iowa. Any nation whose people are known for scrubbing sidewalks will certainly disinfect their own houses and husbands when given the opportunity.

When I return to my seat, I think I hear the smiling flight attendant ask, "Do you want any more sugar?" (She actually said pastry)

"No thank you."

In a few minutes she returns with a hot face cloth served with tongs, indicating that we're going to get more food.

Heather pleads, "Please Dad, Don't repeat that comment to her again about 'her not wanting us to lose weight on this trip.' You say it every time she brings food and it's getting a little tiring."

Heather never understood my philosophy of telling jokes over and over again in the faint hope that someone, somewhere will laugh. "If I tell a joke and no one laughs, I feel obligated to try it again. That hasn't changed since the days we traveled together twenty years ago. You may have matured, but I haven't."

"Believe me Dad, she's only being kind when she laughs." I miss the days when she was a child, and everything I said was funny.

A map on the TV monitor shows our progress. Familiar map colors of blue for water, green for land, brown for mountains, black for the equator, and yellow for dessert are logical until we fly over the Sahara Desert and it is pictured green. Can I trust this map? And if I can't trust the map, can I trust anything on this airplane, like the pilot and navigator?

Rome, Athens, and Cairo are behind and we progress south over Addis Abba, Mogadishu, and Khartoom, towards Nairobe.

The screen also shows that it is 39 degrees outside the plane. I think some of those 39 degrees must have penetrated our cabin because I'm cold. I will not wear shorts and a T-shirt on the return trip. Everyone wraps one of those amazingly thin airline blankets around themselves. It's not long enough to cover both my feet and shoulders. I have to choose, shoulders or feet. It's too thin anyway to offer more than a tease of comfort. Mountain climbing clothes are suitable for these air conditioned flights. My thermal underwear is checked in with my luggage.

The screen tells us it is one hour a forty seven minutes to our destination. I can jog for an hour so I should be able to tolerate the overly efficient air conditioning for that long. I've heard about the "bad air" on airplanes. Maybe they are trying to freeze the bacteria. During another bathroom break, I ask a beautiful woman, "How are you doing?" Her silent, confused response makes me wonder if she is wary of me (yes), or doesn't she speak English (I hope)? Despite her rejection, I hope that she is one of our twelve unknown traveling companions. She isn't. I'll never see her again.

When I return to my seat, the always smiling red headed hostess offers a hot towel at the end of a pair of tongs. I wipe my face and hands and then wait while nothing happens. "Heather," I ask, "Where's the food? We get a towel and no food. Is this towel like the carrot and the stick to keep us pacified or are we going to get another meal?"

"Dad, relax. We'll get our food first because we're in the back of the plane. They're probably serving first class before us."

"First class is a different world. They don't count. I'm hungry."

I'm reminded again that this is a Dutch airline when the hostess brings a warm finger cloth before dinner and then a little gadget wrapped in paper for a final after dinner, end of the trip, cleaner.

A sign that this has been a "good" nine hour flight is that I haven't taken my earphones out of their wrapper. Sleeping, eating, some reading, but mostly, conversing with my daughter, has made the time pass with ease. We leave behind the hot towels, the TV monitors, the carbohydrates, and disembark into the Kilimanjaro Airport. We are in Africa.

What to Do about Sara?

I volunteer as an English teacher in an orphanage school in the West African country of Ghana. Ghana was colonized by the British. English is their national language, but most conversations are in one of many local or tribal languages. They need help with their English to get a better job and to make their life easier. On my second day there, I was teaching in a mid-level class and noticed one girl, named Comfort, constantly had her hand in the air, giving correct answers to all questions. She was interested in everything. I was impressed with her and was disappointed when, the next day I was asked to teach in a lower level class.

Here, the students were learning the ABCs and numbers. Most of them could recite the alphabet, "A, B, C, D, E, etc," but they couldn't recognize letters when I wrote them on the blackboard. I wrote, D, E, F, and then asked for someone to write what was next. No one could complete the exercise except for one very dignified, tiny little girl named Sara. She got the correct answer every time and then, when it was time for students to draw on their own slates, most just scribbled a few forms resembling letters, but Sara showed me her work with every letter, A through Z, written neatly and perfectly. This got my attention.

When we worked on numbers, I again wrote, "1, 2, 3…." and then asked for volunteers to write the next number. Sara was the only one who could do this consistently. During a break, she came to the blackboard at the front of the room, said nothing but wrote all numbers, 1-30, by herself. This was way beyond the rest of the class, who at that time were struggling to count to ten on their fingers.

I watched while another teacher introduced the class to shapes, circles, ovals, squares, rectangles and triangles. These children have no books, papers, or pencils but write with tiny bits of chalk on well worn slates. I went over to Sara and asked, "Sara which of these is a triangle, etc?" She immediately identified each shape and went on to draw, by herself, each one when I asked. I was shocked. If students were rated 1-100, and the average was about 7 or 8, one boy, Felix would get maybe 12 and Sara would be at 100. I was impressed and wanted to help this gifted girl.

The teacher in charge of the school had only been there two days and wasn't yet familiar with the students. I told her about Sara and recommended that she be promoted several levels to where this special person could be taught and challenged. The teacher, named Elizabeth, agreed and talked with Sara. She asked her to bring her mother to school the next day to discuss her precocious daughter.

The next morning, a short, well dressed woman, sat in a plastic chair in front of the school while Sara sat dutifully behind. I introduced myself, told her how impressed I was with her daughter's ability to learn, and complemented her on being such a good mother. She spoke little English but managed to tell me about her other daughter, named Comfort. I said, "Comfort is your daughter? I know her. I taught her when I first arrived. She also is very smart. With daughters like that, I know that you also have to be smart and an excellent mother." She smiled like she understood

Elizabeth, the head teacher arrived and also complimented the mother. She translated for me that Sara's father had a stroke, can't work, and so the mother is the only financial support to her husband and daughters. The mother never attended school, can't read, or write. The sole family income is from the mother taking in their neighbor's dirty laundry. She worries that Sara and her sister may need to drop out of school because the family can't afford the $30 per year school fees.

Ghana is a poor country. Many, like Sara and her family, live on less than a dollar a day. They struggle not only with school fees but to put a bowl of rice on the family table. Sara's family is not unusual. For many of our fellow human beings, poverty dominates their life. Sara's gifted intellect is unusual but the desperate poverty is not unusual. It is accepted as a normal human condition. One of the slogans for raising college funds in the United States warns, "A mind is a terrible thing to waste." It is beyond terrible, it is tragic. A tragedy for us all. Sara is the future of her country and our world. We need to nurture brains like hers . Maybe she would someday write great books or help us with issues that must be solved like global warming, peace, or hunger. In this era of globalization, our world shrinks so that Sara's problems become our problems. We all need Sara and right now, today, Sara needs us. What do we do about Sara?

United Planet

Ten days in the big city of Accra giving polio immunizations was a nice introduction to volunteering in Africa. I stayed in a fancy hotel with ninety Rotarians from the United States and Canada, giving immunizations in the poor areas of the city each day and then back to our comfortable hotel at night. We ate western type food, listened western type music performed by a talented piano player, and retired to our soft bed at night. Before I left the USA, an NGO called United Planet had arranged for me to stay an extra two weeks and teach English in an isolated African village. As the Rotarians returned home, I went on to Biakpa in the Volta Region. Thus began one of the best two weeks of my life.

I stayed in a lodge overlooking a pristine mountain range, without electricity, but with an abundance of love and excitement. I returned each afternoon to the lodge after teaching in the nearby school. After a light lunch, and maybe a short nap, I'd sit outside and wait for other guests to congregate. By 4 PM vacationing Peace Corps volunteers, people from all over Ghana, Europe, and the United States met for stimulating conversations. Because there was no electricity, it was dark by 6 PM but we sat talking by candle light, well into the night. The local beer was excellent

Each morning I walked one kilometer through the village to the school. The townspeople waved, smiled and said "welcome," as I passed on the dusty road. Within days I felt at home in the lodge and village. The Ghanaian teachers were on strike so I was put to work immediately. I taught English to three different class levels. The students were highly motivated, respectful, and supportive. When I assigned homework to "tell me about yourself," one girl described how much she liked to read, tell stories to her younger sister, how she hated gossip, and liked to play a certain game with her friends. These were middle school aged children but her well detailed essay showed a lot of writing sophistication. I was impressed by the students and thought about organizing a pen pal program between them and some American high school children. My United Planet Quest lives on in the U.S.A.

My stay in the Volta region coincided with the funeral for a tribal chief who died two years before. Every morning I woke up to the sound of magical African drumming, muskets firing from nearby villages, and an occasional cannon resounding over the pastoral mountains. Tony Fiakpa, my host at the Mountain Paradise Lodge, did everything possible to immerse me in the total African experience.

On third day there, he offered to drive me to school to meet the new chief. In town, I shook hands with a regal, handsome man about forty years old. He sat with his elders around a pot loaded with herbs, bottles of incense, and smoking embers. They were starting the funeral for his predecessor. He invited me to participate while they opened the ceremony by preparing the departed chief's journey to the afterlife by sacrificing a chicken. I watched as someone plucked a few feathers from the neck, prayers were chanted in unison, while a tribal leader sliced the neck with a machete, and then dripped the blood over the simmering herbs. We ended the ceremony by sharing local gin, first pouring a drop on the ground to communicate with our dead ancestors. The sun was just rising as put down my empty shot glass and left the ceremony to enjoy another day of teaching at the school.

We spent one day at Tony's ancestral village where they were celebrating the anniversary of their church. I met his family and friends and soon felt like I was one of them instead of a visitor. I shook hands with his tribal leader, who introduced me to his interpreter. The chief spoke English well but used an interpreter because a leader is presumed to be faultless. If a mistake was made, the interpreter could be blamed instead of the chief. I joked that I wanted an interpreter also.

Another day I talked with a voodoo man. He was a retired educator but practiced voodoo like his ancestors. He sat in an easy chair beside a shrine and directed me to sit alongside. Behind me was an empty looking house that was reserved for ghosts and ancestors. No living person lived there. We talked about his traditional African religion. He explained that there was one superior being, above all others, who used agents as helpers. He said this is similar to our Christian religion where we believe in one God, Jesus Christ as our lord and savior, but may a have angels, like their agents.

I asked if he referred some cases to medical clinics when necessary. He said he did and used the example of his wife's high blood pressure. He first treated her with his traditional remedies but when the problem persisted, he referred her to a medical clinic and would do the same for any patient. He added that often area medical clinics might refer clients to him. When asked about marital or family issues, he responded like a trained psychologist the United States. We talked for hours and I was honored that when we parted he called me "a godly person."

One Saturday, we arose early and drove to the neighboring village of Vane, which was the focus of that day's funeral festivities. On the way we passed men and women, walking along the road, wrapped in bright red tribal clothes. Bright red is the mourning color in Ghana. They were all headed to Vane, where a large crowd was already assembled. Men poured black gun powder into their long muskets and compacted it tightly with metal ram rods. The air was clouded with gun smoke from muskets already fired. Each village grouped together and marched, danced, shuffled to the beat of the rhythmic drumming into the town square. One overwhelmed woman, yelling, crying and throwing herself on the ground, had to be led away and comforted by her friends.

We followed the procession towards a central arena. Each village marched separately to the stage, danced, fired their muskets, performed a warlike drama, and then retreated to allow room for the next village. The frenzy increased with louder, faster drumming, I glanced off to the side of the road and saw a very old woman, bent over from age, staggering with a cane, steadied by a younger man assigned to help her. She somehow balanced a pot of water on her head. She was leading her villagers towards the stage to the beat of the drum. She walked past me a few steps, hesitated, turned back, looked me in the eye, bowed, and raised her hand in a two fingered salute like Winston Churchill in World War II. I felt the eyes of the crowd were on me and didn't know what to do. I returned her bow, raised my two fingers like she did. She nodded to me, then continued ambling towards the stage. When she arrived at the center, she listened as the drums reached a feverous beat, then threw down her cane and danced to the music.

After a few minutes of dancing, she sat watching the others, and then as if on cue, picked up her cane, took her aid's hand and walked off the stage. She again led her villagers past me, turned back, repeated her two fingered salute, bowed and then tipped her head so water poured from the pot, onto my feet. I again bowed and returned her salute. She nodded back and continued her retreat from the crowd. When she shuffled beyond the sound of the drums, she reverted to the posture of an old woman, more stooped over, and more dependent on her aid for support.

I rushed over and asked Tony, "Hey, did you see that? What was that all about? Why did she give me that salute? And spill that water? What's going on?"

Without hesitation, Tony said, "She acknowledged you as a godly person."

Now I don't think I'm any more or less godly than anyone else. I think we all are capable of being godly or hellish and one of our challenges is to be more good than bad, but I appreciated the gesture.

I thank United Planet, Tony, and most of all, the people of Ghana for making my quest one that I will never forget.

I love Ghana and the African people. I'm returning in May for the third time and hope to make these visits a regular part of my life.

A Changing Attitude

I had never seen an adult beat a child with a stick. Ebenezer, the nineteen year old teacher, strutted in front of young children, whacking the cane against his free hand, threatening the class. "You better behave or I'll introduce you to my stick," he warned. He told me he had graduated from high school but had run into "financial problems," so he took this teaching job, only to earn money. This frustrated scholar, with little training, was responsible for educating these precious youngsters.

He stood over six feet tall, towering over the frightened children who were crowded together on benches before him. He was slender, able to tuck his shirt tails into his pants without loosening his belt. He wore a clean, ironed white shirt, frayed around both sleeves and collar. His shoes were polished but one sole flapped where it was no longer attached at the toe. He strutted more than walked, back and forth, up and down the classroom, waving that horrible cane, always ready to whack it against the hands, head, or body of the cringing orphans. "This guy is a sadist," I thought as I sat in judgement in the back of the room. "He likes to beat little kids. He loves it."

Whack, whack went the cane against his free hand, a stern warning to pay attention. He stopped strutting long enough to beat the cane off Victoria's head when she failed to recite the ABCs, or against Freda's outstretched hand when she hesitated over two times four, or against Rubby's back, when she said "people is," instead of "people are." His cold icy stare never changed as he roamed the room, cracking his cane against delicate body parts, demanding perfection. "I've got to talk to the administration about this guy," I thought, remembering that Mother Vivian encouraged me to discuss anything with her.

I did notice, however, that the children listened to him and when my turn came to teach, they would sit politely as long as he was in the room but when he left, there was instant chaos.

One day Freda was bitten by a dog when she was out in the field going to the bathroom. Ebenezer saw what happened and immediately rushed from the room and escorted the frightened child to the nurse's office. While he was gone, I strode to the front, anxious to teach the students. I wrote personal pronouns on the board, thinking this would be a shortcut to their mastery of English

Singular	Plural
I	we
You	you
He, She, It	They

By the time I got to "we," I noticed commotion behind me. The steady murmur of young voices soon escalated to a roar. I turned around in time to see Tetter pulling Dominic across the room by his arm, Victoria dancing with no one in the middle of the room, and everyone talking, laughing, and teasing each other while I frowned.

"Hello," I yelled, thinking this was enough to regain their attention.

"Hello," they responded politely but then went on with their monkey business like I wasn't there.

I tried to stand tall, erect, hands on my hips, striking up an authoritative pose. I failed. Instead, I paced, pointed and finally, pleaded, "Don't you want to learn this? I came all the way from the USA to try to help. Can't we work together?"

Several shouted in unison, "Yes, Let's work together," but the anarchy continued.

I was relieved to see Ebenezer come back to the room, leading a now smiling Freda, who was holding a band aid on her shoulder where the dog had attacked her. She sat down, Ebenezer picked up his cane, whacked the hand of the child closest to him and the room instantly became silent. There was order. Everyone returned to their seats, closed their mouths, and leaned forward, like angels.

Class soon ended for their break time and my trembling hand told me that I needed it as much as anyone. The children ran from the room, yelling, pushing, and laughing. I tried to brush past Ebenezer who stood in the exit door but he blocked the way. "Oh, how is Freda?" I asked more to relieve tension than out of concern.

"Oh, she's fine, a little scared, that's all," His face seemed to soften when he wasn't pacing in front of the students. "Charlie, after the break, would you tell them a Bible story?" I wasn't yet ready to befriend this child beater. I was confused, disappointed in my performance in leading a class, and wondering if I really had a function in this very different world. "And now, a Bible story in school?" I wondered.

I said, "Sure, I'll be glad to," and then asked, "Will you stay in the room? They seem to behave much better when you're here."

"I'll be here," he answered, maintaining his stoic stare. I didn't feel like friendly small talk, smiling, or shaking hands. I needed help if I was going to survive in this classroom with him for three more weeks.

I sought out Kinga, the beautiful German girl who lived most of her life in Romania and had been volunteering at the orphanage for three months. She was a graphic designer but was changing professions and needed this time in Africa to reorganize her life. She had a constant smile, a beautiful face, and fit in at the orphanage like she had lived there forever. On our first meeting, two days before, she sat with a one year old on her lap who immediately vomited all over her. She excused herself and calmly strolled off to the bathroom to clean herself and the child. She never said a word of protest and I was very impressed.

"Hi Charlie, how is your morning going?" she asked. I approached holding hands with an orphan at each side and a third one hugging my pant leg from behind.

"I'm doing great. I feel like the most popular kid in the first grade," I joked, looking down at the happy faces of the children surrounding me. "This is what I came for and it's worth the money and the long plane ride just to be with these kids.

"You're doing well," she reassured with her with her calm voice and characteristic smile.

"This is great, but I don't think Ebenezer and I are working well together." I sat down next to her while the kids ran off to play with their friends. "He uses that cane all the time. I could never do that, but when he leaves the room, everything disintegrates. There's no learning. No teaching. Just chaos." She sat silently, waiting for me to continue.

"Ebenezer and I need to work together, but we're not. I feel like I have a lot to contribute, but I'm not being used well. We're not a team at all." The whininess in my voice reflected the morning's frustration.

She stooped down to help a child climb up on her lap and gave her a hug. She spoke in a soft voice, full of emotion. "Many volunteers come here for a few weeks, think they are doing the Ghanaians a big favor. They want to change everything. Make it like it is back home. Ghana is a young country. They're doing fine. They don't need us. Look at their tragic history. They've been enslaved, colonized and exploited. We white people have been terrible to them."

She continued, "They've been independent for only fifty years. Fifty years. Think about it. Give them a chance."

"I agree with that," I said. "I couldn't agree more." I was aware that my voice sounded weak and needy. "But I'm not being used. I came here to contribute. I want to feel useful, but I don't. I hate to my waste time."

"Be patient," she answered almost like a scold. "Be patient. We have our way of doing things, they have theirs. We're intruding on them. Ebenezer has his lesson plans and different volunteers interrupt as they rotate through here. He adjusts the best he can. Their way works for them. Ours works for us." She leaned towards me like she was talking to a child, "Be patient and maybe you'll find your way."

"Patient?" I protested, "That's not me. I'm not patient, .I have no patience. I want it done now." I smiled at my obvious weakness.

"That's the Western way, especially in America," she continued. "Do the job, accomplish, then go on to something else. But that's not here." She hesitated to let the words soak in. "Work on your patience while you're here. Relax. Sit back, relax. You'll get your chance."

I looked at her beautiful face, alive with emotion, pleading with me to slow down. I was moved by the sincerity in her voice. I looked at her, absorbed in what she was saying and felt less sure of myself than when our conversation began. I prided myself in not judging others, in not being arrogant, in not letting my own cultural background interfere with my appreciation of someone else's, but that's exactly what I had done. I had projected my values on another culture instead of embracing them and trying to learn.

I excused myself and walked slowly back to the classroom where students and Ebenezer were waiting for me to enlighten them with a Bible story. My head was down, I shuffled my feet. I didn't feel up to the challenge.

Who is Your Neighbor?

I had been warned that Ebenezer would ask me to tell a Bible story so I spent part of the previous night rereading "The Good Samaritan." I had to read by flickering candle light because the electricity was off but I had heard this famous story so often that I felt prepared.

Ebenezer was already pacing in front of the blackboard, waving his cane at the students who were sitting in place, attentive, waiting for Uncle Charlie to give his talk. He retreated to the back of the room and I shuffled to the front. I wrote words on the board like "Good Samaritan, Bible, neighbor, and priest." I spoke of the priest, representing religious people, the Levites as businessmen or rich people. The Samaritans were the poor, the people who no one liked, the rejected, unloved part of society. I don't know how accurate that is but it added to the drama of the story. I took regular pauses to let Ebenezer translate my words into Tui or Ga, their local traditional languages because they were not familiar with English. When he translated, he paced in his usual manner but carried his cane with less enthusiasm than before. I talked, he translated, and the students listened. I felt like we were a team. I had a function, we were working together. I thought I saw a faint smile forming at the corners of his mouth.

When I came to the part about loving your neighbor, I asked for his help. The students were confused by the word "neighbor" so I asked him to stand beside me. I reached up and put my arm around him. "This is an example of a neighbor," I explained. "One week ago I was in the United States, he was in Ghana. We were separated by endless miles of ocean. I didn't know Ebenezer. He wasn't my neighbor. Now I am here in your wonderful country. I am near him. He is my neighbor and my friend. This Bible story tells me how to please God and how to be happy while we're alive. I must love my neighbor. Ebenezer is my neighbor so I must love him, and help him if I want to be happy here on Earth. God through this story instructs me to help him, to care for him like the Good Samaritan cared for the victim in the story.

The rest of the class went very well. Students delighted in asking questions about "How can you help your neighbor? Why did the rich man pass by the wounded man?" I assured them that in my short time in their classroom I had seen many instances of being a good neighbor, like when someone needed an eraser and a friend lent it to him without hesitation, or sharing your lunch, or playing games together.

The class ended much too soon. This was fun. I walked towards Kinga, trying to be cool, but my wide eyes and broad smile reflected my mood change. "How did it go?" she asked.

"Oh, OK. I think we made some progress," I answered, trying to control my enthusiasm. With Kinga's advice and my patience, I now felt like I could be a useful teacher in Ghana.

"Sometimes it just takes a minor adjustment," she smiled. "A little change of attitude."

First Day

Cuban Doctors

I was not happy having to spend a night in a Ghanaian hotel rather than go directly to the orphanage from the airport. The $50 hotel fee could have been used to buy supplies for the school and I didn't like delaying my reunion with the children. *This is Africa*, I thought, *and things work differently here. Slow down, enjoy yourself; this is a different pace than the United States. Be patient.* I made the best of a lonely hotel stay the night before when I talked with a Cuban psychiatrist in the lobby. His partial understanding of English matched my confusion with Spanish but we managed to pass a pleasant hour together and say "Good night," and "Buenos noches," as friends.

I didn't see him the next morning but noticed many Spanish speakers scurrying around the lobby, getting ready to depart and begin their day. A middle aged woman casually dressed in a tank top, shorts, and sneakers smiled as I approached. "Buenos dias, senora. Esta cubano."

"Yes," she answered in English, realizing immediately that we would get no place with my Spanish. She ignored my bilingual attempt and spoke English like a Yankee. "My name is Vilma. We are all Cuban doctors, working in Ghana. Are you from the United States?"

"Si.. errr….Yes, I am. How did you know?" I asked.

"Call it a lucky guess." She giggled, eyeing my New Balance jogging sneakers, and my standard middle class haircut, neither long nor short, parted to one side. She was maybe thirty five years old, slender like an athlete, and wore the wire rimmed glasses of a philosophy professor. She took a step back, shifted her weight, and looked away for a second then intensely at me. "You look like a nice guy," she stated, "Maybe you can help me. I don't see many people from your country. There are none over here. Please tell me, 'Why does your country hate us so?'" I was shocked by her question but refreshed by the way she came right to the point, no small talk, just, "Why do you hate us?"

I became instantly defensive, "Hate you? We don't hate you. I know I don't. My friends don't." I came closer, wanting her to understand. "That's political, unfortunately and I'm not a politician. I don't even watch the news on TV. I don't think the people hate each other. It's our leaders. I don't understand it any better than you do."

She agreed, "It's never the people who hate each other, only the leaders. After that storm, was it Katrina? We offered 300 Cuban doctors to come to the United States, to help you. We were refused. Why?" I shrugged my shoulders, stuck for an answer. She leaned forward, gaining momentum. "The United States is a strong country. You do well. That's great. Your way works for you, but it's is not the only way to do things. We're doing fine too. You could have used our help in that storm, we were anxious to give it, maybe break some barriers between our countries but we were refused."

She turned to her friends who were lined up behind her, listening, "You know Castro has outlasted nine of your presidents. We like what he's trying to do. In five years or so, I think our economy will be stronger. If we didn't have faith in him, he'd be gone." I doubted that statement but kept silent to let her continue, "Cuban doctors go all over the world to help. We do it because it's expected of us, not to gain political support, not for some *religious* reason. We go where we're needed. It's the thing to do if you're a doctor. I don't care if you're Cuban or from the United States. It doesn't matter. If you're a doctor, you go where you're needed. "

The fire in her eyes and passion for her work were obvious. "I don't know much about Cuba. I'm sure we get only limited information about your country. I've heard that your health care and educational systems are good. We could make some changes in the United States, especially in delivering health care."

She almost interrupted, "We could help. We have an abundance of doctors. They're well trained, highly motivated. Students from all over the world come to Cuba for training, even some from the United States. They go through our med school, work for our government for six years, and then return to their own country. It works for them, works for us."

She hesitated to make sure I was listening, and continued in a low voice. "I've been in the northern region of Ghana for a year. It's hot. It's the poorest area of the country. People have nothing up there, but I like it." She went on like devoting a year of your life to help in one of the poorest areas of the world was a normal thing to do, hardly worth talking about. I felt like a school boy being scolded by his teacher but remained quiet. "There are over 300 Cuban doctors here right now. They want to be here. We're paid fifty Ghana

CDs (about $50) a month. That's nothing. We could help in the US if you'd let us. Why can't we be friends? It would be better for both countries. We could help each other instead of the way it is now. Maybe the United States is paranoid about Castro. I don't know. There's been a lot of inflamed rhetoric from both sides, I'm sure." She was making this a one way discussion but I was content to listen.

She thought Jimmy Carter was a good US president. I asked her about Clinton. "No," she said, "In 1994, the US flew spy planes over Cuba and three times we begged them to stop. The fourth time, when Cuba shot it down, the flights stopped. If the situation was reversed and one of our planes got anywhere near your border, it would be shot down the first time. No warning, just shot down." I forgot the incident until she reminded me. An important incident for Cuba was soon forgotten in the United States.

She picked up her luggage of one small duffle bag and joined her friends who were loading a pickup truck with their suitcases and boxes of medical supplies.

"Do you contribute all this?" I asked.

"Yes, we contribute this ourselves, it's not much. These people need help. We can give it." I thought about the Bible lessons like The Good Samaritan, and thinking these non-Christians, probably Communist atheists, were happy, living the lessons our religion teaches.

She added that she writes daily in a journal about her African experience, but when I asked her to email some of it to me, she hesitated. She took my email address but shook her head sideways, like that would not be possible. I wondered, *does that reluctance come from the Cuban government censure or just her wanting to keep her thoughts private?*

I took a photograph of the group, posing in front of the over loaded truck and one of her, my new friend, who I almost certainly will never see again. One of the male doctors joked to me, "You're in trouble, recording good things about Cuba. You'll lose your job and your house." I thought, *we don't do things like that in the United States.* I waved goodbye, they honked their horn and drove through the hotel gate, off to their next clinic.

My taxi came within minutes of their departure. I threw my two bags in the trunk and relaxed in the back seat while the driver weaved through the crowded streets of Accra, heading to the orphanage where I would live and teach for the next three weeks.

The Negotiation

The taxi turned off the paved highway onto the dirt road that was so familiar to me when I taught at the school months ago. I jumped out of the cab when I saw the welcoming sign "Christ Faith Foster Home." I opened the gate to let the cab pass through and Priscilla, the loveable seven year old orphan girl, ran to me with arms wide opened and a huge smile on her face. "Priscilla, you're beautiful," I yelled and bent down to receive her exuberant hug. She wrapped her arms around my neck, held tight, and we pranced around, cheek to cheek. All the time and money was worth it to see Priscilla again. I had joked with Lorrie while still in The States that I was going to bring Priscilla home with me and she might as well make the spare bedroom ready for this wonderful little girl. I was half serious about bringing her home because I thought of her often. I was thrilled to see her looking so well and to have her be the first one to greet me.

Behind her, Victoria Abraham, the administrator of the orphanage reached out to shake my hand. She is maybe sixty years old, overweight, forces wry smile that she uses to conceal her underlying, serious, business side. She gave me a quick hug, kissed my cheek, and said, "Oh Charlie, it's so good to see you."

I protested when she grabbed my largest luggage and strode towards the dormitory where I would be staying. "Victoria, let me carry that. It's heavy." She walked on like I had said nothing and led the way into a small room with two bunk beds against each lateral wall. A long table sat in front of two windows, opposite the entrance.

"Here's your room. It's all yours. You can sleep in that bed that the kids have made up for you." She opened the curtains and then pushed open the two windows. The sunshine filled the room but the opened windows did nothing to improve the stagnant air or the musty smell from being too long enclosed.

"Come on. Let's have a seat in the living room." She pushed past me and I followed her down the semi dark hallway to a room with two couches and another table like the one in my bedroom. A small Gideon Bible rested on the otherwise empty table. "Charlie, thank you so much for the $250 you sent me. My daughter is sick so we used that money for her hospital bills." I said nothing but wondered why the money went to her daughter rather than the orphanage. I had had a garbled long distance call with her months ago, telling her that the money I was sending was to allow me to lodge and teach at the school. I thought I heard her give a verbal okay and assumed the issue was settled. I was aware of Victoria's reputation as an unscrupulous business woman, who often sought opportunities to line her own pockets while supervising the school's finances.

"We're so glad you came back Charlie. The kids are thrilled and so am I. How long will you be able to stay?" she asked. Victoria always came right to the point and usually had money on her mind.

"Stay," I responded. "I'm not sure exactly. We'll see how things go but I'm hoping to be here for three weeks."

"That's fine," she said, "Stay as long as you like." She glared at me, "I suppose you want to know how much it'll cost." She hesitated a few seconds like she was adding figures. "For three weeks, it will be $200." She stared while I looked around the room.

Two hundred dollars, I sent her $250 already. A very generous donation and now she wants $200 more? I shifted in my chair, looked at the one dim over head light, the soiled cushions on the couches, and the torn rug held together with duck tape. "Victoria," I said, trying to be firm, "I thought that money I sent was for my stay here. I didn't bring much money with me. I thought we were all set." She maintained that intense stare but kept silent while I squirmed. I rose from my seat, paced the room, her eyes followed. "I don't have much money," I whined, "I didn't expect to have to pay more than I've already sent. How about $150? Will that be OK?"

Too quickly she replied, "Yes, that's OK."

Despite my anger over the $250, I felt guilty negotiating at all about giving to the orphanage and the children I loved. "Are you happy with that?" I asked.

"Yes, I'm satisfied. You can have whatever you want." Her tone softened but she kept staring. "We want you happy." Her lips formed that familiar smile. "What do you like to eat?"

I remembered the favorite national dish, fufu, made from pulverized cassava root, was dipped in animal fat, and eaten with the fingers. Here it is prepared adjacent to the latrine, while dogs and chickens pooped and fornicated nearby. "Just bread and water, maybe some cocoa for breakfast. I like spaghetti or rice with vegetables for lunch, I don't need much dinner." Last time I lost five pounds in the month I was in Ghana. Beans, rice, and spaghetti, hopefully free of parasites, were my staples. Everything cooked.

"That's no problem," she added then got up from her seat, attempted an awkward hug, and said, "Welcome to the orphanage, Charlie. We're all happy you're here."

Mary, Like Jesus' Mother

Despite my unexpected loss of the $150 and the realization that the $250 I had previously sent wound up in Victoria's pocket instead of with the children, I put the incident behind me. I had come too far and had planned too long to let one person ruin my day. Everything looked the same as when I left months ago. The six foot high wall surrounding most of the school was open at one end so anyone could come and go as they pleased. This gave the whole complex an open, friendly atmosphere, not locked in by walls like a prison. Two school buildings with straw roofs and cement floors were brightly painted with children's art, A for apple, B for box, C for car. The circular structure doubled as a class room and a meeting place for teachers during break time. The rectangular one next to it was for older student's classes during the week and housed a children's church service on Sundays. The three main classrooms remained in the cement block building just inside the welcoming gate. I assumed I would teach in one of those rooms.

I excused myself from Victoria, returned to my bedroom, turned on the fan, and laid down on the lower bunk bed for a rest. I removed my shoes, stretched out, and decided to not allow the unpleasant negotiation ruin my time in Africa. I was glad to be here. The bed was comfortable, a breeze from the floor fan soothed my face, and I had a room to myself. I savored the moment, but I didn't come all these miles to rest in bed.

I was anxious to explore the village surrounding the school. I knew the neighbors would be friendly because that is the nature of Ghanaians. Warm hospitality is as much a part of their culture as fufu and family togetherness. Whether I was in a small village like Baikpa or in the metropolis of Accra, I loved their warm smiles and their traditional, "welcome," greeting. I knew I would get the same in this family neighborhood surrounding the school.

I arose, downed a bottle of water and a handful of chocolate cookies, and strolled up the dirt road away from the orphanage. Holes in the red clay road were deep enough to break an ankle or misalign any passing car. Puddles of stagnant water from the recent rain provided a perfect breeding ground for the malaria causing anopheles mosquitoes. Only the female spreads this killer disease and she only bites at night so I walked on confidently in the daylight. Someone's well tended front yard, dominated by pink bougainvillea, stood next to a dump site with abandoned plastic bags smoldering in the ashes. A faded sign leaning over it, pointed to "Glory to God Car Repair."

I said, "Hi," to a group of four or five teenagers, who were roasting corn to sell from their road side stand. A young man held up his bleeding hand and asked if I could help. A deep gash in his right hand oozed blood but didn't look serious to me. "You look like you're from the United States, will you help me?" he asked. This was the second time today that my citizenship was immediately identified by a stranger. *Is it the way I walk*, I wondered. When I inquired what happened, he joked that one of the young ladies standing alongside had cut him on purpose.

I asked in jest, "Well, What did you do to her to make her angry?" His girl friend held up a small knife, making a stabbing motion like she had used it as a sword. Her "sword" was hardly big enough to shave the cornels off the corn cobs and definitely not designed for self defense or to injure anyone. He admitted that he had slipped with his own knife while cutting the corncobs and not the victim of a lover's quarrel. I laughed and advised him that if he just kept pressure on his wound, the bleeding would stop, and he would be healed enough to make up with his girlfriend. They all laughed with my parting advice, "and be nice to her. Don't make her angry again."

I walked on a few paces and a pretty woman approached, formally dressed in brightly colored church clothes. She stopped, looked me over, smiled, and exclaimed, "Welcome. You're back." I studied the familiar face and soon recognized the delightful lady who cooks rice in her home each morning, then brings it to school to sell to the children. This loving woman lifted everyone's spirits and her exuberant greeting assured me that she hadn't changed. She hugged me, took my hand, and half pulled me down a side path, away from the road. "Come on," she urged, "I'm taking you home." She held my hand like we were dating. "How are your two children? She asked." I wondered, *How could she remember that I had two kids and what am I getting into now?* "Come on," she repeated, "I'm taking you home. My house is just over that hill."

I looked at her beautiful face, alive with joy and warmth. "I'm sorry, I forgot. What is your name? I may have forgotten your name but certainly not you."

She mumbled something. I couldn't understand so I asked again, "My name is Mary," she responded with deliberation. "Mary, like the mother of Jesus."

"Oh Mary, of course. I'm sorry I forgot your name but I'll never forget you. You're one of those gifted people who spread joy like a farmer spreading his seeds. And you're beautiful."

She ignored my compliment, kept walking, keeping her tight grip on my hand. Her vibrant expression lit up her face and drew me to her, but I wanted to know what was expected of me by this pretty African lady, leading me to her house. "Who do you live with?" I asked.

"I live with three of my kids and my husband." With the mention of her husband, I breathed easier. "I have five kids, three are married, two live at home. Come on. I'll introduce you."

"Mary," I stopped and looked at the smooth skin on her face, her slender well proportioned body, and bright eyes, excited like a child, "I can't believe you have married daughters. You hardly look old enough to be married yourself."

She laughed. "I'm fifty two," she volunteered, which shocked me because she looked more like twenty five. "God is good to me. I'm healthy, have a great family, and a wonderful life."

We were only two minutes into our reunion but I was already enamored by her charm. I stopped, wrapped both arms around her and burst out, "It's so good to be back and see you. Of course I remember you. And to get a greeting like this, Wow!" We reached her house and I got another greeting from her teen age daughter, Dorlene. She still held my hand. The cinder block house was modest but clean, chickens roamed outside in the yard and inside the house, while two dogs barked and wagged their tails. Dorlene brought out a plastic chair for me, offered a coke, and talked with us. I sat comfortably, excited to be back, and reassured by this loving family. She wanted to know everything about my life in the past year, how long I was planning to stay, and where I was going to live.

When I stood up to go home, she took my hand again to lead me back through the path. I said, "Mary, in my culture, when two people hold hands like this it's a sign of romance, reserved for couples in love."

She said, "I love everybody and I want to show it. If neighbors talk bad about me, that's their problem not mine. I'm a Christian and I'm going to heaven someday. I want to show my love for everybody." I squeezed her hand and thought *I love these people; especially this woman and I want to learn as much from her as possible while I'm here. I love Ghana and people like her.* She continued talking and smiling as we walked, "The Bible says that we're all supposed to love each other. Holding hands feels good to me. It doesn't matter what people think." The longer I was with her, the more I wanted to prolong our meeting, but too soon, she pointed out the main road, gave me another hug, and waved goodbye, "See you tomorrow in school , Charlie. Welcome again. Bye for now."

I watched her walk away, anxious for our next meeting, feeling at home on African soil and wishing I could be like her, "Love everybody and don't be afraid to show it."

I walked on and sidestepped a car parked at the intersection of the path and the dirt road. The driver sat with his arm out the open window, "Hi, Where are you from?" he asked.

I answered proudly, "The United States. Ahh, South Carolina."

"Oh," he said, "I lived in Boston, in Jamaica Plains, for twelve years."

"And I'll bet you missed Ghana and came back," I interrupted.

"Yes," he said, "I missed it here. People are nice and this is my home. Too many people in the US are rude." I nodded like I understood and felt sad for the way he may have been treated in my country.

"Are you a Red Sox fan?" I asked trying to change the subject and lighten the mood.

"Yes, a little, but I can only get scores here on the internet." The female companion he was waiting for stepped into the passenger seat of the car. He introduced her, then waved, and started the engine, "I built a house just down the street. I'm happy, happy to be home." I understood his preference for the dirt road, the warmth, the charm of the people versus the fast pace, competitive USA. I walked back to the orphanage, happy with my first day, ready to go to bed early.

Music to Put Me to Sleep

By 8:30, it was dark. I was in bed, teeth brushed and content, thinking about all that had happened that day, like the conversation with the Cubans, reunion with Priscilla, the unpleasant negotiations, and especially, walking with Mary, as in "Mary, like Jesus' mother."

My thoughts were interrupted by a group outside my window, singing church hymns, reciting prayers in a local language, clapping hands, stamping feet, and beating drums to African rhythms. I got up and asked Victoria about the enchanting sounds. She said, "Oh yes. They're Pentecostals, having a church service. You can join them if you want."

The light from their small fire outlined seven or eight Ghanaians holding hands in a circle, dancing and singing as I approached. I asked, "What are you singing?"

A young man answered in a soft voice, "We're not singing, we're praying. Please join us." Two women dropped their hands to make room for me. I listened while the woman to my right translated that they were asking God for forgiveness and seeking how to best serve Him. I couldn't imagine how such humble but dignified people needed to ask forgiveness for anything. I joined them, clapped a little, tried to sing, and prayed silently to be spared the night time bite from the female anopheles mosquito. After 5-10 minutes of trying to feel part of their group, I excused myself, and returned to my room.

I turned off the lights, laid on my back, smiling, contemplated the joy of the day, while the continuing African sounds outside lulled me to sleep.

Hiking in Ghana

Five of us sat at the outside dining table at the Mountain Paradise Lodge. I looked across the table at Agnes, the beautiful young Ghanaian college student, who was also an overnight guest at the lodge. The morning sun glistened off her black skin. She looked up at me, smiled, and asked, "What are you going to do today Charlie?"

"I don't know," I answered, "I could just sit at this table all day and admire the scenery."

"I know what you mean, it's beautiful here but you look like the active type. Not someone who could sit around for long."

"You're right there Agnes. I like to keep busy but this breakfast is a nice relaxing start to the day." I spread the mango jam over a slice of toast, cut the vegetable ohmlet in pieces, and watched the crisp local vegetable mixture of onions, tomatoes, red and green peppers gush out onto the plate. I sipped some strong coffee brewed from beans from the village and looked out over the porch to the mountains. Lush green bushes and trees covered the sheer peaks before us. A cell phone tower at the top was the only indication of human intrusion into the pristine scene. There was no noise, not even the squawk of a bird or the rustle of leaves on a bush. Bright yellow bougainvillea decorated the garden alongside the lodge.

A woman dressed like an experienced mountain climber spoke up from the nearby table. She was one of the three volunteer health care workers from McGill University in Montreal. "You two might want to go on a hike to Kaluga Falls. We did it yesterday. It was quite a workout with ropes on the steep trails but you both look in good shape. You could do it."

I shuttered, remembering the difficult hike I struggled through two years ago to those same falls. I told myself at the time that it was a nice challenge but I was pushed too hard and I decided then that I would never get trapped into a repeat performance.

My mind was made up until Agnes smiled and spoke with such excitement, "Hey Charlie that sounds like fun. This place is so much like the village where I grew up in the Northern Region. I'd love to do it. Come on let's go. Let's do it together." *Look at that face, I thought. Damn women and those beautiful faces, they can make me do the most ridiculous things.*

I looked at her wide eyes, alive with enthusiasm, pleading with me to join her. I could not disappoint, but how about my swollen knee? I had contemplated cancelling my trip because it ached, pained, and was stiff for my last month in the US. It had been okay for the first two weeks in Africa but this hike would put stress on it that I had tried to avoid. "Let's go," I said. I couldn't be responsible for turning that happy face to sadness. "As I remember, there are a few forks on the path that could get us lost. Do you think we need a guide?" I asked the Canadian girls

"Absolutely yes," the youngest one replied. "You could get lost out there and never find your way back. It will only cost you a few dollars and Prince here is a really good guy. Please, take advantage of him. It's worth it."

"Okay," I said, "It sounds like a good idea. I don't want to get lost, but I didn't come to Africa to sit around, so let's go." I pushed myself away from the table. Prince was hovering nearby ready to lead us into the forest. I thought he took a long look at my gray hair and wrinkled skin but was grateful when he said nothing. Ghanaians are hospitable, tactful people and would never insult a guest.

Soon we were hiking down the dirt road towards Fume. After about a mile Prince took a sharp turn onto a foot path that we would follow to the river and waterfall below. I never would have found the path in the dense underbrush without his guidance. We took about ten paces on the steep slippery decline, saturated with wet leaves and loose mud, when Agnes admitted, "I can already see that it was a good idea for me to rent these sneakers. I know I couldn't have made this in my sandals or bare feet." Even Prince, the guide, wore hiking boots.

We slid, caught ourselves, ascended, descended, tried to steady ourselves on tree branches and pushed on. Prince looked back at me, slowly picking my way down the mountainside that my two young companions had just passed through. "Do you want this hiking stick Charlie?"

I saw that their hands were free and my inclination to get along without help made me first say, "No, I'll be okay," but then I saw the vertical drop in front of me, "Yeh, I'll take it. I'll take all the help I can get." I also remembered from two years ago that we were still on a relatively easy part of the hike. The steepest inclines and the most treacherous footing were ahead of us.

Within a few steps, I realized the walking stick was a necessity, like water and fresh air. This was not like a work out at a health club where if I misstep I might get a backache or a sore leg for a few days. Here, it was different. A careless step, a slide, or a slip could send me over the edge, writhing in a ditch, or worse. I had thought once that dying in Africa appealed to my romantic side but I wasn't in any way ready to accept that now. I was confident that if I concentrated, watched where I stepped, and took my time I would make it. I cautiously planted the stick in solid earth, each step avoiding loose dirt that would not support me. I stepped over the wet leaves, the unsupported stones, and the slippery mud.

I declined Agnes' offer to go in front of her. I didn't want her to see me so timid. I was comfortable bringing up the rear of our threesome and was determined to take my time and get home safely. The steep descents and sharp climbs ranged from ridiculous to horrible. I knew we had a long way to go but already my clothes were drenched in sweat. Perspiration ran off the end of my nose, down my chin, soaking my t-shirt and pants. The crotch of my pants cut sharply into my privates.

I was glad to finally reach the ropes. I hung on tight like a sailor grasping a life ring and stood waiting to catch my breath. A bug flew up my nose. My reflex was to swat it away but I didn't want to let go with either hand. I sniffed and hopefully expelled the intruder. My shoulders and arms are strong. I can hang on, pull myself along, trusting my upper body. It's my left knee that's the problem, my weak link. I could pull up to ascend and let myself down in descent, while tucking my walking stick under my arms. I didn't want to let go of that either. I knew I was falling behind the other two but didn't care. Those ropes were my pacifier and life line.

My entire body was drenched in sweat, mud, and filth. I thought of the book I recently read, "The River of Doubt," about Theodore Roosevelt's excursion up the uncharted Amazon River. I was so inspired by his bravery and survival skills that I went on the internet from the safety of my home, to find an ecotour that would lead me into that Amazon Jungle. I came to Ghana instead and now this hike has cured me forever of the notion that I need to challenge nature in settings like this. I fell farther behind, getting more tired, more cautious. *"How do guides always make this look so easy?"*

Prince and Agnes were waiting for me as we reached the last vertical drop to the falls. Prince had a too serious look on his usually placid face. "I'm going to go first. Charlie you leave your stick here and hang onto the rope with both hands. Come down backwards and I'll yell up to you where to place each foot and hand as you come down." I was glad when he added, "Agnes you come only after I've reached the bottom. And Charlie after we're both down there, I'll call up to you."

It took him maybe ten minutes to reach the river. Agnes followed, panting, sweating and occasionally looking up to me as if to ask, "What the hell are we doing this for?" I had already asked myself the same question and couldn't come up with a reasonable answer. She reached the bottom in half an hour and spread herself out over a bolder. She took a minute to catch her breath, then yelled back to me, "Charlie, that's far enough. Wait there. Don't come any farther." Finally someone said something sensible. I concurred. We still had to climb all the way back. I told myself, *"I did this two years ago. I don't have to do it again, and I don't care how pretty she is. She offered me a way out and I accepted.*

I could hear the loud roar of water falls and see the spray rising through the underbrush. That was enough. I waited, hung on to the ropes, rested, and tried to regain my strength. They were splashing and talking below. I turned back by myself, knowing they would soon catch up to my slow progression up and down the slopes. I never did let go of my precious walking stick. I pulled myself up by tree roots, choosing the green ones solidly attached to trees. I crawled around ant colonies, dreading what African ants could do to my body. Prince and Agnes caught up and I followed them back. After hours of sweating, straining, slipping, sliding, pushing and pulling, we reached the dirt road where we had begun our descent. Agnes collapsed in the middle of the road. She stretched out and gasped, "Charlie, don't you want to lie down?"

I thought of ants and other crawly things and how hard it would be for me to get up after lying down. "No. I'm OK. I don't want to have to get up once I lie down." Ten minutes later we trudged on back towards the lodge. The road was a mixture of solid and loose clay eroded from the heavy rain falls. It was barely wide enough for a car to pass. I don't know what would happen if two cars met going in opposite directions but chances of cars meeting in this isolation were remote.

We climbed and stumbled. No one spoke until Agnes shrieked, "Look out for the snake!"

I stepped towards the dormant black serpent lying by the roadside, but Prince cautioned, "Stay back Charlie. I'm not sure if he's dead or sleeping." He threw a rock and the four foot long snake didn't move. It was dead.

I breathed again. "What kind of snake is it?"

They each answered in unison, "A cobra."

"Is it poisonous?" was my next city slicker question.

"Yes very poisonous. They bite, you die." Agnes hunched up her neck to show how a cobra enlarges its head and neck before striking, She made a hideous hissing sound for emphasis

"Are there many of them around here?" My innocent questions continued. They discussed their opinions in Twe, the local language but I never did get a response in English. Maybe I really didn't want an answer. I followed them back to the lodge where the three of us, even Prince, collapsed on couches. I didn't want to move. I dreamed of a soft bed and a cool shower with lots of gushing water and soap lathering all over my body.

Instead, I was wakened too soon by a gentle tap on my arm. "Charlie, I just wanted be sure you understand." It was Tony, my friend, Ghanaian brother, who would do anything for me. He was the always hospitable, administrator of the lodge. I struggled to open my tired eyes in the bright mid day sun. "I told you when you arrived we would be full one night while you were here. This is the night. But I also promised we could arrange something for you. And we have. You can sleep in a tent tonight. The guys are putting it up now. No problem."

A tent I thought, in Ghana. In the jungle, with cobras around hunching their necks up and hissing before they kill you. And anopheles mosquitoes, that bite at night, injecting their malaria causing bacteria into any handy bloodstream.

I chuckled, still groggy from my nap. "No problem Tony. A tent will be fine. Just let me know if a room does free up. Okay?" and closed my eyes again.

A few more dreams of my three bedroom, air conditioned house in the USA, with juice in the refrigerator, and drinkable tap water. This time it was Agnes who was shaking me awake. "I didn't want to wake you but I want you to know how much I enjoyed our hike together this morning."

"Ah, Yes, I'm glad I went. It was also nice having breakfast together. You have to go?"

"Yes, I've got a class tonight that I can't miss. It'll take me an hour to hike to Fume, then five hours by bus to get to school. I've got to go." I again looked up into her bright face and without any thought said, "Here, let me walk you down the road to Fume. I'm fine." *Well I wasn't fine and the last thing I wanted to do was walk that dusty, slippery trail to Fume. Women. Am I ever going to outgrow this compulsion to impress a lady? She's not even in distress. She's in a lot better shape than I am right now. She's younger, healthier, and completely capable herself. But, she's also very nice and very pretty. And I'll probably never see her again. Damn.* "I'd like to walk with you" I lied. "After what we went through together this morning, we're a team." I continued my macho facade. I knew we weren't a team but I really didn't want to say goodbye so quickly. I assumed I would never see her again.

"Oh you don't have to," she said with the same smile that started the Trojan War and distracted Mark Anthony from his missions. "But if you really want to, I'd love the company."

Before I knew what happened, I was back on that road, hiking to Fume as a favor to a woman I hardly knew. I staggered most of the way down the mountain before I stopped, "Hey Agnes, This is ridiculous. You've got to get to a class and I know I'm just holding you up. You can get to Fume a lot quicker without me. You go ahead, I'll go back to the lodge."

She didn't protest at all which made me think she was glad to go on by herself. She was worried about me on the hike and still probably wondered why this old guy wanted to escort her to the bus stop. "Okay," she said, "I'll be fine. You go back and rest up." I was too sweaty and dirty to hug her so we just smiled and wished each other well.

I turned back up the road, glad to be able to now shuffle along slowly. I wasn't afraid of falling, just exhausted. I thought about her, the hike, my snail like progress back to the lodge, and the approaching night with me sleeping in a tent, with cobras and killer mosquitoes free to attack me at will. *This is crazy I thought. I could be on Hilton Head sitting on the beach.* I put one foot in front of the other, trudging and sweating some more, ready to accept whatever fate dealt me at night.

I reached the lodge and collapsed on the same couch I had given up for my walk to Fume with Agnes. I was exhausted. I leaned back on a soft cushion, feet up on a chair, grateful to be alone. *It's 4:30 in the afternoon and I already feel like I've had a week's worth of physical and emotional stress in one day. I'm tired, sweaty, and filthy but too tired to sponge myself off. "What's the use?" anyway in this heat?*

This time I dreamed of orange popsicles, root beer floats, and soft mattresses. I thought about last night's dinner conversation with Sandra, the young Danish medical student. She described how she had ridden a horse up a mountain in Mongolia that was forbidden to women, and trekked for three weeks in New Guinnea, and now was headed to an isolated village in Ghana to do medical exams. A missionary added how he was caught in crossfire in the Congo during a coup de tat. Next to their experiences, sleeping for a night in a tent alongside the lodge was pretty tame.

I smiled, thinking about telling friends at home of my wild time in Africa. I could hear many people moving about into their rooms at the lodge. I was resigned, almost looking forward, to the adventure of spending a sleepless night in the tent.

I heard my name called, "Charlie, Charlie, it's me Tony. I just thought I'd let you know. We have freed up a room. You can have it."

I jumped up, "You mean I don't have to sleep in the tent?"

"No, you don't. We've got a room. Someone will help you move your luggage."

A reprieve: No matter how I rationalized my night in the tent, I now was thrilled to be inside, with a roof, four walls, and a hard floor. My room was just large enough for a small bed and a place to put down my luggage. It was beautiful. It was dry, almost free of bugs, and no hissing snakes.

Mama's Dinner

I walked down the dirt road away from the orphanage hoping I would run into my new friends in the neighborhood. I met Diamond a few days ago, soon after I arrived at the school this year. She was twenty years old, friendly, and had a habit of tilting her head downwards when she talked, almost like she was being coy. She looked up through sparkling eyes that drew me to her. She always greeted me with enthusiasm and I looked forward to our daily visits. She introduced me to her heavy set sister named Peace who was equally friendly but not so pretty.

They lived with their parents, three younger siblings and two or three cousins, crammed together in a house about the size of one of our trailers. The house was constructed of blocks made of a combination of sand, mud from clay, and dung. They were held together by another mixture of mud and dung. There was never a covering of wood or siding. Every house was gray.

This day, Diamond and Peace were waiting for me in their front yard. They were fascinated by my white skin and the way I talked like an American. When I talk with someone from another country with different accents, like all Ghanaians, I slow my speech and try to enunciate each word so they can understand. It has become my habit from years of teaching English to immigrants in the United States. Diamond often said, "I like the way you talk."

I readily accepted their invitation to come onto their porch to meet their Mama who was preparing dinner for the family. Peace brought out a plastic chair so I could sit in comfort and watch Mama prepare supper. It started innocently enough with Mama chopping some green leafy like things and dropping them into a large pot of water. She was preparing soup. She then took some fresh tomatoes, sliced them, and mashed them into a wooden bowl, and dropped the mixture into the cauldron. Peace and Diamond smiled at me making sure I saw every move. "Mama is a great cook," said Peace with pride. I was anticipating a dinner invitation and thought that green leafy vegetables and tomatoes might be a welcome break from my steady diet of beans and rice at the orphanage.

Mama then reached into her large garbage bag and pulled out a rolled up leathery thing with a rubber band around it. She took off the bands and cut up the leather into strips and dropped them into the pot. "What's that?" I asked as politely as possible.

Peace thought for the correct English words, "The skin of a (how you say) oh yeah, a cow. It is the skin of a cow. Did you ever eat one of those?"

"No," I answered, "I haven't." I tried not to show my revulsion for their meal as Mama kept slicing and shaving the skin. She scrapped off some gut like residue and dropped it on the floor where an emaciated dog lapped it up. I felt sick.

Next she reached into the same bag and pulled out a handful of small fish with heads, fins and tails still attached. Mama held one of the tiny fish in her left hand and used her two foot long machete to deftly pluck out a miniscule piece under the fish's belly. I asked' "What are you taking out?"

This time it was sister Diamond who struggled for the proper English words. "You know Charlie, when a fish eats, things go in its mouth then down to here," she said pointing to her throat.

"Oh, I see, the fish's stomach. That's what she's cutting out."

"Yes that's it. The stomach, we no eat that." I was glad to hear that but watched while everything else, eyes, fins, tails, gills, every organ, internal and external, was dropped into the bucket. Mama picked up some more undersized fish, flicked off the same piece, no larger than an eraser at the end of a pencil, and added the rest to the soup.

They have no refrigeration so I asked. "Did you buy these fish today at the market?"

"Oh yes today. They smoked." The fish parts didn't smell like a fish off a Cape Cod boat, but more like the inside of the hull that hadn't been cleaned of last week's catch. Both Peace and Diamond smiled and pushed out their chests, proud that we could converse and that I was lucky enough to witness Mama's culinary talents.

She then reached deeper into the endless garbage bag and withdrew five or six slightly larger fish and dropped them straight into the pot. I didn't want to seem impolite but I thought if I saw one more dip into the bag, I would get sick right there on the porch. I stood up, forced a smile, and thanked them for being so nice. "I've got to get back," I said, "It's my dinner time at the school."

Diamond walked me to the dirt road in front of their house. "You're lucky." I said, "You have such a nice family." And I meant that. They are a nice family and I'm saddened that they like so many others have to eat and live in those conditions. Nine people were crowded into two bedrooms in a trailer type house and ate like food that would be discarded in our country.

As I walked up the hill, the thought of me eating anything seemed like the ultimate challenge.

A few minutes later, for my dinner I forced down some plain rice and picked around some fishy smelling reddish sauce. I knew it had been prepared outside over an open fire next to dogs pooping and chickens reproducing. I rethought my intention to next time bring a friend, like Lorrie, with me to Ghana.

Coaching Basketball in Africa

Outside the classroom, beyond the mango tree, a solitary pole slants from the ground, supporting a metal basketball backboard, and a rim with no net. I have been teaching at the school for almost two weeks but have never seen anyone playing. This is soccer crazed Ghana, more enthused than ever after their recent World Cup victory over the United States. The rim is approximately ten feet tall but it's hard to tell because the court is not level. A jump shot from the right corner might face an eleven foot challenge, while it could be nine from the top of the key. The court surface itself is a mixture of clay and hard packed sand, with an occasional tuft of grass, strong enough to survive the daily trampling of little feet chasing a soccer ball. Deep ruts and puddles lie waiting to twist or sprain an ankle.

This typical hot, humid day is the first time I've seen anyone playing basketball. Three teenage boys dribble an over inflated ball, with its rubber bladder protruding from a tear in its cover, like a man's hernia. Despite the lopsided ball and the uneven surface, I watch them dribble behind their backs, between their legs, switching hands with ease, like a big college point guard. One fakes a pass, pulls it back and flips it behind to his other friend, a move the Harlem Globetrotters would have been proud of in their prime.

While Ebenezer is teaching I leave the classroom and approach, marveling at their excellent ball handling skills. "Wow! I'm impressed. Where did you guys learn to do that?"

They stop, smile, come towards me, and offer me a shot. The tallest one, possibly their leader strains to answer in English, "American man teach us. You want try a shot?" they ask.

I accept their offer, take a shot and watch it fall two feet short of the rim, retrieve it, then hand the ball back. "How long was he here? You guys are good. Did he live here?"

"He here two months. He showed us," said the tall one.

"You sure learned a lot in two months." I take a few more shots, alternating with them, each time becoming more aware of my sixty five years and their youthful energy. Trying to maintain my dignity, I ask, "Did he show you how to shoot too?" I used to think of myself as a decent high school basketball player and an excellent shooter.

They look at me confused. Their conversations are in their tribal language and when someone speaks to them in English, it's usually with a British accent, not from the eastern United States. I persist, "Here, let me show you how I shoot." I must be teaching too long because I really think I can instruct these guys in the technique of shooting a basketball. I take the ball and demonstrate how the ball has to roll off your finger tips, "See like this," I say, "Not off the palm of your hand. Just like dribbling, Fingers only, No palms." I demonstrate again, clanging my attempt off the rim. "See? Not a good shot but fingers only. See?"

"I think I understand," says the one wearing glasses. He takes the ball and without much effort, guides it right through the rim. I can't say he "swished it," because there is no net, but the shot from beyond the foul line, clearly was good. His friends take their turns, same result, most going through the hoop, the majority of those that fail, are my attempts. "Swish, swish, swish, clang, swish, swish, swish, clang," goes the imaginary sound as the three of them score and I miss my attempt. I retrieve one of my errant shots, headed into the weeds, throw it back, and try to excuse myself with dignity, "Hey, Thanks a lot. I've got to get back to class. Thanks for the game," I yell, aware that I have been put in my basketball place.

One shouts back, "We come back tomorrow. You come too. Teach us more."

I didn't respond but in an hour, they quit and walked by my classroom. I rushed out the door, trying to be one of the guys, "Thanks for letting me play with you. You are all very good. Wow!"

The leader says, "Thanks for teach us. We come back tomorrow. More show us."

I watched them walk up the road flipping the ball between them. I thought that these guys who probably share basketball genes with Michael Jordan don't need basketball advice from a slow, gray haired, white guy. I know where I belong; teaching English to little kids, not coaching basketball in Africa.

Victoria's Greeting

Victoria was my favorite student last year and a big reason for me returning to Ghana again. She is nine years old, with huge bulging eyes that light up over everything. Her constant smile and enthusiasm for life drew me to her immediately. At first I felt sorry for her. She was always getting caned by the teacher for talking when she should be silent, dancing when she should be sitting, constantly teasing her classmates, always laughing. She could be an annoyance to them but always a delight to me.

One day she was poking around my ears and despite my pleadings to stop, she pulled out my hearing aid. She ran around the room waving it in the air, "Hey everybody, look what Charlie has." By the time I retrieved it, everyone knew about my hearing loss. She had such fun doing it that I couldn't get mad.

After class, many days I'd walk her part way home, pleading with her to behave so she wouldn't get punished so much. She laughed as if to say, "Why would I ever want to stop having fun." We strolled along the dirt road, holding hands, singing in full voice, "I love you, you love me, we are friends as friends should be, with a great big hug and kiss from me to you, then you'll know you love me too." I can't think about her and that song without laughing. Her consistent lesson to me was to not take life seriously.

This year, she was not in my class. She had been promoted to the next level to a classroom across the compound. On my first day teaching, I went looking for her. Three or four children were holding my hands, exploring the strange white skin on my hands and arms. I looked ahead and saw Victoria running across the field, full speed, running over anyone in her path. She jumped over the kids hanging onto me, wrapped her arms and legs around my neck and torso. We laughed cheek to cheek as I spun her around in an exuberant dance. In a minute, she climbed down, stepped back, looked me over and uttered her first words, "You have beeg (big) stomach." My big stomach ached from laughing with her again.

The Storm

The storm hit with a sudden crash that made me drop the chalk to the floor and look to teacher Florence for help. I had been in Ghana for a week in the middle of their rainy season but had seen no daytime rain like this until it hit mid morning. It teems, lets up for a few seconds, then attacks again like the end of the world is near. The raindrops, huge and heavy, like weighted ping pong balls, bomb the tin roof, making the school room sound like the inside of a drum. I have stood next to a jet plane reving up its engine in a confined space and had the same panicky impulse to escape this deafening roar. Despite my hearing loss, I want to cover my ears, hide under a table, but there is no place to run. I'm reassured by seeing no daylight through the rusted tin roof or any puddleson the floor.

I had been teaching pre- primary schoolers with Florence, who a few years ago sat in this same class herself as a student/orphan. I have never seen her show any emotion, although I know that her feelings run deep. She is twenty two years old and when not teaching, she lives in the dorm, as a sort of house mother to the orphans. I asked her once if she would like more privacy, maybe a night free of the thirty girls she watches over. Her laconic response of, "I love the children," told me all I needed to know about Florence and her ability to love.

Despite her compassion, outward stoicism is her way of dealing with the world and a valuable asset in surviving in this harsh environment. I look to her now for guidance and see the same blank look that has become her trademark. She sees my eyes wide open, searching the room, arms outstretched, pleading for help. She wisely took over the class. She raised her arms to get everyone's attention, then lowered them, signaling to the children to put their heads down on their desks. This was a new experience for me but a regular occurrence for them. No one rebelled. Like a well trained army, every head went down, eyes closed, no panic, just a deep acceptance of nature's onslaught.

The dignified way the Ghanains like Florence and the children face daily crisis, like the storm, again showed me how much I can learn from them.

Heads down their world at peace

All angelic to say the least.

I bid them all a quiet adieu,

To see what's happenen' in room two.

Here the students are two years older and much bolder than the angels I just left. They were running around yelling, chasing, and enjoying the freedom brought on by the thunderous storm. The teacher, Miss Elizabeth, sat at her desk, reading a magazine , ignoring her teacher's duties and the chaos in front of her. She looked up occasionally, said nothing, maybe shuffled a few papers, but made no attempt to restore order. I left her with her paper shuffling and went next door to room three.

Ebenezer, the teacher, greeted me with a warm smile and an excited look on his face, "Charlie, it's raining. We're dancing. We're singing. Come join us."

"This is more like it," I thought as I walked into the darkened class room, noisy with children's laughter and singing. These were happy sounds in contrast to what I just left. The exuberant joy of the children and teachers took the threat out of the thunder outside. Ebenezer and his teaching partner Micheal, clapped and stamped their feet to a rhythmic tune sung in the local language. Children with broad smiles clapped their hands, drummed on the desks, following the lead of the two teachers. They cheered, chanted, clapped and stomped to the rhythm of the song in their native tongue. There was so much enthusiasm and joy permeating the room that my feet automatically started tapping, my hands clapping to this wonderful African rhythm. Those on the floor jumped to join those already dancing on the desks making a stage and theatre of the room. I became part of the chorus line, dancing like a child to their music.

After two or three more vibrant songs, they turned to me and Ebenezer asked, "Mr. Charlie, can you teach us a song." He had watched me lead the "Hockie Pockie," and "the Mexican Hat Dance," the previous day out in the field. I couldn't do that again. I don't know where it came from, I'm not a musician or a singer, but following the mood of the room, I started, "Goom Bye Ah, My Lord, Goom Bye Ah." Soon everybody was laughing and singing it in unison, "Goom Bye Ah My Lord…" We sang and laughed through the song together two or three times, when Ebenezer asked, "What do the words mean, Charlie, what does Goom Bye Ah," mean?

"I don't know really. Maybe it doesn't mean anything. It's just a fun song." Everyone agreed and continued singing. After a while, tired voices rested and Micheal asked again about the meaning of the words..

I responded, "Like I told Ebenezer, it may mean nothing, but someone in my area of the United States suggested that it was an old slave song and it was sung to fool the white masters. When their lives were especially tough, the slaves were trying to sing, "Good Bye my lord (meaning the master) we're leaving, going back to Africa, while the duped masters interpreted it that they were paying homage to them." I don't know if it's true or not but it made a good story and pleased everyone that the slaves could trick the masters.

The laughter, singing, and stomping inside, blended with the life sustaining rain drumming the roof, sounded like a symphony of celebration. I felt at home and as welcomed as the rain.

PART VI

Fiction, Poems

Learning from Mice

NEWS FLASH: We can be young again! A new study shows that Resveratrol, the wonder drug, reverses the aging process in mice and may do the same for humans. It also protects against certain forms of cancer, is an anti-viral and is a neuroprotector. We can expect a lower the risk of Alzheimer 's disease and dementia.

This study showed that mice injected with reservatrol, lived longer and lived better than the control group without the injections. The resveratrol enhanced group kept their hair longer, maintained a youthful appearance, were stronger and had better stamina on a treadmill. If these benefits could be transferred to humans, we too could live longer and enjoy our lives more along the way.

Resveratrol is one of the chemicals found in some red wines. It is therefore easily accessible, cheap and does not require a prescription. My wife, Lorrie, and I both want to have longer and healthier lives so we decided to give it a try. One problem is that the dosage injected into the mice was the human equivalent of thirty two bottles of red wine each day. We decided we had better get started if we were to gain the benefits before our demise.

Lorrie has been a moderate drinker all her life. She seldom, if ever, has more than one glass of wine in the evening. Unlike the pure Lorrie, I am more seasoned, nurturing the drinking art started in college fraternity parties, to my present form as a quiet social drinker searching for purpose in retirement.

We both share the common dread of growing older and are willing to try almost anything to remain young. We once drank five gallons of water each from the Fountain of Youth in St. Augustine, Florida. We only wound up bloated and flooded all the bathrooms on the drive back to Hilton Head Island. In contrast, this wine study wasn't superstition, like Ponce de Leon's fountain. This was cold, hard, factual science and we were hopeful.

On the first day of our new life, we bought fifteen cases of red wine from Sam's Club. That about depleted their supply but we did not care. We were determined in our pursuit of eternal youth. We showed our seriousness by exercising and watching our food intake throughout the day. At 4:30 in the afternoon, I uncorked our first bottle of a moderately priced California red wine. Our choice of Robert Mondovi 2007 Pinot Noir was full bodied, with nice legs, and pleasing aroma. Lorrie brought out tumblers, much larger than the common red wine glass, signaling that we meant business. By 4:51, when we drained the last of that bottle, I noticed her wrinkles had disappeared and her cheeks took on a red, youthful appearance.

We sat on the couch and snuggled. I took her hand and said, "Lorrie I had forgotten how blue your eyes are. And your hair glows like when we were dating. "

She smiled, turned her head coyly to the side and winked at me. "Oh Charlie, I think you're feeling the wine." She swiped her lips with high gloss lipstick and laid her hand on top of mine. Her red lips and blue eyes accentuated her blond hair and alabaster skin. "That shirt brings out the deep color in your eyes, Charlie. You have that youthful sparkle, but we can't delay our mission. Shall we attack that second bottle?"

At 4:59, I uncorked a bottle of 2006 California Merlot. Neither of us gave a damn about its bouquet or legs. We threw our cherished tumblers into the fireplace, giggled as they crashed against our white birch logs from Maine and gulped the Merlot from pint beer mugs. We had to drink fast if we were to gain the full health benefits. I sang the "Love Song" from *Romeo and Juliet*, in Italian, which I had never spoken before. She glided over our bare kitchen floor like a teenager as she danced her first ballet.

"Jeesh, honey, I didn't know you were sush a good dansher," I exclaimed.

"I din't either," she slurred. "And hey Charlie, You're looking younger every minute." She was sexy even when she stumbled.

I was now singing, "All I Ask of You," from *"Phantom of the Opera."* She joined me, as Christine, my romantic partner. Neither of us had realized we were so talented. Her eyes were beginning to glaze over but we knew we had to persist if we were going to get young again.

At 5:21 I wrestled, twisted and somehow uncorked our third bottle. It was some kind of red stuff. Although the outside temperature was 39 degrees, we opened all the windows. We wanted to share our newfound talent with the neighbors.

"Hey, honey, you shing like you did twenty yearsh ago when you were a sholoish in church."

"You're right there, Chuckie boy. I am better now. Aged to perfecshon jush like thish red wine."

The details now get a bit fuzzy, but we woke up at 8:39 P.M., sprawled out on the living room couch, hugging and assuring each other that we indeed seemed younger. We managed to stagger into bed, stumbling over the empty third wine bottle along the way. Being young and healthy can take a lot out of a person. The next day and the day after that we slept, medicated our headaches with aspirin, and reexamined our quest for youth.

Beach Day

Ellen left her car in the parking lot, climbed the wooden staircase to the boardwalk, and passed the shower on her right where she noticed a tall blond woman rinsing sand from her young son's feet. The woman wore heavy eye makeup and bright red lipstick. Large breasts exploded from her tiny yellow bikini.

"Roger," she said, "we've got to wash this sand off. You're not getting in the car like this. Your Dad would kill me if he finds sand in his brand new Mercedes."

She grabbed the boy's arm and jerked him under the shower. The boy, slim, about six years old, a frown on his face, protested, "Yeh, but Mom, that water's cold. A little sand doesn't hurt anything."

"I wish just once you wouldn't give me a hard time." She waved a finger in the boy's face and screamed. "I bring you to the beach, sit out in the hot sun for hours and all you do is complain. I get so sick of this. Can't you help for a change?" She ran her long fingers, with nails brightly painted, up and down Roger's shivering legs.

Ice cold water gushed from the shower head, soaking the boy from his blond brush cut to his feet. His lower lip turned down. He wiped a tear from his face with his wet, sandy hand. "I hate the beach. I hate you."

The woman ignored the comment, as if she had heard it so many times that it no longer meant anything to her. She continued scrubbing the boy's legs.

Ellen stood by, quietly watching the mother's face turn redder as her voice got louder. "Excuse me ma'am. Can I help you?"

"What the hell do I need your help for?" The woman rose to her full height, hands shaking, feet spread apart as though she was ready to defend her turf against the world.

Ellen took a step back. "I'm sorry, but I hate to see the boy unhappy, especially over a few grains of sand."

"A few grains of sand, huh." The woman stepped towards Ellen and continued. "My husband works hard. He just leased a brand new Mercedes, and now this little monster is determined to turn it into a piece of junk." She stopped, thought for a moment, "Besides, what's it to you? I don't remember asking you for advice."

"Please ma'am," said Ellen," I don't mean to interfere but the boy is hurting. Surely a few grains of sand aren't worth the boy's tears"

"O.K. now, let's get this straight. This is my kid, my Mercedes, and nobody needs your lousy advice. Why don't you keep on walking down to the beach, cool off, and stay out of my life. C'mon Roger, let's get out of here."

The boy, still whimpering, looked at his mom, then at Ellen. "Yeh lady. Why don't you leave us alone? Nobody asked you. You stink."

His mother grabbed his hand and pulled him up the boardwalk towards the parking lot. Ellen watched the retreating pair, staring in disbelief at the mother, beach bag in one hand, herding her reluctant son up the boardwalk with the other. Each one seemed accustomed to this misery.

How can any parent be so unhappy about raising a child, she thought.

She turned away from the pair and walked towards the beach. The handrail cast a dark shadow at her feet. She stopped, leaned against the railing, looked out over the tough halophytes firmly rooted into the sand, protecting the dunes against wind and waves. *That's what I need. Some firm footing, a purpose. I feel more like that tall grass that bends with the slightest breeze, or even the dead spartina grass, washed up on the shore, lying dead, useless, ugly.* She continued her walk. *When am I going to stop feeling sorry for myself? It's a beautiful sunny day and I'm stewing in my own misery. Stop it now.*

She stopped at the end of the boardwalk, removed her sandals, and felt the warm sand crunch between her toes. The tide was out, exposing the hard packed tidal flats, already filled with sun tanned bodies. She took a few steps, looked around, saw no one she knew, and unfolded her beach chair. She took off her sundress and sat facing the ocean. The hot sun burned the exposed skin of her stomach *Don always wanted me to wear a bikini. Now I've got one and he's not here to see it. What a waste.*

It seemed that everyone on the beach was with someone except her. Couples read together, occasionally looking up from their books to admire the day. She closed her eyes and tried to calm herself by prayer, but her thoughts ran to past heartbreak worries of the future, today, yesterday, and tomorrow running together, in and out of her mind. The young boy crying in the shower, his angry mother, the Mercedes, the mutual resentment, and then... *the knock at the door, the sheriff, the sorrow in his voice,* "I'm sorry Ellen, there's been an accident, a drunken driver. Your husband Donald, your daughter Gretchen, Killed. No, I'm sorry, they never made it to the hospital." *Then the horror, the empty bed, the deathlike silence of the house, Gretchen's bedroom, friends so kind but unable to fill even a little bit of that eternal emptiness. The loneliness so strong that it was like hunger in her stomach, dominating all thoughts, making any action impossible.* A tear ran down her face, into a corner of her mouth. *I've got to do better than this,* she thought.

With effort she opened her eyes and saw a seagull before her perched on one leg. It hopped ahead a couple of steps, stopped, looked back, cocked his head towards her as if asking for food, then flew away, leaving her alone again.

The rhythmical sound of the waves breaking on the beach was interrupted by two people singing the song, "Zippity Doodah Zippity A-A-A," over and over again. "Zippity Doodah, Zippity A-A-A, My Oh My, What a Wonderful Day."

About ten feet away from her, a man and young boy about three years old, put down their cloth bags and sang that song as though nobody else was on the beach. The boy raised his arms, the man pulled the boy's T-shirt over his head getting it momentarily caught under his chin.

"Where's Aidan?" joked the man.

"I'm in here." responded the child.

The man laughed as he gently pulled the shirt up the rest of the way, revealing blond hair, chubby cheeks, a broad smile and big blue eyes that made Ellen want to yell, "Wow!" After he took off the boy's shoes and socks, sensing freedom, Aidan ran to the water but stopped suddenly when his toes touched the cold ocean. He ran back to his friend, laughing, squealing, running circles around him, yelling, "Richie, Richie, it's a beautiful day. It's a beautiful day," as if that was some kind of mantra between them.

Aidan picked up some sand, examined it, then let it flow through his fingers. "Wheee," he said with delight.

Richie picked up some sand and let it flow through his fingers, "Wheee," he exclaimed with enthusiasm equal to the boy's.

Richie was maybe fifty years old with broad shoulders, graying hair, and constant smile. His short legs and middle-aged paunch made Ellen think that his body was an enlarged version of his young playmate. She sat back in her chair, smiled, and thought, *I think I kind of like these two*

She watched them run up the beach together, in and out of the waves, stopping to admire a pelican flying overhead or a dolphin passing offshore. Soon they turned back, running, splashing, laughing together until they stood nearby. Aidan ran into the water and Richie followed close behind. When Richie crouched down, Aidan leaped up on his shoulders and held tight as they walked into deeper water. Ellen walked to the water's edge, picked up some salty foam, ran it through her fingers, and watched the bubbles disappear in her hands. *What a beautiful day. I'm so glad I came to the beach.*

She looked out in time to see Aidan and Richie, heads covered by an unusually large wave, stand up dripping, startled, but safe, still clutching to each other, now returning to shallower water. Richie put Aidan down and they walked hand in hand to the shore.

"That one sure got us," he said, "Let's go make a castle."

Aidan forgot the fright of the waves and ran past her to retrieve a plastic shovel they had brought with them earlier. Richie walked past without saying anything and picked up his own pail and shovel. They sat together, Richie digging a hole, Aidan trying to help but filling it in, and the incoming waves making the whole effort futile, but they didn't seem to care. Without warning, Aidan stood up, watched Richie dig for a minute then threw his arms around his big buddy's neck and the two of them hugged their sand laden bodies together. Not a word was spoken. Both were laughing.

Ellen kicked away the salty foam that was sticking to her legs.For the first time today, she noticed the deep blue sky, the white crests of the waves, the swimmers splashing and yelling. Out beyond the surf, a pelican dove into the water, then floated on the surface, enjoying the fish dinner as his reward for hard work. Contented, constant, water and bird united, up and down, the building and breaking of the waves, surging and receding, their rhythm beating to the rhythm of life.

She stared as if in a trance, focusing on the ebb and flow of water and life. Behind her the boy and man, laughing, digging with their shovels, throwing away the sand, digging, throwing to this same rhythm. *I've got to meet these two*, she thought. She took a step towards them, hesitated, took a step back ran her fingers through her hair, looked away, then without thinking, approached them. "I'm sorry to intrude, but I have to tell you, I don't think I've ever seen two people enjoy each other as much as the two of you."

Aidan looked up at Ellen, "What did she say, Richie?"

"Oh, it's okay, Aidan. She's just being friendly." Richie looked up from his hole in the sand to her beautiful face. His face turned red, his head turned down, and shifted his weight from foot to foot. He stood up, rubbing his hands together, brushing away the sand. "Well, that's a nice thing to say. I'm Richie," he said, reaching out his hand. "This is my friend, Aidan."

Ellen crouched down until her face was level with Aidan's. "It's so nice to meet you. I saw you playing in the waves. What a big boy you are."

The boy grinned with self-pride and stepped towards Ellen, "We're making a castle."

"I see you are," said Ellen. She scooped up some sand, ran it through her fingers, and watched it blow away in the breeze. "I like to play in the sand. I really don't want to interrupt your fun but I can't tell you how much I've enjoyed watching the two of you."

"Us?" said Richie. "We're just having fun. We come down here all the time. I'd rather come to the beach with him than do anything else."

Aidan smiled. Ellen said, "That's pretty obvious. It's just so nice to see an adult having such fun with a child like that."

"It's funny, but I usually don't think of us as man and child. I just like a lot of the same things he does. I love the beach and being with him gives me license to act like a kid. He's a very special person." Ellen looked affectionately at Aidan, as if already realizing how special he was. "Do you have children?" asked Charlie.

"No," she looked away for a second, beyond them, beyond the beach, to a different time and place. Richie pursued this innocent question no farther.

They both looked down at Aidan and watched him walk away towards a boy about his age who was playing nearby with a toy truck. The boy pushed the truck through the sand, making the "Hmmm, Hmmm" sound of little boys playing with trucks all over the world. Aidan took a step to the boy, paused, and crouched as if he was stalking a prey, then another step forward, another crouch. He picked up a nearby truck and started making his own "Hmmm, Hmmm," sound. Within minutes, they were playing as though they had been friends for years.

"We adults can learn so much about having fun by watching kids. I love it." Ellen realized she was talking faster, using her hands, her voice loaded with emotion, something changing within.

"I had no idea we were being watched. I don't mind. I don't think we're much of a show. Look at that. Now he's playing with a whole bunch of kids. He's such a happy guy. If I wasn't playing with him, I'd probably watch him like you were a while ago. He has that wonderful freedom of a child. No inhibitions."

"What a great way to be. I wish I was more like that," said Ellen. "I don't know how I got the courage approach you. I know I talked to you first but really, I'm pretty shy. I don't know what got into me."

She looked away towards Aidan then back at Richie, trying to avoid eye contact. He touched her arm. She didn't want to step away but felt she should. His touch was gentle. He dropped his hand to his side. "Would you mind if I sat with you? We could watch Aidan and his friends together," he said.

"I'd like that." Her quick response revealed her enthusiasm. "My stuff is right here. I can't offer you a chair."

"That's OK. I never bring a chair. The sand is fine." She sat facing the boys. Richie plopped in the sand beside her, hands clasped, forearms resting on his knees.

Her heart was pounding but she felt a calmness that was unfamiliar to her. "I usually don't walk up to guys. Try to pick them up on the beach. I don't know what got into me."

"Sure you do," Richie joked. "I know your type. That sweet innocent act doesn't fool me." They were both laughing. "The only thing is, I know if you had your choice, you'd rather be playing with Aidan than sitting with an old guy like me."

"He is a doll. I can't believe those big eyes. They were the first thing I noticed about him."

"I can't compete with him," said Richie. "He's excited about everything. I find myself staring at him too. He comes over to my house every day, always happy, 'Wanna play trucks Richie?' He talks and I melt. Whatever he wants to do, I do it."

"Do you mean he's not your son? From the way you were both acting, I assumed you were father and son."

"No, it just feels that way sometimes. Actually, I'm his neighbor. His father died. His mother works. I watch him whenever I can."

"That's pretty nice of you," said Ellen staring into his face.

"Not really. It's a pleasure. Some days I'm with him for eight hours, his mother comes home form work, takes him. I miss him immediately. He's an unbelievably good person."

Ellen stifled her reflex to say, *I think you are too.* Instead, she said, "I guess there are worse things than bringing a kid to the beach every day."

"There sure are. I used to be a dentist. Thirty years. Twenty five were good but the last five.. I was ready to quit."

She touched his hand and withdrew it quickly, "You don't look like a dentist."

Richie wrinkled his forehead, trying to look hurt, but he couldn't hide a broad grin. "OK. Now you've said it. What does a dentist look like?"

Ellen's brown eyes sparkled, "I don't know. I guess I never thought about it. Serious, I think. They're always serious. And glasses and gloves and masks. And combed hair, polished shoes. You know, a dentist."

"You know, I never, ever wear gloves or mask to the beach. A drill maybe, but never a mask. And I stopped combing my hair when I retired. Never again will I comb this hair. I may rinse the sand off, maybe, but comb? Never."

She felt a laugh explode that had been lying dormant for too long. She sat up in her chair, reached over and touched his hand.

"You know, I'm probably the only person in the world without a dental story. I've never had a cavity. Never needed anything but a cleaning."

"Well, that's good for you, I guess, but how about me? If everyone was like you, I couldn't have made a living. No retirement, I don't mean to make you feel guilty but you really didn't do your share."

"I guess I never thought of it that way. Me being selfish because I didn't have any problems. Hmm."

He looked at her tight curly hair, the way her mouth turned up at the corners in a natural smile, her flashing eyes that sparkled with every word. He sighed, "It looks like you're perfect. No cavities, no dental horror stories."

"Yes, I am perfect. And I'm shocked it took so long for you to notice." They were both laughing. Their hands touched and instead of withdrawing, they intertwined and stayed together.

They smiled at each other but looked up to see Aidan walking towards them, struggling to carry a huge red plastic truck, almost as big as he was. He peeked out from behind, eyes bulging, breathless, "Richie, Richie, Look at this. Look what I found. A truck, a truck, a big red one."

Richie responded, "Wow, Aidan, you and me, Buddy. I guess we both got lucky today."

Alagash

I knew that the six hour ride from Cape Cod to the Alagash River would be a challenge when I saw the Volkswagen Beatle waiting for me in front of the house. I trusted Peter, the responsible psychologist to arrange the whole trip, while I did nothing. I couldn't blame him. He flashed his familiar smile, greeted me, and introduced me to Graham and his 16 year old son, Lucifer. "Excuse me, "I said, "I'm hard of hearing, I thought you said 'Lucifer.' What is your name?"

"There's nothing wrong with your hearing, Charlie. My name is Lucifer, but please, please call me Luke. You'll see on this trip, my Dad has an unusual sense of humor. Who else would name their only son Lucifer and plan trip like this with four big people stuffed in a Volkswagon Beatle?" Luke might be only 16 but his broad shoulders indicated countless hours of weight lifting in a gym. Fortunately, his father was short legged and skinny so the two of them could ride with tolerable agony in the back seat.

I threw my duffle bag in the trunk up front, and obeyed Peter's plea to "C'mon, Let's go." Was everything on this trip going to be backwards and ridiculous like this little car, trunk in front, engine in back, stuffed with four big people, traveling six hours to Maine? I sat beside Peter in the front while Luke somehow contorted his body to slide in beside his Dad in the back. They were intertwined like teenage lovers on a sofa. I thought of the old circus routine where an endless row of clowns flowed out of a trick car to the amazement of the crowd.

Peter, the doctor, always in control, immediately began pontificating about how the Republican Party was ruining the country, and we all had better beware or the right wing reactionaries would lead us to war and eternal damnation. As his voice got louder, the veins near his temples bulged out and pulsated. He waved his right hand in the air to emphasize that we were all doomed if we didn't listen to him. The car swerved onto the shoulder of the highway, a car behind tooted his horn. Without apologizing, Peter returned both hands to the wheel and steered us back in line. I heard a sigh from the back seat. "Hey Peter," said Graham. "Could you spare us the political diatribes and watch the damn road? We're not going to be able to vote for anyone if we wind up dead in a ditch."

"Sorry," said Peter. "I didn't realize you guys were such sissies. Don't worry, I'm in complete control."

"Why do you think we're all up tight, Peter. It's because we realize you're in control." He paused for a minute, seeming to fixate on Peter's ear that was inches from his face. "Peter you ought to do something about all that hair growing out of your ears. You look like a bear. What the hell does your wife have to say about that? I always wondered what a psychologist was like in his own marriage. Do you practice what you preach, or is all that stuff just for your patients?"

"I'm a perfect husband," said Peter, keeping both hands on the wheel but his eyes darted back and forth between the road and the rear view mirror, watching the passengers in back. "If I had only married the right woman, I'd have a perfect marriage. It's not my fault we fight all the time. Obviously, I'm flexible, sensitive, and understanding. She's damn lucky to have me. I shudder to think what she'd be like without me."

"Bullshit," said Graham. "I'll bet if Gloria said anything about that forest coming out of your ears, you'd pout, get angry, and retaliate just like the rest of us. You psychologists are one screwed up bunch. Marriage counseling. What a racquet that is. I should know I've had enough for two lifetimes. It never did any of my wives any good. They couldn't change. They just didn't get it. All it did was take money from my pocket and put it into yours. And please, watch the road."

Then the psychologist surfaced in Peter. "I've often wondered if part of the problem with marriage is that we all hear too well. Maybe we'd be better off if our spouses missed half of what we say. It's possible that our highly developed sense of hearing puts our marriages at risk. We've all regretted saying certain things. I'll bet our problem is that we all hear too well. Even you, Charlie."

"I don't know about that. The most common word in our house is me saying, 'What.' It drives Laura crazy"

"I'm sure that's annoying," continued Graham, "but at least you don't have to hear all that whining and nagging. I agree with you, Peter, poor hearing isn't all that bad. It's like if you turned the sound off on the TV, it might actually make some sense. I know it's silly with the sound on. It's better when I push that mute button. Maybe the rest of the world would fall into place if we couldn't hear each other. Mute everybody. Except, of course, everybody in this car. I wouldn't want to miss anything here."

"You know something, Dad," Luke spoke up for the first time. "I think you're all crazy. I really do. Deafness is good, me cramped in a Volkswagon for five more hours. What's going on, anyway? Is this some kind of a joke you old guys play on innocent kids like me? You're supposed to be my role models. Well, forget it. I'm going to play football, love up the ladies when they let me, and that's it. I don't believe any of this crap."

"You're wise before your time, Son," added Graham. "You will definitely not learn anything of value with a bunch like this. Love the ladies, have fun, and everything else will fall into place. Of course you may not want to listen to me either. I have been married four times, you know. Four times in love , three times to the judge to explain why we can't live one more day together. I don't understand it. I'm so reasonable. So nice. There must be something in the damn wedding cake that makes them so weird from that point on. I'm great at honeymoons. I could give lessons. It's just what follows that I haven't completely mastered."

"Maybe if you had a steady job, or a career. it might help. You've done more things than any five people I can think of. Or your inventions. Your investments. How much did you lose on those soybeans in Bolivia?"

"Don't ask. Please., Please. Don't ask. It wasn't my fault about that coup. Who would have ever thought a government, anywhere would nationalize soybean production. Soybeans. Why would anyone even think of such a thing, let alone do it. Soybeans, I never want to hear that word again."

The soybean subject was dropped, but Graham entertained us with stories about his love affairs, past Plymouth, through Boston into New Hampshire. The common thread of all his tales was that they were willing lovers until he married them and then their lust turned to dust. I thought he was insensitive to talk so freely in front of his son about lovers other than Luke's mother but he never lost a beat.

The trusty engine had purred along the highway despite its heavy load. Peter had stayed in the left lane passing cars through three states and colorful tales of Graham's love life made the time fly by until the sign welcomed us to "America's Vacationland." After a few more stories and just before my back became permanently deformed from the cramped car, a large red and blue sign pointed us down a dirt road to, "Mulligan's, Best White Water Rafting in the World."

We left towns and highways behind. I expected to be nose to nose with a Maine moose around the next turn. Peter had to downshift the car into second and third gear to negotiate sharp turns and avoid deep holes in the dirt road. It was nearly noon. The hot sun and slow speed turned our joy ride into a prison sentence. Graham's stories continued but became tedious and annoying. I wanted to get out and run alongside the car, do anything to escape the confinement. I cranked open my window for relief but instead the hot air made us more uncomfortable. Peter said, "Maybe if I speeded up, we'd fly over these potholes like they weren't there. Maybe I'm too cautious. I'm going to speed up and see what happens."

No one offered an argument so he shifted into third, then fourth gear and we were on our way again. We did seem to fly over everything until suddenly Peter yelled, "Oh shit!" The car rocked to the left, hesitated for a second and then a violent crash. Screams from the backseat drowned out my own. Our little car had flipped over on its side. I was hung up by my buckled seatbelt, looking down at Peter's frightened face. The world turned ninety degrees, dust flooded the car, Graham groaned and swore, "Holly shit Peter, What happened?"

"Yeh Peter, What the hell happened?" said Luke. "We've got to get out of here. I'm crushing my Dad. Is everybody OK?"

"I think so. Maybe I can climb out this window, open the door and help everybody out," I said. I twisted my body, unbuckled the seat belt and contorted again to push upwards. I stood on Peter's hip and pulled myself out through the opened window. I then opened the door and helped Peter. Luke and Graham followed.

"What the Hell happened?" asked Luke again.

"I think I went too fast around that last turn," answered Peter.

"I guess you did," added Luke and Graham in unison. Long faces stared at the wreck of our only link with civilization. Peter walked away with his head down. The rest of us stretched and checked out our body parts. My back ached but that was normal after our long confinement. Luke and Graham appeared OK. They walked around, assessing the damage to our recently reliable transportation now lying worthless on this isolated road. The dust settled. A squawking crow broke the silence of the Maine woods. "We're lucky. No one seems to be hurt," I said in an attempt to break the spell.

Luke paced around the wreckage and said, "C'mon, Lets flip this thing over and see what happens. We might be able to drive it away." His optimism spurred us to come together, reach under the car and lift it back to its upright position. It bounced twice on its tires before it landed. The whole left side was caved in, twisted, gnarled, windows broken, the door unusable, the outside mirror cast off into the nearby weeds.

"Oh shit," was all I could say.

Graham looked around at the mangled left side and said, "Hey, You can't kill a Beatle. This thing has nine lives.

We've still got eight left. The body is shot, but maybe it'll still go. Peter, get in there and turn that key. I'll bet we're OK." Anyone who had suffered through three failed marriages and still had the courage to try for four, could see hope in anything.

Peter obediently opened the passenger side door, climbed over the gear shift, sat back into the driver's seat and turned the key. The familiar sound of the engine humming brought cheers from us all. "All right. Bring on to the rapids," said Luke, his optimism showing that he was indeed his father's son. A few minutes later, any residual tension disappeared when the wounded but not defeated Voltswagen turned into Mulligan's Rafting Center, our destination. The owner, his face outlined by a long gray beard, watched the four of us climb out of the wreck. He shook his head, thumbed his suspenders, and spit a wad of tobacco juice, just missing Peter's shoe. "Looks like you fellas have already had your adventure. Rafting might bore you after a flip in a car like that. I don't know if the car or you guys are a bigger mess."

None of us was amused by his attempt at humor but we shook hands and paid our money. He introduced us to our guide, another block of granite named Fred. He apologized to us for issuing wetsuits on such a hot day but assured us they were necessary. "I know it's hot today but the water is still freezing. If we go over, these things could save our lives."

Five of us wearing the bright orange suits boarded the rubber raft and were soon being swept down the fast flowing Allagash. The accident was forgotten. Huge boulders loomed in front of us but Fred's expert steering left them safely in our wake. The loud roar of the river drowned out our screams of excitement. We were like kids on a roller coaster who yell for the ride to stop but at the same time hope it will never end.

Occasionally we came to a quiet, deep pool that would be a welcome respite from the excitement and give us a chance to admire our surroundings. Clear blue skies capped the tall pine forest growing from the rock canyons on all sides. A trout rose to the surface to snatch a fly and was gone with a flick of his tail. With the roar of the river left behind, we breathed in the fresh air, listened to the lullaby of the water flowing over rocks, felt the warm sun on our faces. After a short break, we paddled on for another run at the rapids. A few more thrills brought us safely to the last calm pool and the end of our ride.

It was hot. The wetsuits now felt like we were wearing long underwear on a summer day. We wanted to peal our orange skins and drop into the water. No matter how cold it was, it had to be an improvement over these constricting suits. Dousing cold water over our heads was like an invitation to jump. Fred understood when we unzipped each other and stripped to our bathing suits. I looked around and thought I saw everyone else in the water.

I jumped in, but my plunge came to an abrupt end when my bathing suit hung up on the air intake valve of the raft. My head and feet were trapped under water, only my rear end was out, pinned to the raft. I couldn't raise my head out of the water to take a breath. I was hung like clothes on a line. I kicked and tried to jerk my head up, but couldn't. I kicked, flayed my arms, kicked some more. My heart was racing, my lungs about to burst, my stomach aching from holding my breath. The image of my two beautiful kids waiting at home, far away, made me kick franticly. No result. Was I going to die in this stupid way? I jerked my head up again but it was hopeless. I couldn't raise my head out of the water. I thought, "One breath of water and it will be all over. Fast. I'll give one last kick." Suddenly, my bathing suit ripped free. I took a couple of strokes, came to the surface, and gulped in that life saving air. The sky was blue and I was breathing. I swan away breathing deeply, again and again. I joined the others swimming around the raft as if nothing had happened. We laughed and joked and agreed that this is the way to live. The icy water cooled our overheated bodies.

In a few minutes, I climbed back aboard the raft and looked around for an explanation of what had happened. Peter strolled over, looked down at my torn suit, and casually asked, "Charlie, were you in trouble over there?"

"I sure as hell was," I answered.

He continued, "I decided not to swim. I was still feeling shitty from flipping the car over. I just wanted to be alone. I was strolling the deck when I saw you kicking in some weird way. Your bathing suit hung up on that valve. I thought you were struggling, so I ripped your suit off that valve. Are you OK?"

I hugged him and said, "Yeh, I'm OK. I'm great as a matter of fact. But Peter, I think you just saved my life. Maybe you didn't realize it but I was completely helpless. I couldn't raise my head out of the water. I couldn't breathe. You did. You saved my life."

He stepped back, looked me in the eye, thought for a minute, smiled, said nothing, and then walked away. He began joking with the rest of the guys, like he did before the accident. He was readmitted to the group. No one else knew what had happened and neither of us talked about it. Why hadn't he dived into the water with the other three guys? Why? It was never mentioned on the long ride home or at any of our later reunions.

That was over twenty years ago, never brought up again, almost forgotten. But when I lay sleepless, in the middle of the night, it comes back to me. The water, the panic, the question, my kids, the feeling of being freed, that first gasp of precious air, the relief. I hug my pillow, take a deep breath, feel it fill my lungs and give thanks.

Lobster Love

"Aw damn, I'm trapped."

My feelers undulated between the wooden slats, my claws ripped at the nylon netting, my tail flapped in the mud. Nothing helped. The cod head that I had chewed on an hour ago was reeking. "I'm screwed," was all I could say. I struggled, cursed some more, then made a deal with God that, if He chose to get me out of this mess, I would change my ways. No more being controlled by passions. Eating and sex had been my weaknesses and now I needed His help.

Suddenly the whole world started shaking. I was being lifted from my familiar mud up towards the surface where I hadn't been since I was a larva, twelve years before. "Good bye Cape Cod Bay," was the last thing I remember saying before being hauled out of the water onto that filthy boat where they stuck those wooden pegs in my carapace. I was completely helpless. They threw me on the ice, hauled me on that hour truck ride over the bumpy beach to the market and my life changed forever.

That was two months ago. That night I was airlifted to Florida and for three weeks I rested in one of those glass cages with Larry, Leroy, Lolita and Louise. All those damned humans were staring at us. The worst were those kids tapping on the glass. I'd have liked to have gotten one those little brats in the water with me and seen how smart they'd be then.

Larry disappeared first. Two big human hands came and lifted him out. We never saw him again. Leroy and Louise went together, then it was just Lolita and me.

Me, Oh sorry, I'm Louis. Louis the Lobster. Sorry I took so long to introduce myself. My roommate was Lolita, a real sweet kid, but not my type. Her tail was too small. And huge claws. I couldn't get near her if I wanted to. And what a personality! Soo aggressive and nasty. I was afraid to go to sleep. Afraid she might eat me.

I was almost relieved when a few days later those same hairy hands grabbed me, put me on the scale, stuffed me in that paper bag and jammed me into that ice chest. He carried me aboard his yacht like I was a piece of meat. The guy had no respect.

"We're sailin' out to The Keys," he said to someone. "The Keys," he repeated. "We're sailin' out to the Keys."

What the hell are the Keys, I wondered. It doesn't matter. He had one of those long haired humans with him. One of those things that talks so sweet and sashays around like she was a queen. But hey. No distractions. Not this time. They were drinking and carrying on, propagating their species something fierce. They got that yacht really rocking. But I knew I had to concentrate. No distractions. This was serious.

Despite everything, it was great to be back at sea. I felt better. I liked that rocking and rolling of the boat, almost like home. I felt the change in the air. I was energized. Confident, borderline cocky even.

"I've got one chance," I said to myself, "One chance and that's it. When that drunken lover boy lays a hand on me, he's going to get one giant pinch on the face. He'll feel pain like he's never felt before. I've got to do it right clawed, It's the only one I could free from that awful peg. A horrendous pinch and hopefully, he'll be so angry, he'll howl and panic and throw me overboard. I'll be free. A long shot sure but it was all I could think of at the time. Here's what happened.

Things got serious real fast. He lifted me from the bag. I saw daylight, reached out and grabbed his red, obnoxious, bulbous nose. I squeezed hard and miracle of miracles, he yelped, fell forward onto the guard rail and the momentum hurled us both into the sea. He belched, burped and puked. I let go his nose and swam like mad. I never want to see him again. Ever.

Ow-w, I just hit bottom. It's not soft mud like Cape Cod Bay. It's hard sand and rocks and corals and clear water. I can see twenty feet away. It's beautiful down here, with all those pretty colors, but hot. I just feel like going to sleep. Even that glass tank was cooler than this, but it's sooo pretty. That yellow, purple, and red coral, I've never seen anything like this. Those prickly, black sea urchins look mean though. I don't want any part of them. And those barracuda, such sharp teeth. I've got to watch my butt around here.

But Wow! What do we have here? All pink and pretty, and a huge tail flapping at me so nice. And Look! No Claws. She is CUTE and I mean cute. A lobster with a huge tail and no claws. And she sees me. She's coming over.

OH, now I've got it. That incident with the trap, the pegs and the glass case. That was my passage. I'm cooked, no, not cooked. Bad expression. I'm dead. Real dead and this is heaven. This is it, I know it is. Heaven. The coral, the warmer water, the slower pace and now best of all, this ravishing babe with gorgeous eyes, sexy tail and no claws is coming on to me.

"Hi there handsome," she says in that slow Southern drawl while twitching her protruding eyes, "I'm Lola. I haven't seen you around before. Do you come here often, Big Boy? Where have you been all my life? Where have you been hidin', you macho guy you. And look at those claws. I'd like to have them wrapped around me some night. I'm smitten."

Well, that was the end of my freedom. I took one look at her and was trapped by her seductiveness. Now I'm a prisoner of love. Lobster love. A victim of my own desires, just as helpless as being in that cage. But I admit, it's a lot better here with Lola than in that cage. There's no comparison.

"I'm coming dear. Sorry to keep you waiting. And of course darling, I'll even shed my carapace for you. Any day, all day, any time. Yes, you're right dear, I will be more careful with my claws. Yes, dear. Sorry dear, I'm coming."

Mrs. Grayson

Everybody liked Mrs. Grayson. She lived across the street from us in a white shingled house, with green shutters, and an enclosed in porch with big bay windows. She kept her front blinds open all the time so we could look in at her and she could watch us play kick ball in the street. My parents called her, "a pillar of the community." She went to church every Sunday and had a kind word for everybody.

Ever since I was little, she had a candy waiting whenever I knocked on her door. I didn't go too often because her daughters were older than me and I felt like I was in the way.

She looked like Doris Day in that movie I saw with my sisters. Her happy face radiated joy and made me think of happy things. Her eyes sparkled and her broad smile was centered on flashing white teeth. She wore glossy red lipstick like a movie star. I used to think of her as just another friendly neighbor until I progressed into Middle School and then I couldn't stop thinking about her. When I was a kid, I just ran up to her and got a peppermint and thought nothing of it. Now I found it hard to talk around her. My face turned red and my head went down. I couldn't look right at her. She was too pretty.

Her daughters were getting older. Donna would go to college next year, to the same school Elinore had gone the year before. I seldom saw her husband because he worked two jobs and golfed on weekends. Her next door neighbor, old Mrs. Shutsle gossiped that Mr. Grayson drank too much and was violent but I was quickly herded away when such talk began. Nobody listened to Mrs. Shutsle anyway. She talked bad about everybody.

I was playing mumble-t –peg in the front yard one sunny day, when my best friend Graham stabbed the knife through his foot and ran home crying. "Sorry Graham, I hope you're Okay." I shouted as he limped up the street. Mrs. Grayson happened to drive into her driveway and heard him whimpering. He whined about the blood spurting from his foot and he was sure he was going to die.

"What happened Freddie," she shouted as she got out of her car. "Is Graham Okay?"

"I'm sure he is, Mrs. Grayson. He takes a few drops of blood pretty seriously."

"I'm glad you're not like that, Freddie. You always seem so brave to me."

"Thanks Mrs. Grayson," I replied. She smiled above the bag of groceries she was carrying into her house. "Can I help you?" I asked, thinking this would be a good excuse to get a closer look at her and maybe find out why I became so weak around her.

"Well yes, Freddie that would be wonderful." She handed me the bag and I followed her into her kitchen. Her floor was shiny clean and smelled like the same chemicals my mother used in our house. "You know Freddie, I've been wanting to talk with you for a long time." She smiled, leaned over, and my eyes raced to the place where her chest mounds separated and disappeared under her blouse. Her perfume smelled better than the flowers in the corner florist shop. She took a seat and looked right at me. I only put my head down a little bit. I don't think I had ever been that close to a lady before and she was even prettier than I imagined.

"Freddie," she said, "you used to come over here all the time, we were buddies but you don't come any more. Why? What's the problem? Have I done something wrong?"

"Oh no Mrs. Grayson. Nothing's wrong. I think you're wonderful." Now I was sweating. I had never talked to a grown up person like this. I wanted to run away but I couldn't. I wanted to tell her everything about movie stars and school and how pretty I thought she was but I couldn't say anything. My mouth was dry. I kind of stammered something but it made no sense.

"Well Freddie," she said, "I'm glad we don't have a problem. I like you a lot and I don't want anything to mess up our friendship. Do you understand?"

I shifted my weight to my other foot and tried to look up at her. Her blouse hung down low like the ladies in pictures and I could just imagine what was underneath. I managed to look up and was glad she wasn't laughing at me. "That's good Freddie. I miss your visits. Please don't stay away. Okay?"

"Okay Mrs. Grayson. I won't stay away." I wondered what was making me talk like this. I kept beaming and smiling. "Mrs. Grayson. You don't even have to give me a candy," I burst out without thinking. Her closeness made me say things that just popped into my head."

She smiled, hesitated then continued, never taking her eyes off me. "What grade are you in now Freddie? You're getting to be such a big boy."

"I passed five, Mrs. Grayson. I'll be going into six next week."

"Wow, sixth grade and it seems like you were so young just yesterday." She held my two hands in her beautiful fingers. It felt great and I smiled right up into her face. I noticed she had those funny little lines at the corner of her eyes and her eye lashes were painted dark black like those actresses in the movies. One eye was red and had a fading bruise mark around it like she might have walked into a door or something.

She let go and stepped back. "You know Freddie, I often watch you out my front window. You really are becoming well developed, very fast." She looked up and down my whole body. My privates were feeling uncomfortable like my pants were shrinking or something was getting bigger inside.

"Thanks Mrs. Grayson. I can do thirty five pushups now and not even get tired."

"Wow, Freddie, thirty five pushups. I'll bet I can't do five. You're so strong. Can I feel those muscles of yours?"

I flexed my arm like Charles Atlas in the comic book advertisements. She chuckled, looked at me again and then came closer. She felt my muscle then ran her fingers over each of my shoulders and started rubbing the back of my neck. I wanted her to keep doing it but instead, I brushed against her and ran out of the house. I didn't even think to stop think or get a peppermint or anything else. It felt so good and so strange that I had to run away.

I stayed away for a couple days, but daydreamed only about her. I could hardly eat and my teacher yelled at me at school for not paying attention. I imagined myself rescuing her from her mean old drunken husband and taking her away to some lakeside resort with cottages and a swimming pool and a restaurant where people wear neckties and drink out of those funny shaped glasses.

Two days later, I couldn't stand it any longer. My chest thumped hard when I rang her doorbell. She answered after two rings. She opened the door and held her arms wide opened, "Freddie, you've come back. Come on in." She laughed, hugged me, and danced me around in a circle. She took my hand and led me into her now familiar kitchen. She sat on a stool, reached out, leaned over and gave me a big kiss on the cheek with her bright red lipstick. The next thing I knew my arms were tight around her neck and I was telling her everything. I told her about the kids at school, my favorite teachers, how some of the kids were playing "spin the bottle" but didn't invite me because I was too shy, and why I had really stayed away all that time. I couldn't stop talking.

Finally, I slowed down a little bit and she rested her hands on each of my shoulders. "Oh Freddie," she said, "I'm glad you think I'm beautiful. Grownups don't say nice things like that to each other. Not often enough anyways." She glanced off in the distance like she was thinking of a different time and place. She looked back at me and whispered, "Sometimes they can be so cruel to each other."

She took a deep breath, smiled, and continued, "Freddie, I'm so glad you're here. It's nice to feel close to someone again."

She started rubbing the back of my neck with her painted fingernails like she did on my last visit.

This time I didn't run away.

Mrs. Grayson's candy became a steady diet for me until one day about a month later, when my mother took me aside, held my hands, and said, "Fredrick, I have some bad news." She was whispering. I had never seen her so serious. "Our friend Mrs. Grayson, across the street, won't be with us anymore." She paused and swallowed hard. "Mrs. Grayson died last night. We're all in shock. She was such a kind person and a good friend. She never hurt anyone. I just feel so bad for her family. I know she was your good friend too, Fredrick." Her tears fell against my face.

I was too numb to react. I pulled away, withdrew my hands, and walked out of the room. I said nothing. I felt nothing.

Weeks later I found a newspaper article, hidden in my parent's dresser drawers, reporting on the death. There was a picture of the Clarrisa Street Bridge with an arrow pointing to a spot where a woman had jumped into the river and drowned. They didn't give a name but I knew who it was. She had done a suicide.

No one talked about it and no one knew why this beautiful lady suddenly decided she couldn't stand one more day on Earth. It caught everyone by surprise. Our house was pretty quiet for a while, everyone retreated into their own way of dealing with misery.

Most conversations ended when I walked into a room. I did overhear my parents say, "You just never know what's going on in other people's mind," or another time, "You never can tell what goes on in someone else's house."

Hiding

I never did anything like that before. I've always been a model citizen, coached Little League, was a Cub Scout Leader, was a long standing member of the town council, even a deacon in my church. That all changed one night when two friends dragged me into a strip club and bought me drinks. Soon I was up on stage dancing with naked ladies, completely losing my barrings.

My friends ushered me out of the bar after midnight but when I drove home I saw that fateful blue light flashing behind me. I pulled over, the cop asked for my license and registration, and then made me step out of the car. I stumbled and he immediately put the cuffs on me. I spent the night in jail. That was a month ago. The next day I was featured on page four of our local newspaper. "Local Dignitary Arrested for Drunken Driving after a Night at a Strip Show." That was only the headlines. The rest of the article implied that this one night extravaganza was not unique. They planted rumors about my lechery and wild second life. They were wrong. That was my one and only debauchery and now I'm paying for it, big time. People stared and pointed at me when I walked the streets of town. I was an outcast. My wife was furious and started divorce proceedings before she heard my side of the story. So much for that "till death do us part," oath.

I had to get out of town fast. I hated lawyers and the constant humiliation. I had some money squirreled away and needed a new identity. I contemplated a face lift, maybe getting my finger prints sanded. I needed a complete makeover. A trusted friend suggested Provo, Utah. It was far away and offered a new life. I was on the next plane, spent three nights in a seedy motel, dyed my hair, grew a mustache, and then on Sunday morning wound up in a Mormon Church. They preached forgiveness and love and I felt like I had found a new home. A couple days later, this guy named Jonathan, wearing a black hat and suspenders, approached, bought me some bottled water, no coffee here, and preached to me about all the pitfalls of that conventional church. He listened to my story, sympathized with me, and urged me to come to his town where the "true" Mormons lived.

I looked at Liberty, Utah as the perfect place to hide and establish a new identity. It was small, isolated by surrounding mountains, and the people were welcoming. They all look alike. They don't drink, smoke, watch TV, or listen to rock and roll music. They pray and smile all the time and there are children everywhere. The patriarch of the town is an eighty seven year old polygamist named Joseph Brigham Smith. He's nearsighted, rumored to be impotent, and moderately demented. He brags that he hasn't shaved in forty years and his beard hangs down to his knees.

He has thirteen wives, fifty seven children, countless grandchildren and longs to get married again. He took a shine to me on our first meeting, proposed on the spot, and tomorrow, I will become the fourteenth wife of Joseph. The downside is I'm not gay. The obvious upside is that this is a perfect hideaway. In this isolated village, I could easily hide under his beard if I had to. No lawyers or cops will ever find me here. And Joseph, he's not really a bad guy. The poor old visionary suffers from halitosis, continuous flatulence, and is toothless except for one prominent central incisor that hangs out over his lower lip, but heck nobody's perfect. It's really a no brainer. I've got no choice, I'm in.

Illegal

Stretched out on the hammock in the shade of the pine forest, I was vicariously transported from this pastoral scene to the deserts of Ethiopia while reading Paul Theroux's Dark Star Safari. My safari was interrupted when my girl friend, Sheila started rubbing the back of my neck. She wanted to play and I wanted to escape. I tried to swat her fingers away like a troublesome horsefly but she persisted. "Damit, Hon, can't you see I trying to read?"

"You're always reading. There's nothin' to do out in this place. I'm bored."

I could feel my neck muscles tense up. She withdrew her hands and started cracking her gum. *I hate the way she cracks that damn gum. How did I ever get into this mess? Big tits and empty brains have gotten me into more trouble.*

She ignored my attempt to get back to my book and said, "That guy is going to let that little fish die." I tried to ignore the comment and continue my journey, but instead, took a deep breath and listened. She continued, "See that fish lying on the ground. He keeps kicking it. It's going to die."

I swore to myself and decided that my African adventure would have to wait. I sat up and watched a young man about 20, wearing an orange baseball cap, kicking a small trout around the bank of the stream. He stopped when his other fishing pole bent double, indicating a fish was on that line too. I stood up and watched one fish flopping on the shore and another one stripping off line trying to free itself. I tried to be sociable by reluctantly asking Sheila, "Do you want me to go out there and see what's happening?"

She answered, "Yes." with such emphasis that I knew I should rescue the suffering fish and leave the Ethiopian Desert for later. The distant lodge was full of people but I was grateful that our modest camp offered privacy on the bank of the Kayoga River. Tall pines trees stretched to the sky, their shimmering branches complimenting the sound of the gurgling water for this pastoral symphony. The trout were running in the stream but I was content to sit with my book, enjoying the cacophony of sound while vicariously traveling through Africa.

I put the book down and swore again. *Shit. She won't leave me alone for a minute. If we can't relax together here, there's no way I'm going to move in with her.* I walked over the wet grass, continued down the rock laden steps to the stream where the young man was now reeling in his second fish. I saw the small rainbow trout that Sheila had complained about lying helplessly on the ground. After a customary, "Hi, How are you," I asked the guy, "That looks like a rainbow trout. Don't they have to be ten inches long?"

He pulled back on the bending pole and answered, "I'm not sure, eight inches I think." He eyed the dying fish on the ground and continued reeling in his other line.

I looked at the fish with the characteristic stripes on its side lying dormant in the grass, "That little guy doesn't look ten inches to me. They've gotta be ten inches my friend. "

He became defensive and in a desperate voice said, "I was going to throw it back, but it swallowed the hook. He was floating; I was going to throw it back. He was going to die, anyway." He took out his tape measure with the hand not holding the rod and sloppily stretched the tape from half way back of the fish's mouth to the tail. "See, ten inches." His voice was shaky and hard for me to hear.

I grabbed the tape out of his hand and this time stretched it from the tip of the mouth to the tip of the tail. The fish barely measured eight inches. It flipped his tail and opened his gills as if to prove to me that it was still alive but not doing well.

"What the hell. Are you afraid to touch a fish?" I asked. "We watched you kicking it around like you were afraid to touch it. Here, let me show you." Before he could answer, I picked up the fish by the underbelly, gave a slight twist and threw back into the water. We watched it swim away. The fisherman gave his pole a big jerk and the next fish came writhing and struggling onto the grass. I grabbed the fish and gave it a cursory measurement. It might have been ten inches but I said, "Too small again. Too bad," and took it off the hook and threw it back into the water. I walked away a few paces then came back to him, "I hate to see illegal fish killed in this beautiful place. You should thank me. I may have just saved you from a two thousand dollar fine." I now stood inches away from his face, staring into his eyes. Neither of us blinked. I felt the blood rush to my head. I was breathing hard like I was running a race. "This really pisses me off, Shithead. If you're too scared to take a harmless fish off the line, what the hell are you doing out here fishing? I'm going to call lodge security and tell them that you're keeping illegal fish."

As I walked away, he smiled and said, "Go ahead, mister, those guys are all friends of mine. And you have no proof."

I wasn't listening to that obvious logic. I stormed back to my camp, muttered something to Sheila, who had watched the whole thing, but said nothing. I grabbed the phone. "Hello, security. This is Mr. Monroe from camp thirteen. There is a guy here keeping illegal fish." I heard him whisper to someone about this guy whining about illegal fish being taken from the stream.

Sheila said nothing. Not a damn word. I jammed the phone in my pocket then went outside and yelled to the fisherman, "I've called security. They'll be here in a minute."

He yelled back, "That's great. They're friends of mine. I'll tell him how you threatened me. You swore at me. And where's the fish? You threw it back." He was regaining his courage and I realized that the evidence was now swimming away in the pond with a very sore mouth.

Ten minutes later the security guard, about the same age as the fisherman, sauntered over with his chest puffed out proudly displaying his shiny badge. "What's the trouble, guys?"

"This guy is threatening me. He swore at me. He's crazy," the obnoxious fisherman shouted while pacing back and forth.

I stared back and countered with, "He's keeping illegal fish."

"Where are they?" asked the officer.

"I threw them back. They were undersized and dying. Even he said that he tried to throw it back but claimed that it floated belly up. 'It would die anyway' were his exact words."

"I don't want to hear that," said the fisherman, denying everything and now feeling confident with the appearance of his friend, the security cop.

"Did you throw his fish back?" the policeman asked me.

"I sure did. It was undersized and dying. He's keeping illegal fish."

The cop walked towards me, pointing his finger in my face, "What you did is worse than what he did. You had no business throwing back his fish. You should have called security. Now you need to apologize to me and to him."

I said, "There's no way I'll apologize this obnoxious little brat, but maybe I could have called security but if I did there'd be two dead illegal fish lying on the ground. Now they're alive in the water.

I was calming down until another vacationer walked over to see what the fuss was all about. I recognized him as the man we had lunch with an hour before. He spent the whole lunch hour bragging to us about being a councilman from a small city nearby. He spoke up, "I know this young guy," pointing to the fisherman. "He works in the kitchen. He seems like a nice guy to me."

He then reached out and shook my hand like a politician running for office. I reluctantly shook it as the guard thanked him but asked him to keep moving. He shrugged his shoulders and spread his hands to show his innocence, "I just wanted to say 'hi.'" He gave everyone a broad smile, another handshake, and then walked away into the woods.

I realized I was helplessly outnumbered and justice would not prevail today. I retreated to my camp and watched them all scatter in different directions. Sheila, who had witnessed the whole disaster from her reclining chair, picked up a magazine as I approached and casually leafed through it while fervently cracking her gum. Now she was trying to focus on her magazine and avoid the whole issue while I bristled. I pleaded my side of the argument and waited for some commiseration, but got none. Her silence hurt more than the guard, the fisherman, and the passing politician combined.

I went into the hammock and tried to go back to Dark Star Safari, but now even reading about Africa offered no solace. I slammed down the book, stormed into the tent, fumbled in the ice chest for a beer. I almost never drink in the woods but I needed one now like I needed my next breath of air. I felt its coolness penetrate my throat and thought, "S*o much for movin' in with that bitch Maybe it's time to join the Peace Corps. The African Desert might be a step up from this little piece of paradise."*

A Dream

To ROB and HEATHER:

Last night I had a dream I'd like to share with you.

In this dream, I was walking along a bustling beachside resort, holding hands with a young boy and younger girl. I thought the boy was Aidan and I didn't recognize the girl. The crowd was happy and so was I. I was mostly admiring and loving the two little kids I was with. We made our way through the crowd, heading for a meeting point where we would find Lorrie. The problem was, it was now 8:30 and we were supposed to meet her at 8:00. I was confused because Lorrie didn't show and I was left with these two beautiful children. I realized that I wasn't only holding hands with these two kids but our arms actually grew into each other. It was hard to tell where my arms ended and theirs began. I felt good throughout the dream- people were happy and mostly I felt an extreme admiration and pride to be with the two children.

I woke up, understood it was a dream, and joked with Lorrie, "Where were you?"

I realized that the woman that didn't show, the one we were looking for, was not Lorrie but your Mom and the two kids that I admired so much, and felt so inseparable to, were the two of you. Rob and Heather, I will always be joined or bonded to you, always admiring you, but wondering, "Where's Mom? What happened?"

In the dream, we, and the rest of the world, were happy but I was confused about "What happened to Mom? Why isn't she here?"

I'm sorry your Mom missed growing up with you two great people. She would have had a lot of fun and been so proud. I am.

The Progression

My mother hugged me, laughed, and bounced me up and down on the sidewalk, like she was giving me a dance lesson. I had never seen everyone so happy. Our house with four young children was a normal gathering spot for kids in the area but this was different. Every child in the neighborhood seemed to be there and even grown up people hugged each other. Everyone was laughing, dancing in circles, and singing together. My sister Flora even took her thumb out of her mouth to scream, "Its VJ Day Charles. Don't you understand?"

"No I don't. What's BEE Jay Day?"

"No," explained my oldest sister Liz, "VJ means victory over Japan. The war is over. We won."

My mother let go of me long enough to hug our cousin Jean who lived next door. "Now maybe my brother Alex can come home. I miss him so much."

"He'll be home. They'll all be home. They're all heroes." Suddenly four planes roared overhead, flying low, shaking the earth and making me dash into my Mom's arm. "It's OK Charles. Those are B-29s. That's what won the war for us. They're bombers."

"Yes," replied Marcia, "and here come those fighter planes. See how fast they are? Wow!"

"They're fast all right. They had to protect the bombers before the Japs or Nazis shot them down."

"What are Nazis?" I asked, "Are they the bad guys?"

"Yes, They're real bad guys. Worse than the Japanese."

"Nobody's worse than the Japanese," Marcia responded as if casting her vote on who truly represented the biggest evil.

"The Nazis put people in ovens. Baked them and ate 'em." Chimed in Florence.

"They didn't eat them," argued Liz, as if she was the final authority on all things good and evil. "Nobody eats people anymore."

"They do too. The Japanese eat people all the time."

"I don't think they do kids." Interjected my Mother. "Anyways it's all over now. We're safe. Nobody's going to eat anybody or drop bombs on anybody else. We're safe, the war is over. We won the war in Japan and Europe. The Germans surrendered a while ago and now the Japanese quit too."

"What's a German?" I asked no one in particular.

"That's who we fought against. They were dropping bombs on everybody even England so we bombed them. They quit. When we dropped an A bomb on Japan, they quit too."

"Yeh," interjected Liz, "We bombed Hiroshima and Nagasaki. It served them right. They deserved it."

Everything was happening so fast. I snuggled closer to my Mom "What's an A bomb? Does it kill people?"

"It kills everybody. It's the biggest bomb in the world and we have it." Liz was the oldest sister and seemed to be the only one who stopped celebrating long enough to give me a straight answer.

My mom put me down and told my sisters. "You girls watch your brother. Don't let him run out in the street. Your Dad will be home soon and he's going to be so happy. I'm going to make a special dinner tonight. I think we'll have a meat pie, his favorite. What a special day this is. It's about time we all celebrated. There is peace in the world."

Dinner that night revolved around the excitement of the day. "Who did most of the fighting, Dad? The Army, Navy, or Marines."

"They all worked together, Hon. We needed them all. They all did a great job."

"Is General Eisenhour going to be president someday. How about MacCarthur?"

"Who's president now?" I asked. "And what's a president? Does he fight too."

"No Charles, The president is different. He doesn't fight. He just tells everybody what to do."

"Oh kind of like Liz? Is she a president?"

Everyone laughed except Liz. "I don't tell everybody what to do. I just try to help. I am the oldest in the family you know except for Mom and Dad."

"Of course you don't." said my Dad. "You're not bossy. Are You?"

"She told me that my friend Olga Fisher was a German. That I shouldn't trust her. Isn't that being bossy Dad?"

"Maybe a little bit but it doesn't fit anyways. Olga's parents came from Germany, kind of like I came from Scotland. They're just as American as we are. Her parents came from a different country. That's all. We're all Americans now. We won the war. It's time to celebrate, not hate. The war's over."

"I still think she's bossy," whimpered Marcia.

"I am not. And besides, you eat too much. You'll get fat."

"Okay, that's enough," said mother. "If we can't get along as a family, how do you expect countries to get along. We have to love each other. That's what the Bible says."

Marcia leaned over and whispered to Florence, "I still think she's bossy."

I heard her and wondered if they were going to start another war right here at the table. *Isn't that what Mom just said? If we can't get along, how can we expect countries to? I don't want to start another war, War is bad, I guess, everybody is so happy when it's over.*

Five years later we sat at the same dinner table. I was in fifth grade and knew pretty much everything there was to learn about the world. I could add four figure columns in my head as long as I didn't have to carry from one column to another, I knew my times tables all the way up to 12 times 12 equals 144, and the capitol of our state was Albany, not New York City as most people thought. Liz and Marcia were both in high school and Florence was heading there the next year.

Liz as usual started the dinner conversation. "Dad, some kids at school were talking about our Army freezing in someplace called Korea. There's another war there and this time we're fighting the Russians or somebody. Where is Korea?"

"It's in Asia, Liz, but our soldiers have already relanded at Inchon. Now they're trying to push the North Koreans back where they came from. It looks pretty good. General MacArthur is leading our troops and hopefully the soldiers will be home by Christmas, I just hope the Chinese don't enter the war. Or the Russians. That could start another world war."

I asked, "I thought the Russians and Chinese were on our side. My teacher told us they helped us fight the

Germans and Japanese in the last war? Why are they going to fight against us now?"

"They're a bunch of dirty Communists. We have to kill them or they'll come and bomb us. Isn't that why we hide under our desks, Dad, during an air raid drill?" interrupted Florence."We're supposed to put our hands over our heads and scrunch under our desks. That's going to protect us if the Russians bomb us."

Marcia responded, "The Lotoffs are building a bomb shelter in their back yard. Maybe we should build one."

"We don't need a bomb shelter. No one's going to bomb us today. Let's enjoy dinner. Pass the gravy, Marcia."

"Yes but Olga said the communists that are trying to take over the world. Hitler is dead. Now the Germans are our friends and they help us against the communists."

"Uh ah. Not all Germans are good. The East Germans help the Russians. The West Germans are on our side. They're the good ones."

"How do you tell if a Germans is West German or East German? One's bad the other good. Do they look different?"

"No. that's what makes it so difficult. They look alike but one is communist and the other one is on our side."

"What's a communist?" I asked.

"It's someone who wants to bomb us. That's why we have to hide under our desks."

"Oh," I answered, "Let me get this straight. North Koreans are bad, South Koreans are good. East Germans are bad, West Germans are good."

"Now you've got it Charles. You learn fast."

Fifteen years later, I had just graduated from medical school and would soon head for Army duty at Fort Jackson, in South Carolina. My sisters were all married, living far from home. My mother had died two before so I sat in the same kitchen alone with my Dad. His advanced age and the constant grief from my mother's death left him confused and sometimes out of touch with reality. His hands shook, his steps were slow and unsteady, his speech sometimes got lost in mid sentence, and other times he appeared as lucid as ever. I often wondered how much he understood.

"You look great in your uniform, Charles. Those captain's bars are pretty impressive I can't wait for your Mom to see them, Where is she anyway? Why isn't she here?"

I said nothing but held his hand. He looked up at me with a sad look on his face. "Oh yeh, now I remember." His mouth quivered as I squeezed his hand. "Anyways, I'm sorry you might have to go to Vietnam, where ever that is, and leave your wife and little boy."

"It's in Asia Dad. The North Vietnamese are attacking the South Vietnamese. They need our help. We have to stop communism from spreading. If they conquer the South, Communism might spread from country to country."

"Oh, I guess I understand. You'll be fighting for the South against the North, someplace in Asia."

"That's right Dad. This time we're fighting for the South against the North."

"However it turns out, I'm sure you'll do the job, son. This country has been very good to us since we came from the old country. I guess it's time to pay back. I wish I could go in your place."

"You can't Dad. It's my turn now."

Street Scenes

In Haiti, children play in a pool
The water is fed by streams loaded with feces, garbage, and decay
A man rushes out, invites me into his house
It's of cement block, the finest in the neighborhood
I can't see anything, mud floor, no windows, who knows how many live here?
I don't, it's totally dark in mid day sun.
Finest in the neighborhood, rest live in tin or cardboard shacks
Outside, a woman comes to me.
Holds out her baby, she loves the daughter
But offers her to me, "Take," she says
"A rich American," she thinks.
"My daughter, I no can feed her."

At Mother Teresa's Home for the Dying
A nun with a smile, cleans the open sores of a man
I see the exposed bone of his buttocks, his legs,
No skin, no muscle, just white bone.
He's dying with dignity, because he's finally met his angel.

Later she cleans a toilet, the fowlest place imaginable.
Humans dying, pooping, waiting for her touch
She's smiles all the while, grateful for the chance to do God's
work.

I later ask, "How do you do it?" she smiles
"We pray two hours in the morning, work, pray some
more
Work, pray that's how we do it."
This nun is the most beautiful, happy woman
"How does she do it?
"She works, she prays, she gives thanks." and radiates joy.

In Ghana, a woman has two daughters, Sara and Comfort
Both gifted, smart, stimulated, best in the class
The mother takes in laundry, their only income,
The father sick, affords no medicine.
Mama may have to take the kids out of school.
"Thirty dollars per year, too expensive, no cedi's," she says.

In class, a teacher asks, "What is your idea of heaven?"
The students agree, "A bowl full of jeloff rice, that's what
heaven will be.
Bowls full of jeloff rice for my family and me.
That's what heaven will be."

In America, I sit at home, three bedrooms, two vacant
Three baths two unused, Refrigerated loaded,
Grapes, oranges, and apples too
Fish, rice, and left over stew,
Milk, orange juice, two loaves of bread,
"Can't eat too much," goes through my head
"Might get fat." Why am I restless?

Communication

Teen agers face each other in a booth,
Talking on cell phone to someone distant
About lipstick, nails, or shopping sales
One is depressed, she thinks no one cares
Her friend is there ready to listen
Both fill their time gabbing of nothing
Each wants to help, to bond, instead
The cell phones keep them apart

A young woman pushes the old man in his wheel chair
His fingers are scared, a war hero he
Saved his plane, all hands aboard,
World War Two, like the Pelopenesian War to the young
girl
She talks of boyfriends, things she likes to do
Not realizing he was a hero in WW II

A young Korean woman waits at the checkout
She watches the cashier joke with the customer in front
They laugh, talk, and have a good time
She's next, the cashier looks at her, straight faced, serious

"I wish she'd make jokes with me," she thinks
As she passes through the line in silence

They play tennis together, share many lunches
Good friends they are, He a judge, him a Doc
They laugh and play and carry on, till the judge dies
The next day in the paper he reads
ATuskeegee Airman was he
He never disclosed it, I wonder why

They sit down to dinner, just the two
Anxious to talk of the day, delights, victories.
She turns on the tube, "Rape in the city,
Tsusumi, suicide bombing across the world
Stock market up or down here."
What's the difference? The day's joys not shared.

TVs, Cell phones, computers,
To help us communicate, is it working?
People long to unload, to help, and disclose
Instead we talk with our brains
Not from the heart. Strangers we've become
Isolated by our devices

Joy

It's a beautiful mornin'
It's a beautiful day
Got that wonderful feelin'
Things are goin' my way

To sing happy songs, sing 'em out loud.
Buds on the trees, a white fluffy cloud
People together, smiles on their faces
A cool breeze, in quiet places.

I'm feelin' fine, never better in fact
A walk on the beach, I lie on my back
The smell of an orange, its juice down my chin
The neck on a heron, it brings me a grin
The eye of a sparrow, a hummingbirds wings,
I can't get enough of my favorite things

I skip down the stairs, two at a time
Because for today, all is in rhyme
Leaves in the wind, the laugh of a child
The roar of a lion, out in the wild

Snowflake on an eyelash
A fifty yard dash
Church bells that ring
The azalias in Spring
Plenty of sunshine outside for play
Seize the moment, it's the only way